THE MYTHS OF
GREECE & ROME

A Bacchante

Lord Leighton

Fr.

THE MYTHS OF GREECE & ROME

By

H. A. GUERBER

AUTHOR OF "MYTHS OF THE NORSEMEN"
"MYTHS AND LEGENDS OF THE MIDDLE AGES" ETC.

Revised by

DOROTHY MARGARET STUART

WITH FORTY-NINE REPRODUCTIONS FROM
FAMOUS PICTURES AND STATUES

LONDON
GEORGE G. HARRAP & CO. LTD.
SYDNEY   TORONTO   BOMBAY   STOCKHOLM

First published 1907
by GEORGE G. HARRAP & CO. LTD.
182 *High Holborn, London, W.C.*1

Reprinted : December 1907; *July* 1908; *September* 1909
October 1910; *May* 1911; *December* 1911; *December* 1912;
September 1915; *December* 1917; *February* 1919;
May 1920; *October* 1921; *January* 1923; *June*
1924; *June* 1925; *June* 1926; *June* 1927;
February 1929; *March* 1931;
November 1934

NEW EDITION, REVISED, *first published* 1938
Reset and Reprinted June 1943
Reprinted: November 1944; *July* 1946; *June* 1948

THIS BOOK IS PRODUCED IN
COMPLETE CONFORMITY WITH THE
AUTHORIZED ECONOMY STANDARDS

Composed in Plantin type and printed by William Clowes & Sons, Limited,
London and Beccles

Made in Great Britain

PREFACE TO THE
REVISED EDITION

DURING the thirty years which have passed since the publication of the first edition of this book many once widely accepted theories concerning the origin and meaning of Greek and Roman myths have been discredited, and much new light has been thrown upon their archæological background; but the importance of classical mythology from an educational standpoint has never been more generally recognized than it is to-day.

It is not only in the field of literature that the myths of Greece and Rome constantly appear and reappear; they are implicit in the everyday speech of educated men and women all over the civilized world, and even in the most casual and ephemeral branches of journalism we find the song of the Sirens, the shirt of Nessus, the vultures of Prometheus, and the heel of Achilles. In the field of art, architecture, and sculpture ignorance of classical legend makes much meaningless which would otherwise be charged with familiar significance; and in commerce also the old gods are made to serve modern ends.

Guerber's work has now been carefully revised; more frequent use has been made of the original texts of Theocritus, Ovid, and Apuleius, and the English summaries of the *Iliad*, *Odyssey*, and *Æneid* have been brought into closer accord with the epic narratives of Homer and Virgil. The English literary allusions have also been overhauled and greatly augmented.

The Greek in preference to the Roman form of names—*e.g.*, Zeus rather than Jupiter—has been adopted in this edition. This will serve to remind the reader that the Greek gods were the forerunners and progenitors of the Roman.

Several publishers have courteously given permission for the inclusion of passages from works not yet out of copyright. Unless otherwise stated, English versions of Greek and Roman texts have been specially made by Miss M. Bruce.

THE MYTHS IN
SONG AND STORY

7

THE MYTHS IN
PAINTING AND SCULPTURE

9

CHAPTER I

THE BEGINNING

MYTHOLOGY is the science treating of the legends and fables of the ancient world. Though we now call these 'myths,' which is practically the same thing as calling them fairy-tales, we must not forget that to the Greeks and Romans they were part of their religion. Among all the pre-Christian races who were sufficiently advanced to think, speak, and write about their religious beliefs the Jews alone claimed to have received a direct revelation from God, and the Jews alone declared that there was but one God, eternal and almighty. Other nations " deemed either fire, or wind, or the swift air, or the circle of the stars, or the violent water, or the lights of heaven to be the gods which govern the world "; and to those gods they gave a great diversity of names, and round them they wove an immense variety of fables.

These fables were handed down by word of mouth, from one generation to another, long before the art of writing was invented. Many of the earliest show that men soon began to wonder how the world around them, the sky over their heads, the birds, the beasts, all the wonders of Nature, and especially they themselves, came into being. They were not slow to realize that none of these things 'just happened,' and their ideas upon the subject were clothed in mythical language.

A Greek poet called Hesiod, who lived about eight centuries before Christ, wrote down many of the myths current among the Greeks of his time.

Among the Romans, at the beginning of the Christian era, a poet called Ovid put into verse the views then generally held by thoughtful pagans:

> Ere land or water was, or circling sky,
> Throughout the world Nature was uniform,
> What men call Chaos, shapeless and obscure,
> Where seethed the germs of things as yet to be.
>
> Not yet the pure light of the sun shone down,
> Not yet the moon renewed her crescent horns;

No globe hung poised in the enfolding air,
Nor did the sea with its long arms embrace
The margent shores.   Such was this vague, dark world:
Nor earth nor water yet, nor hot nor cold,
Nor soft nor hard, but indeterminate.

Over this shapeless mass reigned a deity called Chaos, whose personal appearance could not be described, as there was no light by which he could be seen.   He shared his throne with his wife, the dark goddess of night, named Nyx or Nox, whose black robes and still blacker countenance did not tend to enliven the surrounding gloom.

These two divinities wearied of their power in the course of time, and called their son Erebus (Darkness) to their assistance. His first act was to dethrone and supplant Chaos; and then, thinking he would be happier with a helpmeet, he married his own mother, Nyx.   The ancients, who at first had no fixed laws, did not consider this union unsuitable, but recounted how Erebus and Nyx ruled over the chaotic world together, until their two beautiful children, Æther (Light) and Hemera (Day), acting in concert, dethroned them, and seized the supreme power.

Space, illumined for the first time by their radiance, revealed itself in all its uncouthness. Æther and Hemera carefully examined the confusion, saw its many possibilities, and decided to evolve from it a " thing of beauty "; but quite conscious of the magnitude of such an undertaking, and feeling that some assistance would be desirable, they summoned Eros (Amor, or Love), their own child, to their aid.   By their combined efforts Pontus (the Sea) and Gæa (Ge, Tellus, Terra), as the Earth was first called, were created.

In the beginning the Earth was not full of loveliness, as it is now.   No trees waved their leafy branches on the hillsides; no flowers blossomed in the valleys; no grass grew on the plains; no birds flew through the air.   All was silent, bare, and motionless. Eros, the first to perceive these deficiencies, seized his life-giving arrows and pierced the cold Earth. Immediately the brown surface was covered with rich green; birds of many colours flitted through the foliage of the new-born forest trees; animals of all kinds gambolled over the grassy plains; and swift-darting fishes swam in the clear streams. All was now life, joy, and motion.

There was the Heaven and Earth at first,
And Light and Love; then Saturn from whose throne
Time fell, an envious shadow: such the state
Of the earth's primal spirits 'neath his sway,
As the calm joy of flowers and living leaves
Before the wind or sun has withered them.

SHELLEY

Gæa, roused from her apathy, admired all that had already been done to beautify her, and, resolving to crown and complete the work so well begun, created Uranus (Heaven).

This version of the creation of the world, although but one of the many current with the Greeks and Romans, was the one most generally adopted.

Her first-born Earth produc'd,
Of like immensity, the starry Heaven;
That he might sheltering compass her around
On every side.

HESIOD (Elton's tr.)

Another popular version stated that the first divinities, Erebus and Nyx, produced a gigantic egg, from which Eros, the god of love, emerged to create the Earth.

The Earth thus created was supposed by the ancients to be a disc, instead of a sphere, as science has proved. The Greeks fancied that their country occupied a central position, and that Mount Olympus, a very high mountain, the legendary abode of their gods, was placed in the exact centre. Their Earth was divided into two equal parts by Pontus (the Sea—equivalent to our Mediterranean and Black Seas); and all around it flowed the great river Oceanus in a " steady, equable current," undisturbed by storm, from which the Sea and all the rivers were supposed to derive their waters.

The Greeks also imagined that the portion of the Earth directly north of their country was inhabited by a fortunate race of men, the " blameless Hyperboreans," who dwelt in continual happiness, and enjoyed a never-ending springtide. Their homes were said to be " inaccessible by land or by sea." They were " exempt from disease, old age, and death," and were so virtuous that the gods frequently visited them, and even condescended to share their feasts and games. A people thus favoured could not fail to be happy, and many were the songs in praise of their sunny land.

South of Greece, also near the great river Oceanus, dwelt

another nation, just as happy and virtuous as the Hyperboreans—the Ethiopians.   They too often enjoyed the company of the gods, who shared their innocent pleasures with great delight.

Far away, in this same marvellous river, according to the poet Homer, were the beautiful Isles of the Blest, sometimes called the Elysian Fields, where mortals who had led virtuous lives, and had thus found favour in the sight of the gods, were transported without tasting of death, and where they enjoyed an eternity of bliss. These islands had sun, moon, and stars of their own, and were never visited by the cold wintry winds that swept down from the north.

Here is a life that of all is the lightest for earth-born mortals :
Here comes never the snow, nor a violent tempest and rain-storm ;
Here incessantly breatheth the breeze of the soft-voiced Zephyr
Sent by the ocean to bring to the land and its dwellers refreshment.
HOMER'S "ODYSSEY" (*Cotterill's tr.*)

The king of this happy realm was called Rhadamanthus.   He was a son of Zeus and Europa, whose legend will be related in due course.

Erebus and Nyx were deprived of their power by Æther and Hemera, who did not long enjoy the possession of the sceptre; for Uranus and Gæa soon forced them to depart, and began to reign in their stead.   They had not dwelt long on the summit of Mount Olympus before they found themselves the parents of twelve gigantic children, whose strength was such that their father, Uranus, greatly feared them.   To prevent their ever making use of it against him he seized them immediately after their birth, hurled them down into a dark abyss called Tartarus, and there chained them fast.   These giants were called 'Titans,' and we still use the word ' titanic ' to describe something of vast size. Thus early did the giant appear in legend.

This chasm was situated far under the earth; and Uranus knew that his six sons (Oceanus, Cœus, Creus, Hyperion, Iapetus, and Cronus), as well as his six daughters, the Titanides (Ilia, Rhea, Themis, Thetis, Mnemosyne, and Phœbe), could not easily escape from its cavernous depths.   The Titans did not long remain the sole occupants of Tartarus, for one day the brazen doors were again thrown wide open to admit the three one-eyed Cyclopes—Brontes (Thunder), Steropes (Lightning), and Arges (Sheet-lightning)—later-born children of Uranus and Gæa, who helped the Titans to make the darkness hideous with their incessant clamour for freedom. In due time their number was increased by the three terrible Centimani (Hundred-handed), Cottus, Briareus, and Gyges, who were sent thither by Uranus to share their fate.

Dissatisfied with the treatment her children had received at their father's hands, Gæa remonstrated, but all in vain. Uranus would not grant her request to set the giants free, and whenever their muffled cries reached his ear he trembled for his own safety. Angry beyond all expression, Gæa swore revenge, and descended into Tartarus, where she urged the Titans to conspire against their father and attempt to wrest the sceptre from his grasp.

The only one of the Titans who had the courage to obey her was the youngest, Cronus. He was called Saturn by the Romans, and from the resemblance between his name and the Greek word *chronos*, meaning ' time,' was early identified with Time, the devourer of all things. Gæa set him free, gave him a scythe, and sent him forth, bidding him return victorious.

Thus armed and admonished, Cronus came upon his father unawares, defeated him, thanks to his extraordinary weapon, and after binding him fast took possession of the vacant throne, intending to rule the universe for ever. Enraged at this insult, Uranus cursed his son, and prophesied that a day would come when he too would be supplanted by his children.

Cronus paid no heed to his father's imprecations, but calmly proceeded to release the Titans, his brothers and sisters, who in their joy and gratitude at escaping from the dismal realm of Tartarus expressed their willingness to be ruled by him. He chose his own sister, Rhea (Cybele, Ops), for his consort, and assigned to each of the others some portion of the world to govern. To Oceanus and Thetis, for example, he gave charge over the ocean and all the rivers upon earth; while to Hyperion and Phœbe he entrusted the direction of the sun and moon, which the ancients supposed were daily and nightly driven across the sky in shining chariots.

Peace and security now reigned on and around Mount Olympus; and Cronus congratulated himself on the result of his enterprise. One fine morning, however, he was told that a son had been born to him. The memory of his father's curse then suddenly returned to his mind. Anxious to avert the loss of his power, he hastened to his wife, determined to devour the child, and thus prevent him from causing further annoyance. Gladly Rhea placed the baby in his extended arms; but imagine her surprise and horror when she beheld it disappear down his gigantic throat!

Time passed, and another child was born, but only to meet with the same cruel fate. One infant after another disappeared, devoured by 'Time,' which creates only to destroy. In vain the bereaved mother besought the life of one little one: the hard-hearted father would not relent. As her prayers seemed unavailing, Rhea finally resolved to obtain by stratagem what her husband denied; and as soon as her youngest son, Zeus (called by the Romans Jove or Jupiter), was born she concealed him.

Cronus, aware of his birth, soon made his appearance, determined to dispose of him in the usual summary manner. For some time Rhea pleaded with him, but at last pretended to yield to his commands. Hastily wrapping a large stone in swaddling clothes, she handed it to Cronus, feigning intense grief. Cronus was evidently not of a very inquiring turn of mind, for he swallowed the whole without investigating the real contents of the shapeless bundle.

He seems to have had a very powerful digestive system, for he did not realize how he had been deceived, and Rhea then cast about for some means by which she could continue to conceal the deception.

To ensure this she entrusted her babe to the tender care of the Melian nymphs, who bore him off to a cave on Mount Ida. There a goat, Amalthea, was procured to act as nurse, and fulfilled her office so well that she was eventually placed in the heavens as a constellation. To prevent Zeus's cries being heard in Olympus the Curetes (Corybantes), Rhea's priests, uttered piercing screams, clashed their weapons, executed fierce dances, and chanted rude war-songs.

The real significance of all this unwonted noise and commotion was not at first understood by Cronus, who in the intervals of his numerous affairs congratulated himself upon the cunning he had shown to prevent the accomplishment of his father's curse. But all his fears were aroused when he suddenly became aware of the fraud practised upon him, and of young Zeus's continued existence. He immediately tried to devise some plan to get rid of him; but before he could put it into execution he found himself attacked by his son, and after a short but terrible encounter he was signally defeated.

Zeus, delighted to have triumphed so quickly, took possession of the supreme power, and aided by Rhea's counsels, and by a nauseous potion prepared by Metis, a daughter of Oceanus, compelled Cronus to produce the unfortunate children he had swallowed—Poseidon, Pluto, Hestia, Demeter, and Hera (called by the Romans Neptune, Pluto, Vesta, Ceres, and Juno). The stone substituted by Rhea for the infant Zeus also came to light, and was afterwards piously preserved at Delphi.

Following the example of his predecessor, Zeus gave his brothers and sisters a fair share of his new kingdom. The wisest among the Titans—Mnemosyne, Themis, Oceanus, and Hyperion —submitted to the new sovereign without murmur, but the others refused their allegiance; which refusal, of course, occasioned a deadly conflict.

> When gods began with wrath,
> And war rose up between their starry brows,
> Some choosing to cast Cronus from his throne
> That Zeus might king it there, and some in haste
> With opposite oaths that they would have no Zeus
> To rule the gods for ever.
>
> E. B. BROWNING

THE GIANTS' WAR

Zeus, from the top of Mount Olympus, saw the superior numbers of his foes, and, quite aware of their might, cast about him for allies. In haste, therefore, he released the Cyclopes from Tartarus, where they had languished so long, stipulating that in exchange for their freedom they should supply him with thunderbolts—weapons which only they knew how to forge. This new engine caused great terror and dismay in the ranks of the enemy, who, nevertheless, soon rallied, and struggled valiantly to overthrow the usurper and win back the sovereignty of the world.

During ten long years the war raged incessantly, but at the end of that time the rebellious Titans were obliged to yield. Some of them were hurled into Tartarus once more, where they were carefully secured by Poseidon, Zeus's brother, while the young conqueror joyfully proclaimed his victory.

> League all your forces then, ye powers above,
> Join all, and try th' omnipotence of Jove;
> Let down our golden everlasting chain,
> Whose strong embrace holds heaven and earth and main:
> Strive all, of mortal and immortal birth,
> To drag, by this, the Thunderer down to earth.
> Ye strive in vain! if I but stretch this hand,
> I heave the gods, the ocean, and the land;
> I fix the chain to great Olympus' height,
> And the vast world hangs trembling in my sight!
> For such I reign, unbounded and above;
> And such are men and gods, compar'd to Jove.
>
> HOMER (*Pope's tr.*)

The scene of this mighty conflict was supposed to have been in Thessaly, where the country bears the imprint of some great natural convulsion; for the ancients imagined that the gods, making the most of their gigantic strength and stature, hurled huge rocks at each other, and piled mountain upon mountain to reach the abode of Zeus the Thunderer.

Cronus (or Saturn) withdrew to Hesperia (Italy), where he founded a prosperous kingdom, and reigned in peace for many long years. In his old age he seems to have become quite a pleasant person.

Zeus, having disposed of all the Titans, now fancied he would enjoy the power so unlawfully obtained; but Gæa, to punish him for depriving her children of their birthright, created a terrible monster, called Typhœus, or Typhon—" Typhon huge, ending in snaky twine," as Milton calls him. This Typhœus was a giant, from whose body one hundred dragon heads arose; flames shot from his eyes, nostrils, and mouths; while he incessantly uttered such blood-curdling screams that the gods in terror fled from Mount Olympus and sought refuge in Egypt. In mortal fear lest this terror-inspiring monster should pursue them, they there assumed the forms of different animals, and Zeus became a ram, while Hera, his sister and queen, changed herself into a cow.

The king of the gods, however, soon became ashamed of his cowardly flight, and resolved to return to Mount Olympus to slay Typhœus with his terrible thunderbolts. A long and fierce

The Childhood of Zeus
G. F. Watts
By permission of Mr Frederick Hollyer

Enceladus under Mount Ætna
B. Picart

struggle ensued, at the end of which Zeus, again victorious, viewed his fallen foe with arrogant pride; but his triumph was very short-lived.

Enceladus, another redoubtable giant, also created by Gæa, now appeared to avenge Typhœus. He too was signally defeated, and bound with adamantine chains in a burning cave under Mount Ætna. In early times, before he had become accustomed to his prison, he gave vent to his rage by outcries, imprecations, and groans; sometimes he even breathed forth fire and flames, in hopes of injuring his conqueror. But time, it is said, somewhat cooled his resentment; and now he is content with an occasional change of position, which, owing to his huge size, causes the earth to tremble over a space of many miles, producing what is called an earthquake.

This myth is one of several invented by the ancients to explain such natural phenomena as earthquakes and volcanic eruptions.

> 'Tis said, that thunder-struck Enceladus,
> Grovelling beneath the incumbent mountain's weight,
> Lies stretched supine, eternal prey of flames;
> And, when he heaves against the burning load,
> Reluctant, to invert his broiling limbs,
> A sudden earthquake shoots through all the isle,
> And Ætna thunders dreadful under ground,
> Then pours out smoke in wreathing curls convolved,
> And shades the sun's bright orb, and blots out day.
>
> ADDISON

Zeus had now conquered all his foes, asserted his right to the throne, and could at last reign over the world undisturbed; but he knew that it would be no small undertaking to rule well heaven, earth, and sea, and resolved to divide the power with his brothers. To avoid quarrels and recriminations he portioned out the world, allowing each of his brothers the privilege of drawing his own share.

Poseidon thus obtained control over the sea and all the rivers, and immediately determined to wear a symbolic crown, composed exclusively of sea-shells and water-plants, and to remain within the bounds of his watery realm.

Pluto, the most taciturn of the brothers, received for his portion the sceptre of Tartarus and all the Lower World, where no beam of sunlight was ever allowed to find its way; while Zeus reserved for himself the general supervision of his brothers' estates, and the direct management of Heaven and Earth.

Peace now reigned throughout all the world. Not a murmur was heard, except from the Titans, who at length, seeing that further opposition would be useless, grew reconciled to their fate.

In the days of their prosperity the Titans had intermarried. Cronus had taken Rhea " for better or for worse "; and Iapetus had seen, loved, and wedded the fair Clymene, one of the ocean nymphs, or Oceanides, daughters of Oceanus. This last pair became the proud parents of four gigantic sons—Atlas, Menetius, Prometheus (Forethought), and Epimetheus (Afterthought)—who were destined to play prominent parts in Greek mythology. Atlas we shall meet later. His name is very familiar, as it has been given not only to a range of mountains in Africa, but also to books of maps innumerable in Europe and America.

THE STORY OF PROMETHEUS

In the great conflict between Cronus and Zeus Prometheus, unlike his father Iapetus, had ranged himself with the Olympian gods. He was now chosen by Zeus to direct the important task of creating living beings to inhabit the empty though beautiful world. In this undertaking he was aided by his brother Epimetheus. Together they made birds, beasts, and fishes, giving to each gifts of strength, swiftness, beauty, or intelligence according to their different needs, but it was Prometheus who last of all brought into existence the most intelligent though not the strongest, or the swiftest, or the most beautiful of creatures— Man.

From a lump of clay kneaded with water Prometheus wrought an image resembling the high gods themselves, an image standing upright, with its head lifted to gaze upon the stars. But Epimetheus had been so lavish with his gifts to the other new beings that his elder brother decided to endow Man with a gift which should surpass all the rest—the gift of fire. Prometheus soared heavenward and lit his torch at the eternal lamp of the sun. Then he descended to earth and bestowed upon humanity the divine spark which, in the fullness of time, was to flame up into knowledge, art, commerce, and civilization. Hence the metaphor, so dear to poets, of ' Promethean fire.'

Then, according to the ancient poets, came the true Age of Gold, when men were, as they have never been since, happy, sinless, and peaceful. This was the legend in Milton's mind when, speaking of the angels' song " On the Morning of Christ's Nativity," he wrote:

> For, if such holy song
> Enwrap our fancy long,
>   Time will run back, and fetch the Age of Gold;
> And speckled Vanity
> Will sicken soon and die,
>   And leprous Sin will melt from earthly mould;
> And Hell itself will pass away,
> And leave her dol'rous mansions to the peering Day.
>
> Yea, Truth and Justice then
> Will down return to Men,
>   Orbed in a rainbow; and, like glories wearing,
> Mercy will sit between,
> Throned in celestial sheen,
>   With radiant feet the tissued clouds down-steering;
> And Heav'n, as at some festival,
> Will open wide the gates of her high palace hall.

This Age of Gold was in some ways a rather monotonous time. The year was not divided into seasons, and perpetual spring reigned. The men who dwelt in this paradise had neither wives nor daughters—they were like Adam before the creation of Eve. They did not work—why should they, when the earth brought forth everything that they needed? They had no arts or crafts. The plough, the loom, the potter's wheel, were as yet unknown.

Then came the Age of Silver, when Zeus divided the year into seasons, and for the first time mankind suffered the hardships of wind and weather. They took refuge in caves, instead of dwelling happily in the open air. They had to plough and sow instead of harvesting rich crops which had sprung up of their own accord. The discipline of rough weather and hard work seems to have had anything but a good effect upon men. Soon they began to neglect the altars of the Olympian gods, and presently they had the audacity to dispute with Zeus himself, and to claim greater privileges than the All-Highest was disposed to grant.

Prometheus sided with the presumptuous creatures he had made, and, endeavouring to settle one disagreement in their favour, he played upon Zeus a trick which the god never forgot or forgave. The question at issue was what portions of an animal sacrifice should be dedicated to the gods, and what should belong to man. Prometheus divided a sacrificial ox into two, and having stuffed the eatable parts into the skin he slyly put a heap of ugly odd bits on the top; then he covered the bones with what looked like fat, and invited Zeus to choose between the two.

According to one version of the story, the god chose the more attractive alternative, and was very wroth when he found nothing but bones inside; according to another version, he saw through the trick, but pretended to be deceived, in order to have an excuse for punishing the now detested human race. This punishment was to deprive them of fire, but once more Prometheus came to their rescue, and brought the precious flame down from the sky in a hollow fennel-stalk. Such a hollow stalk is still used as a primitive means of carrying a light in some of the isles of Greece.

Zeus inflicted upon the Titan a terrible penalty. Chained to a craggy peak of Mount Caucasus, Prometheus was doomed to have his liver gnawed all day by a vulture. By night what had been devoured grew again, so that the ghastly process should be renewed the next morning. This agony continued for many centuries, until at last Herakles (Hercules) slew the vulture and set its victim free. According to Æschylus the Titan suffered for thirty thousand years.

> Titan! to whose immortal eyes
>   The sufferings of mortality,
>   Seen in their sad reality,
> Were not as things that gods despise;
> What was thy pity's recompense?
> A silent suffering and intense;
> The rock, the vulture, and the chain,
> All that the proud can feel of pain.
>   BYRON: *Prometheus*

Meanwhile the vindictive Zeus had resolved, with the aid and approval of his fellow-gods, to mete out an overwhelming punishment to man. This was the creation of woman!

Having endowed her with beauty, charm, a sweet voice, a graceful walk, an appealing manner, they called her Pandora, the gift of *all* the gods, and Hermes (Mercury), the messenger of the immortals, escorted her down to earth and presented her to Prometheus, who was not then fettered to his Caucasian crag. Distrustful of Zeus and all his works, Prometheus turned his back resolutely on the lovely newcomer; but his more confiding young brother Epimetheus received her with joy.

By way of a dowry Pandora had brought with her, as a gift from Zeus himself, a sealed casket, which she had been solemnly warned not to open. The All-Highest had apparently realized that curiosity would be one of the characteristics of the new creature which he had invented to be the curse of man, for it was his intention that she *should* open the mysterious casket, and before very long she *did*. And then, alack! out flew a swarm of evil sprites, all the bodily and mental ills that ever since have tormented the human race: out flew rheumatism, gout, blindness, and deafness; out flew malice, pride, cruelty, and covetousness, each uglier and more malignant than the last. They darkened the air with their dusky wings, and Pandora recoiled in terror from what she had done. But in the very bottom of the casket there remained one sprite whose wings were not dusky—a little golden being whose name was Hope. Thus did the gods, with a torch of divine pity, light up the shadow which then descended upon man.

After the Age of Silver came the Age of Brass, or Bronze, wilder than the earlier ages, yet not wholly evil. And then came the graceless and sinister Age of Iron, when men's ways were so wicked that one by one the good divinities deserted them, the last to depart being Astræa, the goddess of innocence, daughter of Themis, the goddess of justice. Ancient poets used to prophesy that these goddesses would return to earth when another Golden Age should dawn. This is the idea behind the title of John Dryden's poem on the Restoration, *Astræa Redux.* (Compare the stanzas from Milton quoted earlier in this chapter.)

Zeus had kept a close watch over men's actions during all these years; and their evil conduct aroused his wrath to such a point that he vowed he would blot out the human race. But as he could not decide which would be the best way to do this, he summoned the gods to aid him by their counsels. The first suggestion offered was to destroy the world by fire, kindled by Zeus's much-dreaded thunderbolts; and the king of gods was about to put it into instant execution, when his arm was stayed by the reminder that the rising flames might set fire to his own dwelling-place, and reduce its magnificence to ashes. He therefore rejected the plan as impracticable, and bade the gods devise other means of destruction.

After much delay and discussion the immortals agreed to wash mankind off the face of the earth by a mighty flood. The winds were instructed to gather the rain-clouds over the earth. Poseidon let loose the waves of the sea, bidding them rise, overflow, and deluge the land. No sooner had the gods spoken than the elements obeyed: the winds blew; the rain fell in torrents; lakes, seas, rivers, and oceans broke their bonds; and terrified mortals, forgetting their petty quarrels in a common impulse to flee from the death which threatened them, climbed the highest mountains, clung to uprooted trees, and even took refuge in the light skiffs they had constructed in happier days. Their efforts were all in vain, however, for the waters rose higher and higher, overtook them one after another in their ineffectual efforts to escape, closed over the homes where they might have been so happy, and drowned their last despairing cries in their seething depths.

DEUCALION AND PYRRHA

The rain continued to fall, until, after many days, the waves covered all the surface of the earth except the summit of Mount Parnassus, the highest peak in Greece. On this mountain, surrounded by the ever-rising flood, stood the son of Prometheus, Deucalion, with his faithful wife Pyrrha, a daughter of Epimetheus and Pandora. From thence they, the sole survivors, viewed the universal desolation with tear-dimmed eyes.

In a world of wicked mortals these two had lived righteously; and when Zeus saw them there alone, and remembered their goodness, he decided not to include them in the general destruction, but to save their lives. He therefore bade the winds return to their cave and the rain to cease. Poseidon blew a resounding blast upon his conch-shell to recall the wandering waves, which immediately returned within their usual bounds.

Deucalion and Pyrrha followed the receding waves step by step down the steep mountain-side.

At length the world was all restor'd to view,
But desolate, and of a sickly hue;
Nature beheld herself, and stood aghast,
A dismal desert and a silent waste.
OVID (*Dryden's tr.*)

As they talked upon how they should repeople the desolate earth they came to the shrine of Delphi, the dwelling of a famous oracle, which alone had been able to resist the force of the waves. There they entered to consult the wishes of the gods. Their surprise and horror were unbounded, however, when a voice exclaimed, " Depart from hence with veiled heads, and cast your mothers' bones behind you! " To obey such a command seemed nothing less than sacrilege; for the dead had always been held in deep veneration by the Greeks, and the desecration of a grave was considered a heinous crime, and punished accordingly. But, they reasoned, the god's oracles can seldom be accepted in a literal sense; and Deucalion, after due thought, explained to Pyrrha what he conceived to be the meaning of this mysterious command.

" The Earth," said he, " is the mother of all, and the stones may be considered her bones." Husband and wife speedily decided to act upon this theory, and continued their descent, casting stones behind them. All those thrown by Deucalion were immediately changed into men, while those cast by Pyrrha became women.

Thus the earth was peopled for the second time with a race of good men, sent to replace the wicked beings slain by Zeus. Deucalion and Pyrrha shortly after became the happy parents of a son named Hellen, who gave his name to all the Hellenic or Greek race; while his sons, Æolus and Dorus, and grandsons, Ion and Achæus, became the ancestors of the Æolian, Dorian, Ionian, and Achaian nations.

Other mythologists, in treating of the flood myths, state that Deucalion and Pyrrha took refuge in an ark, which, after sailing about for many days, was stranded on the top of Mount Parnassus. This version was far less popular with the Greeks, although it betrays still more plainly the common source whence all these myths are derived.

CHAPTER II

ZEUS

ZEUS, Jupiter, or Jove, the All-Highest Thunderer, king of the gods, supreme ruler of the universe, the special deity of mankind, the personification of the sky and of all the phenomena of the air, and the guardian of political order and peace, was the most prominent of all the Olympian divinities: the others were obliged to submit to his will, and trembled at his all-powerful nod.

> He, whose all-conscious eyes the world behold,
> The eternal Thunderer sat, enthroned in gold,
> High heaven the footstool of his feet he makes,
> And wide beneath him all Olympus shakes.

> He spoke, and awful bends his sable brows,
> Shakes his ambrosial curls, and gives the nod,
> The stamp of fate and sanction of the god:
> High heaven with trembling the dread signal took,
> And all Olympus to the centre shook.
>
> H O M E R (Pope's tr.)

The Fates and Destiny alone dared oppose his sovereign will, and they continued to issue their irrevocable decrees even after he supplanted his father and began to rule over all.

In common with all other Greek and Roman divinities, Zeus, though immortal, was subject to pleasure, pain, grief, and anger, and a prey to all the passions which rule the hearts of men.

It was he who presided at the councils held on the top of "many-peaked Olympus," and summoned the gods whenever he wished to discuss with them any matter of importance, or to indulge in a banquet, when they ate the celestial ambrosia and quaffed the fragrant nectar.

He is generally represented as a tall, majestic figure, with long curling hair and beard, clad in flowing drapery, his redoubtable thunderbolts or sceptre in one hand and a statue of Victory in the other. Sometimes he is seen wearing a breastplate of storm-cloud "like the skin of a grey goat." The world is his footstool; and the eagle, emblem of strength and power, is usually seen close beside him. His oracle was at Dodona, in an oak-grove, where his priests interpreted the sounds made by the rustling of the branches.

HIS ATTENDANTS

Zeus had his own special attendants, such as Nike (Victoria), the goddess of victory, who was ever ready to obey his slightest behest, and it is said her master loved her so dearly that he generally held an image of her in his hand. His cup-bearer was Hebe.

Jupiter, the Roman form of Zeus, was often represented as being attended by Fama, the goddess of fame, with a trumpet in her hand, or by Fortuna, the goddess of chance, with her wheel.

It happened that Zeus found himself in need of a cupbearer to replace Hebe, who had become the wife of the hero Herakles. He assumed the form of an eagle, and winged his flight over the earth. He had not flown far before he beheld a youth of marvellous beauty, alone on Mount Ida. To swoop down, catch him up in his mighty talons, and bear him safely off to Olympus was but a moment's work; and there the kidnapped youth, Ganymede, the son of a king of Troy, was carefully instructed in the duties he was called upon to perform.

Hephæstus (Vulcan) is also represented as acting sometimes as cup-bearer at the Olympian banquets.

PHILEMON AND BAUCIS

As centuries passed Zeus seems to have become less resentful in his attitude towards the human race. Sometimes he would assume the outward aspect of a mortal and descend from Olympus to mingle unrecognized with mankind. On one such occasion, accompanied by Hermes, also disguised, the All-Highest journeyed through the land of Phrygia. Pretending to be poor wayfarers, they knocked at the doors of many houses, but not one was opened to them. At last, however, they reached the thatched hut of a good old couple called Philemon and Baucis, and there they received a courteous and kindly welcome. Philemon drew forward a bench for them to sit on, Baucis brought them a beechwood bowl of water that they might wash their hands. Then the old woman raked out the fire, heaped on more fuel, and began to prepare a simple supper of pot-herbs and bacon.

The table had one leg shorter than the other three, but a slab of slate was slipped underneath to keep it from wobbling. Baucis wiped the top with some sweet-smelling leaves and then set forth the earthenware dishes and pitchers and the wooden cups, which were all she had. For supper she gave the travellers olives, cornel berries preserved in vinegar, radishes and cheese, and eggs cooked in the hot ashes. Then stewed bacon followed, and, by way of dessert, apples and wild honey. Wine, not very old or rare, washed down the simple repast.

Presently Philemon and Baucis noticed with surprise that as fast as they emptied the pitcher it filled itself up again with wine. Realizing that their guests were not mortals like themselves, the good old couple fell on their knees, craving pardon for the poverty of the meal. The only thing they could think of to make it better was to kill the old—and probably tough—goose, which they kept rather as a pet than with any culinary intentions. But the goose had other views, and strenuously resisted all attempts at capture. Finally it took refuge between the two gods, who declared that it should not be sacrificed. They had less pity, however, upon the inhospitable village where no one had been willing to give them shelter for the night. This they drowned in a deep lake, only the spot where the house of Philemon and Baucis stood being raised above the waters. This house Zeus changed into a magnificent temple, of which he decreed that Philemon and Baucis should henceforth be the priest and priestess. " O, good old man," said the god to them, " and you, woman worthy of such a husband, speak: what boon do you ask of us? " The two took counsel for a short space, and then told Zeus that they had but one wish between them—that their lives might end at " one and the same hour."

The prayer was granted. After ministering in the temple for many years they were suddenly changed into two trees, an oak and a linden. " These trees," Ovid tells us, " the Tyanean shepherd still shows, growing side by side."

Although married to Hera, Zeus often indulged in love affairs with other goddesses, and even with mortal women, whom he wooed in various disguises. The ancients did not demand a high standard of conduct from their gods, to whom they ascribed the

passions and foibles of quite ordinary men; hence it follows that
worship and veneration as the Jew and the Christian understood
them were outside the ken of the pagan world.

THE STORY OF EUROPA

Hera being of a very jealous disposition, Zeus was forced to conduct his courtships with great secrecy, and therefore generally
adopted the precaution of a disguise.   To win Europa, the fair
daughter of Agenor, King of Phœnicia, for instance, he became a
bull.

> The gods themselves,
> Humbling their deities to love, have taken
> The shapes of beasts upon them.   Jupiter
> Became a bull, and bellow'd.
>
> SHAKESPEARE

One day Europa was playing in her father's meadows, gathering
flowers with other young maidens, when she suddenly saw a white
bull coming towards her, not with fiery eyes and lowered horns,
but gently, as if to express a mute request to be stroked.   Delighted, she patted the beast, and decked him with bright garlands
of meadow-blossoms.   Then, seeing him kneel as if to invite her
to mount, she lightly sprang upon his broad back, calling to her
companions to follow her example; but before they could do as
she wished the bull had risen to his feet and galloped off towards
the sea with his fair burden on his back.

Instead of turning when he saw the foam-crested waves, he
plunged into the midst of them, and in a few minutes disappeared,
so rapidly did he swim away.   To reassure the frightened girl the
bull now spoke in gentle accents, bidding her dismiss all fear.

As Zeus swam through the waves dolphins sported round him,
Nereides riding on the backs of sea-monsters rose from the salt
spray, while the Tritons blew a cheerful blast on their conch-
shells.   Europa, clinging to one of the bull's horns, and holding
up the hem of her purple gown lest it should be stained with sea-
water, spoke thus in her amazement: " Whither dost thou bear
me?   What manner of beast art thou, that fearest not the path of
the sea-dwellers?   Surely thou art some god! "

" Fear not, maiden," answered the bull-god. " Lo, I am
Zeus, and it is for thy love that I breast the waves in the shape
of a bull. The island of Crete shall be our dwelling and thy
home."

In Crete, therefore, Europa dwelt, and there she bore three
sons, Minos, Rhadamanthus, and Sarpedon. The eldest became
King of Crete, and after his death, together with the second son,
sat as judge in the land of shadows. The youngest, Sarpedon,
fell in the Trojan war.[1]

Agenor, whose favourite Europa had always been, rent his garments in grief, and bade his sons, Phœnix, Cilix, and Cadmus, go
forth and seek her and not to return till they had found her.
Accompanied by their mother, Telephassa, they immediately set
out on their journey, inquiring of all they met if they had seen
their sister. Search and inquiry proved equally fruitless.

At last, weary of this hopeless quest, Phœnix refused his further
aid. Cilix too lost heart, and settled in a fertile country which
they had reached, hence called Cilicia; and finally Telephassa,
worn out with grief and fatigue, lay down to die, charging her
eldest son to go on alone.

Cadmus wandered on till he came to Delphi, where he consulted the oracle; but the only reply he received was, " There
where you shall see a young heifer stop in the grass build a city and
call it Bœotia."

In deep perplexity he left the temple, and from force of habit
journeyed on, patiently questioning all he met. Soon he perceived a cow leisurely walking in front of him, and, mindful of the
oracle, he ceased his search and followed her. Urged by curiosity,
many adventurers joined him on the way, and when the cow at
last lay down in the land since called Bœotia they all promised to
aid Cadmus, their chosen leader, to found their future capital,
afterwards called Thebes.

Cadmus, desiring to make a sacrifice to the gods, sent his men
to a spring not far away. Time passed, and they did not return.
Armed with his trusty sword, Cadmus finally went down to the
spring to discover the cause of their delay and found that they had
all been devoured by a huge dragon which lived in the hollow.

---

[1] According to some authorities, Sarpedon's mother was not Europa, but
Laodamia, daughter of Bellerophon.

Zeus
Capitol, Rome

Pandora
Harry Bates
(*Page* 23)

The prince raised his sword to avenge their death, and, in the real manner of a hero, slew the creature with one blow.

While Cadmus stood there contemplating his lifeless foe a voice bade him extract the dragon's teeth and sow them in the ground already broken for his future city. No human being was within sight, so Cadmus knew the order proceeded from the immortal gods, and immediately prepared to obey it. The dragon's teeth were no sooner planted than a crop of men sprang from the soil, full-grown, and armed to the teeth. They were about to fall upon Cadmus when the same voice bade him cast a stone in the midst of their close-drawn phalanx. Cadmus, seeing the men were almost upon him and that no time was to be lost, quickly threw a stone. The effect produced was almost instantaneous, for the warriors, each fancying it had been thrown by his neighbour, began fighting among themselves. In a few minutes the number of armed men was reduced to five, who sheathed their bloodstained weapons, and humbly tendered their services to Cadmus. With their aid the foundations of the city were laid; but their labour was not very arduous, as the gods caused some of the public buildings to rise up out of the ground all complete and ready for use.

To reward Cadmus for his faithful search for Europa Zeus gave him the hand of the fair princess Hermione, a daughter of Ares and Aphrodite, in marriage. Cadmus, the founder of Thebes, is supposed to have invented the alphabet, and introduced its use into Greece. Although his career was very prosperous at first, he finally incurred the wrath of the gods by forgetting, on a solemn occasion, to offer them a suitable sacrifice, and in anger they changed him and Hermione into huge serpents.

Zeus was very widely and generally worshipped by the ancients, and his principal temples—the Capitol at Rome and the shrine of Jupiter Ammon in Libya—were world-renowned. His also was the famous temple at Dodona, where an oak-tree gave forth mysterious prophecies, which were supposed to have been inspired by the king of gods; this long-lost shrine has now been discovered.

> Oh, where, Dodona! is thine aged grove,
> Prophetic fount, and oracle divine?
> What valley echoed the response of Jove?
> What trace remaineth of the Thunderer's shrine?
> All, all forgotten?
>
> BYRON

A magnificent temple at Olympia, on the Peloponnesus, was also dedicated to Zeus; and here every fifth year the people of Greece were wont to assemble to celebrate games, in honour of his great victory over the Titans.   These festivals were known as the Olympic Games; and the Greeks generally reckoned time by olympiads—that is to say, by the space of time between the celebrations.   Within the temple at Olympia stood a wonderful statue of gold and ivory, the work of Phidias, one of the most famous sculptors of the antique world.   Its proportions and beauty were such that it was counted one of the Seven Wonders of the ancient world.   It is said, too, that the artist, having completed this masterpiece, longed for some sign of approval from heaven, and fervently prayed for a token that the god accepted his labour.   Zeus, in answer to this prayer, sent a vivid flash of lightning, which played about the colossal image, illuminating it, but leaving it quite unharmed.

CHAPTER III

HERA

HERA (Juno) was the daughter of Cronus and Rhea, and spent her childhood with Oceanus and Tethys in the far-off western regions of the sea. She grew up very beautiful, and when Zeus had usurped the throne of the heavens he decided that she should be his queen. They were married in the garden of the gods, and in honour of the occasion a marvellous tree, bearing apples of gold, sprang out of the earth. These were the apples of the Hesperides, of which we shall hear more later.

Hera was honoured as the Queen of Heaven, and also as the patroness of all marriages, human and divine. In Shakespeare's *Tempest* she is represented, under her Roman name of Juno, as showering blessings on the wedding of Ferdinand and Miranda. Her sandals, her chariot, and her throne were all of pure gold, and the cow, the cuckoo, and the peacock were sacred to her. In art she is represented as a handsome, matronly figure, and Homer refers to her as the ' ox-eyed ' goddess.

Proud, revengeful, and jealous, Hera resented the fickleness of her husband's affections, and was wont to wreak her revenge on any being, mortal or divine, upon whom he looked with too much favour. She had her own messenger, the fleet-footed Iris, whose name means ' Rainbow,' and whose track through the clouds was marked by the colours of her many-coloured mantle as she sped upon Hera's errands.

The Greeks honoured Hera especially at Argos, Sparta, and Mycenæ. Though the family tree of the Olympian deities is often complicated and even contradictory, most mythologists agree that she had three children, Ares (Mars), the god of war, Hebe, and Hephæstus (Vulcan).

THE STORY OF IO

One of the semi-mortals of whom Hera was not unreasonably jealous was the maiden Io, a daughter of the river-god Inachus.

C

Zeus, anxious to elude the watchful eyes of his queen, changed Io into a sleek and beautiful heifer when he saw Hera descending through the dense cloud which he had created to hide his whereabouts.   Questioned as to the beast, he deceitfully replied that he had just created it from the earth; whereupon Hera begged that he would give his newest creation to her.   Even the king of gods dare not refuse such a simple and natural request.   Poor Io, still in the form of a cow, was led away and left to graze on a river bank, in the care of one of Hera's servants, the many-eyed Argus, who never closed more than two of his numerous eyes at one time. Meantime the river-god, her father, had been lamenting the disappearance of his daughter, whom he did not recognize until he noticed the young heifer scratching the name ' Io ' with her hoof on the river-bank.   Unfortunately Argus found the two of them together, and drove Inachus away.

Zeus now decided that in order to release Io it was necessary to get rid of her many-eyed guardian.   This task he entrusted to Hermes, who disguised himself as a shepherd, and, blowing a dreamy air upon his reed pipes, drove his flock towards the pasture where Argus sat watching over Io.   Argus, charmed by the music, listened with delight, but even then would not shut all his eyes at once.   Hermes accordingly hit upon the idea of lulling him asleep with a story instead of with a song.   The story he told is the one relating how the nymph Syrinx, fleeing from the goat-footed god Pan, was changed into a tuft of reeds.   As he hearkened Argus grew drowsy, and at last he had not a single eye open. Hermes, perceiving this, slew him, and set Io free, though he was not able to break the spell laid upon her by the vindictive Queen of Heaven.

Hera, indignant at the slaying of her faithful servant, took the eyes of Argus with which to adorn the tail of her favourite bird, the peacock.   She then sent a fierce gadfly to sting poor Io, who, maddened by pain, plunged into the sea afterwards called in her honour the Ionian Sea.

> In coming time that hollow of the sea
> Shall bear the name Ionian, and present
> A monument of Io's passage through,
> Unto all mortals.

So wrote Elizabeth Barrett Browning.   And Milton, in *Paradise*

Lost, describing the " watchful Cherubim," thus alludes to the myth of Argus:

> Spangled with eyes more numerous than those
> Of Argus, and more wakeful than to drowse,
> Charmed with Arcadian pipe, the pastoral reed
> Of Hermes, or his opiate rod.

Poor Io, after long wanderings, reached the land of Egypt, when at the earnest prayer of Zeus Hera restored her to her human form.

CALLISTO

Another maiden whom Zeus admired and of whom Hera felt jealous was the young huntress Callisto of Arcadia. To her a son was born who received the name of Arcas, and from whom the people of Arcadia claimed descent.

The resentful Hera changed Callisto into a she-bear, and in that form the one-time free and happy huntress led a harassed existence in the wildwood, equally terrified of human hunters and of the wild beasts whom she herself now resembled. At last, after many years, as one of these hunters drew near her, spear in hand, she recognized him as her son Arcas, and opened her arms to embrace him. Arcas, not unnaturally alarmed, raised his spear, but before he could touch her Zeus intervened. Even the king of the gods could not undo the spell worked by the Queen and give Callisto back her original shape; but he could, and did, change both the she-bear and the young huntsman into constellations, groups of stars known to the ancients—and to ourselves—as the Great Bear and the Little Bear. (According to another story the youth became the star Arcturus.)

CYDIPPE AND HER SONS

That Hera was not always represented in mythology as being cruel and implacable is shown by the story of her priestess Cydippe.

This priestess had two sons, Biton and Cleobis. When they beheld the earnest desire of their aged mother to journey into the land of Argos and to venerate the new, magnificent gold-and-ivory statue of the goddess in the temple there, these young men yoked themselves to her chariot and dragged it thither. This they did because they had not been able to provide the white oxen which tradition demanded.

The whole family were received with honour at Argos, and the high priest suggested that Cydippe should draw near the marvellous image and offer prayers before it. This the priestess was glad to do, as it enabled her to beg Hera to bestow upon the two pious youths " the greatest of all gifts." What that gift would be she can hardly have foreseen, for it was death. The goddess descended from heaven and bore away the souls of Cleobis and his brother to the Elysian Fields, the abode of the happy dead.

CHAPTER IV

ATHENE

ALTHOUGH immortal, the gods were not immune from physical pain. One day Zeus suffered intensely from a sudden headache, and summoned all the gods to Olympus to help him to find a cure for it. Their united efforts were vain, however; and unwilling, or perchance unable, to endure the racking pain any longer, Zeus bade one of his sons, Hephæstus, cleave his head open with an axe. The dutiful god obeyed; and no sooner was the operation performed than Athene (Pallas, Minerva) sprang out of her father's head, full-grown, clad in glittering armour, with poised spear, and chanting a triumphant song of victory.

> From his awful head
> Whom Jove brought forth, in warlike armour drest,
> Golden, all radiant.
> SHELLEY

The assembled gods recoiled in fear before this unexpected apparition, while at the same time a mighty commotion over land and sea proclaimed the advent of a great divinity.

The goddess who had thus joined the inhabitants of Olympus was destined to preside over peace, defensive war, and needlework, to be the incarnation of wisdom, and to put to flight the obscure deity called Dullness, who until then had ruled the world.

> Ere Pallas issu'd from the Thund'rer's head,
> Dulness o'er all possess'd her ancient right,
> Daughter of Chaos and eternal Night.
> POPE

Athene, having forced her unattractive predecessor to beat an ignominious retreat, quickly seized the sceptre and immediately began to rule in her stead.

Not long after Cecrops, a Phœnician, came to Greece, where he founded a beautiful city in the province since called Attica. All the gods watched his undertaking with great interest; and finally, seeing the town promised to become a thriving place, each wished

the privilege of naming it.   A general council was held, and after
some deliberation most of the gods withdrew their claims.   Soon
none but Athene and Poseidon were left to contend for the coveted
honour.

To settle the quarrel without evincing any partiality, Zeus
announced that the city would be entrusted to the protection of
the deity who should create the most useful object for the use of
man.   Raising his trident, Poseidon struck the ground, from
which a noble horse sprang forth, amid exclamations of wonder
and admiration.   His qualities were duly explained by his proud
creator, and all thought it quite impossible for Athene to surpass
him.   Loudly the onlookers laughed, and scornfully too, when
she, in her turn, produced an olive-tree; but when she had told
them the manifold uses to which wood, fruit, foliage, twigs, etc.,
could be applied, and explained that the olive was the sign of peace
and prosperity, and therefore far more desirable than the horse,
the emblem of war, they could but acknowledge her gift the more
serviceable, and award her the prize.

To commemorate this victory over her rival the goddess gave
her own name of Athene to the city, whose inhabitants from that
time forth were taught to honour her as their patroness.

Ever at Zeus's side, Athene often aided him by her wise
counsels, and in times of war borrowed his terrible shield, the
Ægis, which she flung over her shoulder when she sallied forth to
give her support to those whose cause was just.

> Her shoulder bore
> The dreadful Ægis with its shaggy brim
> Bordered with Terror.   There was Strife, and there
> Was Fortitude, and there was fierce Pursuit,
> And there the Gorgon's head, a ghastly sight,
> Deformed and dreadful, and a sign of woe.
>   HOMER (*Bryant's tr.*)

The din of battle had no terrors for this doughty goddess, and
on every occasion she was wont to plunge with the utmost valour
into the thickest of the fray.   Poets describe her as being blue- or
grey-eyed.

The Delphic Sibyl
Michelangelo

Varvakeion Statuette
Antique copy of the Athene of Phidias
National Museum, Athens

THE STORY OF ARACHNE

These warlike tastes were, however, fully counterbalanced by some exclusively feminine, for Athene was as deft with her distaff as with her sword.   In Greece there lived in those olden times a maiden called Arachne.   Pretty, young, and winsome, she would have been loved by all had it not been for her inordinate pride in her skill in weaving and spinning.

Arachne, in her conceit, fancied that no one could equal the work done by her deft fingers, so she boasted far and wide that she would not hesitate to match her skill with Athene's.   She made this remark so frequently that the goddess finally was annoyed, and left her seat in high Olympus to punish the maiden.   In the guise of an old crone she entered Arachne's house, seated herself, and began a conversation.   In a few minutes the maiden had resumed her usual strain, and renewed her rash boast.   Athene gently advised her to be more modest, lest she should incur the wrath of the gods by her presumptuous words; but Arachne was so blinded by her conceit that she scorned the well-meant warning, saucily tossed her head, and declared she wished the goddess would hear her, and propose a contest, in which she would surely be able to prove the truth of her assertions.   This insolent speech so incensed Athene that she cast aside her disguise and accepted the challenge.

Both set up their looms, and began to weave exquisite designs in tapestry, Athene choosing as her subject her contest with Poseidon, and Arachne the kidnapping of Europa.   In silence the fair weavers worked, and their webs grew apace under their practised fingers.   The assembled gods, the horse, the olive-tree, seemed to live and move under Athene's flashing shuttle.

> Emongst these leaves she made a Butterflie,
> With excellent device and wondrous slight,
> Fluttring among the Olives wantonly,
> That seem'd to live, so like it was in sight:
> The velvet nap which on his wings doth lie,
> The silken downe with which his backe is dight,
> His broad outstretched hornes, his hayrie thies,
> His glorious colours, and his glistering eies.
>
> SPENSER

Arachne in the meantime was intent upon her swimming bull, against whose broad breast the waves broke, and upon the half-laughing, half-frightened girl, who clung to the bull's horns, while the wind played with her flowing tresses and garments.

> Sweet Europa's mantle blew unclasp'd,
> From off her shoulder backward borne:
> From one hand droop'd a crocus: one hand grasp'd
> The mild bull's golden horn.
>
> TENNYSON

The finishing touches all given, each turned to view her rival's work, and at the very first glance Arachne was forced to acknowledge her failure. To be thus outstripped, after all her proud boasts, was humiliating indeed. Bitterly did Arachne now repent of her folly; and in her despair she bound a rope about her neck and hanged herself. Athene saw her discomfited rival was about to escape, so she quickly changed her dangling body into a spider, and condemned her to weave and spin without ceasing—a warning to all conceited mortals.

Athene, the goddess of wisdom, was widely worshipped. Temples and altars without number were dedicated to her service, the most celebrated of all being the Parthenon at Athens. Only the ruins of this mighty pile now exist; but they suffice to testify to the beauty of this temple, which served in turn as temple, church, mosque, and finally as powder magazine.

Statues of Athene—a beautiful, majestic woman, fully clothed and armed—were very numerous. The most celebrated of all, by the famous Phidias, measured fully forty feet in height. Festivals were celebrated in honour of Athene wherever her worship was held—some, the Greek Panathenaia, for instance, only every four years; others, such as the Roman Minervalia and Quinquatria, every year. At these festivals the Palladium, a statue of the goddess, said to have fallen from heaven, and to have been carried off by the Greeks among the spoils of the Trojan war, was carried in procession through the city, where the people hailed its appearance with joyful cries and songs of praise.

CHAPTER V

APOLLO

THE most glorious among the gods, and the fairest to look
upon, was Apollo (Phœbus, Helios, Cyntheus, Pytheus),
god of the sun, of music, medicine, poetry, and all the fine arts.
He is thus invoked by William Drummond, a Scottish poet of the
seventeenth century:

> Phœbus, arise,
> And paint the sable skies
> With azure, white, and red:
>
> . . . . .
>
> Give life to this dark world which lieth dead;
> Spread forth thy golden hair
> In larger locks than thou wast wont before,
> And, emperor-like, decore
> With diadem of pearl thy temples fair:
> Chase hence the ugly night,
> Which serves but to make dear thy glorious light.
>
> . . . . .
>
> The winds all silent are,
> And Phœbus in his chair,
> Ensaffroning sea and air,
> Makes vanish every star.

THE STORY OF LATONA

Apollo was the son of Zeus and Latona. Before he and his
twin sister Artemis (Diana) were born their mother was driven
forth from high heaven by the relentless jealousy of Hera, who
sent a huge serpent, called Pytho, to pursue her. The unfortunate
Latona could find no resting-place on the face of the earth, for
Gæa, dreading the wrath of the Queen of Heaven, would grant her
none; but at last Poseidon took pity on her, and caused the floating
island of Delos to come to a standstill in the Ægean Sea, and there
the goddess gave birth to her twin son and daughter. Even then
the persecution of Hera was not at an end. Latona was doomed
to leave her island refuge, and go forth as a wanderer once more.

In the land of Caria she was insulted by some uncouth peasants, whom she asked to give her some water from the pool round which they were sitting; but Zeus changed them all into large green frogs, to punish them.

But even the wrath of Hera could not avail to keep the mother of Apollo and Artemis lonely and outcast for ever.   In time she came to be adored, together with her brilliant children, the sun-god and the moon-goddess, and temples in her honour were built at Argos and Delos, and in Egypt.

THE STORY OF ÆSCULAPIUS

Part of the sun-god's childhood was spent in the land of the " blameless Hyperboreans," whom we met in the first chapter of this book.   From his youth he was the most beautiful of all the gods, his radiant head crowned with laurel leaves, a skilful archer and charioteer, a poet who could draw the sweetest music from the seven-stringed lyre to accompany his songs.

From time to time he looked with favour at some maiden of mortal or semi-mortal birth.   Such were Clymene, the mother of Phaeton, and Coronis, the mother of Æsculapius.   Chiron, the most learned of the strange race of beings called Centaurs, was chosen to teach and train the young Æsculapius, who, when he grew up, became a physician of marvellous, almost miraculous, powers.   People travelled from far and near to seek his aid, never in vain.   Once he is said, much to the annoyance of his grand-father Zeus, to have restored a dead man to life.   Temples sprang up in his honour, and for many centuries sick folk would make their way to these temples, there to be tended, and often cured, by the priests of Æsculapius.   Often all that was needful was to sleep for one night in the temple courts, or a touch from one of the sacred serpents which were kept there.

Zeus, who was, like Hera, of a jealous disposition, viewed with misgiving the honours which men were paying to this great master of the healing art, and at his request Pluto hurled at Æsculapius a thunderbolt which ended his life on earth.

Apollo, furious with Hephæstus and the Cyclopes, who had forged the fatal thunderbolt, shot his silver arrows at them to

Arachne
Moreau
(*Page* 39)

Apollo

Bernini

Photo Anderson

43

avenge his son; but Zeus would not permit those useful craftsmen to be harmed, and to punish the god for his deed he exiled him for one year to the world of men, dooming him during that time to serve some mortal there below.

ADMETUS AND ALCESTIS

Apollo descended from Olympus, and entered the service of Admetus, King of Thessaly, who gave him charge of his flock grazing on the banks of the river Amphrysus.

This king soon learned that his shepherd was no ordinary watcher of sheep, and he loved to listen to the songs with which the exiled god whiled away the long hours by the river.

Now it came to pass that King Admetus desired to win the hand of Alcestis, daughter of Pelias, which had been promised to the suitor who should come in a chariot drawn by lions and boars. It sounded an impossible condition, but with the aid of Apollo the king fulfilled it, and won his bride. Not long after Admetus was sick unto death, and his immortal herdsman pleaded with the Three Fates to spare his life. This they agreed to do only if some one were found to die in his stead. To the surprise of the king none of his bravest warriors, none of his most eager flatterers, proved to be willing. Then Alcestis stepped forward, and though her husband was reluctant to accept her sacrifice, the gods took her instead of him. Just as the whole court was lamenting her death Herakles arrived, and on learning the cause of their sorrow agreed to wrestle with Thanatos (Death) in order to decide whether or not the dead queen should return from the land of shades. The hero was victorious, and Alcestis was restored to her husband.

Apollo, after endowing Admetus with immortality, left his service, and went to assist Poseidon, who had also been banished to earth, to build the walls of Troy. The god of music seated himself near by, and played such inspiring tunes that the stones moved into place of their own accord.

Then, his term of exile being ended, he returned to Olympus, and there resumed his wonted duties. From his exalted position he often cast loving glances down upon men, whose life he had shared for a short time, whose hardships he had endured; and, in answer to their prayers, he graciously extended his protection over them, and delivered them from many evils.   Among other deeds done for men was the slaying of the monster serpent Python, who guarded the sacred cave of the oracle at Delphi.   None had dared approach the monster; but Apollo fearlessly drew near, and slew him with his golden shafts.   Thenceforward the oracle was especially associated with Apollo, who was there—and elsewhere —invoked as the Pythian Apollo.

THE STORY OF HYACINTHUS

Although successful in war, Apollo was very unfortunate indeed in friendship.   He had a great affection for a mortal youth called Hyacinthus, and one day they began a game of quoits, but they had not played long before Zephyrus, god of the west wind, passing by, saw them thus occupied.   Jealous of Apollo, for he too was fond of Hyacinthus, Zephyrus blew Apollo's quoit aside so violently that it struck his playmate and felled him to the ground. Vainly Apollo strove to check the stream of blood which flowed from the ghastly wound.   Hyacinthus was already beyond aid, and in a few seconds breathed his last in his friend's arms.   To keep some reminder of the dead boy Apollo changed the fallen blood-drops into clusters of flowers, ever since called, from the youth's name, hyacinths; while Zephyrus, perceiving too late the fatal effect of his jealousy, hovered inconsolable over the sad spot, and tenderly caressed the dainty flowers which had sprung from his friend's life-blood.

> Zephyr penitent,
> Who now, ere Phœbus mounts the firmament,
> Fondles the flower.
>
>   KEATS

THE STORY OF CYPARISSUS

To divert his mind from the mournful fate of Hyacinthus Apollo sought the company of Cyparissus, a clever young hunter; but this friendship was also doomed to a sad end, for Cyparissus, having accidentally killed Apollo's pet stag, grieved so sorely over

this mischance that he pined away and finally died.   Apollo then
changed his lifeless clay into a cypress-tree, which he declared
should henceforth be used to shade the graves of those who had
been greatly beloved through life.

THE STORY OF DAPHNE

One day Apollo encountered in the forest a beautiful nymph
called Daphne, daughter of the river-god Peneus.   He first tried
to approach her gently, so as not to frighten her; but before he
could reach her side she fled, and he, forgetful of all else, pursued
her flying footsteps.   As he ran he called aloud to Daphne, en-
treating her to pause were it only for a moment, and promising to
do her no harm.

The terrified girl paid no heed to promises or entreaties, but
sped on until her strength began to fail, and she perceived that,
notwithstanding her utmost efforts, her pursuer was gaining upon
her.   Panting and trembling, she swerved aside, and rushed down
to the edge of her father's stream, calling out loudly for his protection.   " Help me! " she cried.   " Change my form, or let me
sink into the earth! "   No sooner had she reached the water's
edge than her feet seemed rooted to the ground.   Green leaves
sprouted from her hair and her hands, and a garment of grey bark
covered her quivering body.   Her father had answered her prayer
by changing her into a laurel-tree.

Apollo, coming up just then with outstretched arms, clasped
nothing but a rugged tree-trunk.   At first he could not realize
that the maiden had vanished from his sight for ever; but when
the truth dawned upon him he declared that henceforth the laurel
would be considered his favourite tree, and that prizes awarded to
poets and musicians should consist of a wreath of its foliage.

This story of Apollo and Daphne was an illustration of the
effect produced by the sun (Apollo) upon the dew (Daphne).
The sun is captivated by its beauty, and longs to view it more
closely; the dew, afraid of its ardent lover, flies, and when its
fiery breath touches it vanishes, leaving nothing but verdure in
the self-same spot where but a moment before it sparkled in all
its purity.

Climbing Heaven's blue dome,
I walk over the mountains and the waves,
Leaving my robe upon the ocean foam;
My footsteps pave the clouds with fire; the caves
Are filled with my bright presence, and the air
Leaves the green earth to my embraces bare.

SHELLEY

CEPHALUS AND PROCRIS

The ancients had many analogous stories, allegories of the sun and dew, among others the oft-quoted tale of Cephalus and Procris.   Cephalus was a hunter who fell in love with and married one of the nymphs of Artemis, Procris.   She brought him as dowry a hunting dog, Lelaps, and a javelin warranted never to miss its mark.   The newly married pair were perfectly happy; but their content was viewed with great displeasure by Eos (Aurora), goddess of the dawn, who had previously tried, but without success, to win Cephalus' affections, and who now resolved to put an end to the happiness she envied.

All day long Cephalus hunted in the forest, and when the evening shadows began to fall returned to his home and his wife. Her marriage gifts proved invaluable, as Lelaps was swift of foot, and tireless in the chase.   One day, to test his powers, the gods from Olympus watched him course a fox, a special creation of theirs, and so well were both animals matched in speed and endurance that the chase bade fair to end only with the death of one or both of the participants.   The gods, in their admiration for the fine run, declared the animals deserved to be remembered for ever, and changed them into statues which retained all the spirited action of the living creatures.

In the warm season, when the sun became oppressively hot, Cephalus was wont to rest during the noon hour in some shady spot, and as he flung himself down upon the short grass he often called for a breeze, bidding it cool his heated brow. " Come, sweet air," he would say, " come, sweet goddess of the breeze, come to me! "

Eos heard him, and was fully aware that he merely addressed the passing wind; nevertheless, she sought Procris, and told her that her husband was faithless, and paid court to a fair maid who daily met him at noonday in the forest solitudes. Procris, blinded by sudden jealousy, gave credit to the false story, and immediately resolved to follow her husband.

The morning had well-nigh passed when Cephalus came to his usual resort, near which Procris was concealed.

" Sweet air, oh, come! " the hunter cried; and Procris, with a low moan, sank fainting on the ground. Under the mistaken impression that some wild beast was lurking there ready to pounce upon him, Cephalus cast his unerring javelin into the very midst of the thicket and pierced the heart of his wife. She died in his arms, and the little woodland folk, the dryads, and the fauns, mourned over her.

THE STORY OF CLYTIE

Apollo's principal duty was to drive the sun chariot. Day after day he rode across the azure sky, nor paused on his way till he reached the golden boat awaiting him at the end of his long day's journey to bear him in safety back to his eastern palace.

A fair young maiden called Clytie watched Apollo's daily journey with strange intentness; and from the moment when he left his palace in the morning until he came to the far western sea in the evening she followed his course with loving eyes, thought of the golden-haired god, and longed for his love. But, in spite of all this fervour, she never won favour in Apollo's eyes, and languished until the gods, in pity, changed her into a sunflower.

Even in this altered guise Clytie could not forget the object of her love; and now, a fit emblem of constancy, she still follows with upturned face the glowing orb in its daily journey across the sky.

APOLLO AND MIDAS

Apollo, like his fellow-gods, seems to have resembled mortal men in vanity and maliciousness. He was particularly jealous of his reputation as a musician, and took on one occasion a cruel revenge upon a piper called Marsyas, who had rashly challenged him to a musical contest. On another occasion Midas, King of Phrygia, was so imprudent as to maintain that Pan, the goat-god, was a better musician than Apollo, and the sun-god avenged himself by causing long, shaggy ass's ears to grow on either side of the King's head.

> The god of wit, to show his grudge,
> Clapt asses' ears upon the judge;
> A goodly pair, erect and wide,
> Which he could neither gild nor hide.
>
> SWIFT

Greatly dismayed by these new ornaments, Midas retreated into his own room, and sent in hot haste for his barber, who, after having been sworn to secrecy, was admitted, and bidden to fashion a huge wig which would hide the deformity from the eyes of the King's subjects. The barber acquitted himself deftly, and, before he was allowed to leave the palace, was again charged not to reveal the secret, under penalty of immediate death.

But a secret is difficult to keep; and this one, of the King's long ears, preyed upon the poor barber's spirits, so that, incapable of enduring silence longer, he sallied out into a field, dug a deep hole, and shouted down into the bosom of the earth,

> " King Midas wears
> (These eyes beheld them, these) such ass's ears! "
>
> HORACE

Unspeakably relieved by this performance, the barber returned home. Time passed. Reeds grew over the hole, and as they bent before the wind which rustled through their leaves they were heard to murmur, " Midas, King Midas, has ass's ears! " and all who passed by caught the whisper, and noised it abroad, so that the secret became general knowledge.

ORPHEUS AND EURYDICE

Another famous musician of mythology was Orpheus, the tawny-skinned son of Calliope, the Muse of Epic Poetry. According to some authorities, his father was none other than the sun-god himself. Shakespeare calls the musical instrument played by Orpheus a ' lute,' but it was a seven-stringed lyre.

> Orpheus with his lute made trees,
> And the mountain-tops, that freeze,
> Bow themselves when he did sing:

Apollo and Daphne
Henrietta Rae

48

Clytie
Lord Leighton
By permission of the Fine Art Society, Ltd.

To his music plants and flowers
Ever sprung; as sun and showers
  There had made a lasting spring.

Everything that heard him play,
Even the billows of the sea,
  Hung their heads, and then lay by.
SHAKESPEARE

If he had the power to make flowers open and wild beasts turn gentle it is hardly surprising that when he fell in love with Eurydice, one of the nymphs, he soon won her heart.   Hymen, the god of marriage, joined their hands, but his torch smoked, instead of giving forth a clear golden flame, and this was regarded as a bad omen.   Not long after Eurydice was pursued by a shepherd called Aristæus, and as she fled from him she trod upon a snake, which stung her foot.   She died of the venomous bite, and her spirit went down into the world of shades.

Heartbroken, Orpheus implored Zeus to restore his wife to him, and finally the All-Highest gave him leave to go and seek Eurydice in the dark realm of Pluto.

Orpheus hastened to the entrance of Hades, and there saw the fierce three-headed dog, Cerberus, who guarded the gate, and would allow no living being to enter nor any spirit to pass out of Hades.   As soon as this monster saw Orpheus he began to growl and bark savagely; but Orpheus merely paused, and began to play such an enchanting melody that Cerberus' rage was appeased, and he finally allowed him to pass.

The magic sounds penetrated even into the remote depths of Tartarus, where the condemned shades suspended their toil for a moment, and hushed their sighs to listen.   Even Tantalus paused in his eternal effort to quaff the ever-receding stream, Sisyphus ceased to roll his heavy stone, and Ixion's wheel stayed for a moment in its ceaseless course.

No living being had ever before penetrated thus into the Infernal Regions, and Orpheus wandered on until he came to the throne of Pluto, king of these realms, whereon the stern ruler sat in silence, his wife Persephone beside him, and the relentless Fates at his feet.

Orpheus made known his errand, and succeeded in moving the royal pair to tears, whereupon they consented to restore Eurydice to him.

D

> Hell consented
> To hear the Poet's prayer:
> Stern Proserpine relented,
> And gave him back the fair.
> Thus song could prevail
> O'er death and o'er hell,
> A conquest how hard and how glorious!
> Tho' fate had fast bound her
> With Styx nine times round her,
> Yet music and love were victorious.
>
> POPE

But one condition was imposed before he was allowed to depart; that is, that he should leave the Infernal Regions without turning once to look into his beloved wife's face.

Orpheus accepted the condition joyfully, and wended his way out of Hades, looking neither to the right nor to the left, but straight before him; and as he walked he wondered whether Eurydice were changed by her sojourn in these rayless depths. His longing to feast his eyes once more upon her beloved features induced him, forgetful of the condition imposed by Pluto, to turn just before he reached the earth; and as he did so the form of the wife he had so nearly snatched from the grave vanished before his affrighted eyes.

> No word of plaint even in that second Death
> Against her lord she uttered,—how could Love
> Too anxious be upbraided?—but one last
> And sad ' Farewell! ' scarce audible, she sighed,
> And vanisht to the Ghosts that late she left.
>
> OVID (King's tr.)

All was now over. He had tried and failed. No hope remained. In despair the lonely musician retreated to the forest solitudes, and there played his mournful laments,

> Such strains as would have won the ear
> Of Pluto, to have quite set free
> His half-regained Eurydice.
>
> MILTON

But there were none to hear except the trees, winds, and wild beasts in the forest, who strove in their dumb way to comfort him as he moved restlessly about, seeking a solace for his heavy heart. At times it seemed to his half-delirious fancy that he could discern Eurydice wandering about in the dim distance, with the self-same

mournful expression of which he had caught a mere glimpse as she
drifted reluctantly back into the dark shadows of Hades.

> At that elm-vista's end I trace
> Dimly thy sad leave-taking face,
> Eurydice! Eurydice!
> The tremulous leaves repeat to me
> Eurydice! Eurydice!
>
> LOWELL

At last there dawned a day when some Bacchantes overtook him
in the forest, and bade him play some gay music, so they might
indulge in a dance. But poor Orpheus, dazed with grief, could
not obey; and the sad notes which alone he now could draw from
his instrument so enraged the merrymakers that they tore him
limb from limb, and cast his mangled remains into the Hebrus
river.

As the poet-musician's head floated down the stream the pallid
lips still murmured, " Eurydice! " for even in death he remembered her; and as his spirit drifted on to join her he called upon
her name until the brooks, trees, and fountains he had loved so
well caught up the longing cry, and repeated it again and again.
The Muses buried his remains at Libethra, where the nightingale
sang sweetly over his grave.

Nothing was now left to remind mortals of the sweet singer
except his lute, which the gods placed in the heavens as a bright
constellation, Lyra, also called by Orpheus's name.

THE STORY OF AMPHION

Yet another musician celebrated in mythology is Amphion,
whose skill was reported to be but little inferior to Orpheus's.

> 'Tis said he had a tuneful tongue,
> Such happy intonation,
> Wherever he sat down and sung
> He left a small plantation;
> Wherever in a lonely grove
> He set up his forlorn pipes,
> The gouty oak began to move,
> And flounder into hornpipes.
>
> TENNYSON

This musician, a son of Zeus and Antiope, had a twin brother Zethus, who, however, shared none of his artistic tastes. Hearing that their mother Antiope had been repudiated by her second husband, Lycus,[1] so that he might marry another wife, called Dirce, these youths hastened off to Thebes, where they found the state of affairs even worse than had been represented; for poor Antiope was now imprisoned, and subject daily to her rival's cruel treatment.

Zethus and Amphion, after besieging and taking the city, put Lycus to death, and, binding Dirce to the tail of a wild bull, let him loose to drag her over briars and stones until she perished. This punishment inflicted upon Dirce is the subject of the famous group once belonging to the Farnese family, and now called by their name.

Amphion's musical gifts were of great use to him when he subsequently became King of Thebes, and wished to fortify his capital by building a huge rampart all around it; for the stones moved in time to the music, and of their own volition marched into their places. (Compare the story of Apollo at the building of Troy.)

THE STORY OF ARION

Next to him in musical fame was Arion, the musician who won untold wealth by his talent. On one occasion, having gone to Sicily to take part in a musical contest which had attracted thither the most famous musicians from all parts of the world, he resolved to return home by sea, bearing with him the rich prizes he had won.

Unfortunately for him, the vessel upon which he had embarked was manned by an avaricious, piratical crew, who, having heard of his treasures, resolved to murder him to obtain possession of them. He was allowed but scant time to prepare for death; but just as they were about to toss him overboard he craved permission to play for the last time. The pirates consented. His clear notes floated over the sea, and allured a school of dolphins, which came and played about the ship. The pirates, terrified by the power of his music, and in dread lest their hearts should be

---

[1] Lycus ruled in Thebes during the minority of Laius.

moved, quickly laid hands upon him, and hurled him into the water, where he fell upon the broad back of a dolphin, who bore him in safety to the nearest shore.

> Then was there heard a most celestiall sound
> Of dainty musicke, which did next ensew
> Before the spouse: that was Arion crownd;
> Who, playing on his harpe, unto him drew
> The eares and hearts of all that goodly crew,
> That even yet the Dolphin, which him bore
> Through the Agean seas from Pirates vew,
> Stood still by him astonisht at his lore,
> And all the raging seas for joy forgot to rore.
>
> SPENSER

To commemorate this miracle the gods placed Arion's harp, together with the dolphin, in the heavens, where they form a constellation.

THE STORY OF PHAETON

In the sunny plains of Greece there once dwelt a nymph called Clymene. She was not alone, however, for her golden-haired son Phaeton was there to gladden her heart with all his childish graces.

Early in the morning, when the sun's bright orb first appeared above the horizon, Clymene would point it out to her boy, and tell him that his father, Apollo, was setting out for his daily drive. Clymene so often entertained her child with stories of his father's beauty and power that at length Phaeton became conceited, and acquired a habit of boasting rather loudly of his divine parentage.

Stung to the quick by some insolent taunts from Epaphus, the son of Zeus and Io, Phaeton hastened to his mother, and begged her to direct him to his father, that he might obtain the desired proof that he was indeed Apollo's son. Clymene immediately gave him all necessary information, and bade him make haste if he would reach his father's palace in the far east before the sun chariot passed out of its portals to accomplish its daily round. Directly eastward Phaeton journeyed, nor paused to rest until he came in view of the golden and jewelled pinnacles and turrets of his father's abode.

The sun's bright palace, on his high columns rais'd,
With burnish'd gold and flaming jewels blaz'd,
The folding gates diffus'd a silver light,
And with a milder gleam refresh'd the sight.

ADDISON

Quite undazzled by this splendour, the youth still pressed on, straining his eyes to catch the first glimpse of the godly father, whose stately bearing and radiant air his mother had so enthusiastically described.

Apollo, from his golden throne, had watched the boy's approach, and as he drew nearer recognized him as his son. Timidly now Phaeton advanced to the steps of his father's throne, and humbly waited for permission to make his errand known. Apollo addressed him graciously, called him his son, and bade him speak without fear. In a few minutes the youth impetuously poured out the whole story, and watched with pleasure the frown which gathered on Apollo's brow when he repeated the taunts of Epaphus. As soon as he had finished his tale Apollo exclaimed that he would grant him any proof he wished, and confirmed these words by a solemn oath, sworn on the river Styx.

This oath was the most solemn any god could utter, and in case of perjury he was obliged to drink the waters of this river, which would lull him into a senseless stupidity for one whole year. During nine years following he was deprived of his office, banished from Olympus, and not allowed to taste of the life-giving nectar and ambrosia.

Phaeton, hearing this oath, begged permission to drive the sun chariot that very day, stating that all the world would be sure to watch his course across the sky, and that none would ever dare thenceforward to doubt that he was indeed Apollo's son.

When the god heard this presumptuous request he started back in dismay, for he alone could control the four fiery steeds which drew the golden-wheeled sun-car. Patiently he then explained to Phaeton the great danger of such an undertaking, earnestly begging him to select some other, less fatal boon.

Choose out a gift from seas, or earth, or skies,
For open to your wish all nature lies;
Only decline this one unequal task,
For 'tis a mischief, not a gift, you ask.

ADDISON

But Phaeton, who, like many another conceited youth, fancied he knew better than his sire, would not give heed to the kindly warning, and persisted in his request, until Apollo, who had sworn the irrevocable oath, was obliged to fulfil his promise.

The hour had already come when the sun usually began his daily journey. The pawing, champing steeds were ready; rosy-fingered Aurora only awaited her master's signal to fling wide the gates of morn; and the Hours were ready to escort him on his way.

Apollo, yielding to pressure, quickly anointed his son with a cooling essence to preserve him from the burning sunbeams, gave him the necessary directions for his journey, and repeatedly and anxiously cautioned him to watch his steeds with the utmost care, and to use the whip but sparingly, as they were inclined to be very restive.

The youth, who had listened impatiently to cautions and directions, then sprang into the seat of the golden chariot, gathered up the reins, signalled to Aurora to fling the gates wide, and dashed out of the eastern palace with a flourish.

For an hour or two Phaeton bore in mind his father's principal injunctions, and all went well; but at length he became very reckless, drove faster and faster, and soon lost his way. The moon and the stars were terrified to see the chariot of the sun astray in space. Then Phaeton drove so close to the earth that all the plants shrivelled up, the fountains and rivers were dried in their mossy beds, the smoke began to rise from the parched and blackened soil, and even the people of the land over which he was passing were burned black—a hue retained by their descendants to this day.

Terrified at what he had done, Phaeton whipped up his steeds, and drove so far away that all the vegetation which had survived the intense heat came to an untimely end on account of the sudden cold.

The cries of mortals rose in chorus, and their clamours became so loud and importunate that they roused Zeus from a profound sleep and caused him to look around to discover their origin. One glance of his all-seeing eye sufficed to reveal the devastated earth and the youthful charioteer. How had a beardless youth dared to mount the sun chariot? Zeus could scarcely credit what he saw. In his anger he vowed he would make the rash mortal expiate his presumption by immediate death. He therefore selected the deadliest thunderbolt in his arsenal, aimed it with special care, and hurled it at Phaeton, whose burned and blackened corpse fell from his lofty seat down into the limpid waves of the river Eridanus.

> Why, Phaethon . . .
> Wilt thou aspire to guide the heavenly car
> And with thy daring folly burn the world?
>   SHAKESPEARE

The tidings of his death soon reached poor Clymene, who mourned her only son, and refused to be comforted; while the Heliades, Phaeton's sisters, three in number—Phaetusa, Lampetia, and Ægle—spent their days by the riverside, shedding tears, wringing their white hands, and bewailing their loss, until the gods, in pity, transformed them into poplar-trees, and their tears into amber, which substance was supposed by the ancients to flow from the poplar-trees like tear-drops. Phaeton's intimate friend, Cycnus, piously collected his charred remains and gave them an honourable burial. In his grief he continually haunted the scene of his friend's death, and repeatedly plunged into the river, in the hope of finding some more scattered fragments, until the gods changed him into a swan, which bird is ever sailing mournfully about, and frequently plunging his head into the water to continue his sad search.

THE NINE MUSES

Apollo, as the dearly loved leader of the nine Muses—daughters of Zeus and Mnemosyne, goddess of memory—was surnamed Musagetes.

> Whom all the Muses loved, not one alone;—
> Into his hands they put the lyre of gold,
> And, crowned with sacred laurel at their fount,
> Placed him as Musagetes on their throne.
>   LONGFELLOW

Although the Muses united at times in one great song, they had each separate duties assigned them.

Clio, the Muse of history, recorded all great deeds and heroic actions, with the names of their authors, and was therefore generally represented with a laurel wreath and a book and stylus, to indicate her readiness to note all that happened to mortal men or immortal gods.

Euterpe, the graceful " Mistress of Song," was represented with a flute and garlands of fragrant flowers.

Thalia, Muse of comedy, held a shepherd's crook and mask, and wore a crown of wild flowers.

Her graver sister, Melpomene, who presided over tragedy, wore a crown of gold, and wielded a dagger and a sceptre; while Terpsichore, the light-footed Muse of the dance, was represented in the act of dancing.

Erato, the Muse of lyric poetry, was pictured with a lyre; and Polyhymnia, Muse of rhetoric, held a sceptre to show that eloquence rules with resistless sway.

Calliope, Muse of epic poetry, also wore a laurel crown; and Urania, Muse of astronomy, held mathematical instruments, indicative of her love of the exact sciences.

This glorious sisterhood was wont to assemble on Mount Parnassus or on Mount Helicon, to hold their learned debates on poetry, science, and music.

THE STORY OF COMATAS

A certain goatherd named Comatas used to feed his goats on the slopes of Mount Helicon, and when the nights were warm would stay out all night with them. On one occasion he had thus seen the Muses dancing round the fountain of Hippocrene in the moonlight, and from that moment he was their willing slave.

Not far from this spot was a small altar devoted to the Muses, and Comatas one day took a kid and offered it as a sacrifice.

When his master discovered that one was missing from his flock in a fit of passion he took the goatherd and fastened him in a great chest, intending that he should die of starvation. The Muses, however, would not suffer their servant to die thus miserably, and they sent some bees with honey, which they carried to him daily through a chink in the chest.

Months passed, and one day the chest was opened; but, instead of a heap of mouldering bones, there was Comatas, live and well!

His lord, knowing that honey-bees were the special servants of the Muses, believed that the latter had taken Comatas under their special care, and thereafter treated him with the utmost kindness.

AURORA (EOS) AND TITHONUS

Apollo's favourite attendant was Aurora, the fair goddess of dawn, whose rose-tipped fingers opened wide the eastern gates of pearl, and who then flashed across the sky to announce her master's coming.

> Yonder shines Aurora's harbinger;
> At whose approach, ghosts, wandering here and there,
> Troop home to churchyards.
>
> SHAKESPEARE

This goddess loved and married Tithonus, Prince of Troy, and won from the gods the boon of everlasting life to confer upon him. Alas! however, she forgot to ask at the same time for continued youth; and her husband grew older and older, and finally became so decrepit that he was a burden to her.

> Immortal age beside immortal youth.
> TENNYSON

Knowing he would never die, and wishing to rid herself of his burdensome presence, she changed him into a grasshopper.

At this time the goddess fell in love with Cephalus, the young hunter, and frequently visited him on Mount Hymettus.

The principal temples dedicated to the worship of Apollo were at Delos, his birthplace, and at Delphi, on the slopes of Mount Parnassus, where a priestess called the Pythoness gave out mysterious oracles purporting to have come from the god. The ancients everywhere could not fail to recognize the sun's kindly influence and beneficent power, and were therefore ever ready to worship Apollo.

The most renowned among the numerous festivals held in honour of Apollo were, without exception, the Pythian Games, celebrated at Delphi every three years.

A manly, beardless youth of great beauty, Apollo is generally crowned with laurels, and bears either a bow or a lyre.

I am the eye with which the Universe
  Beholds itself and knows itself divine;
All harmony of instrument or verse,
  All prophecy, all medicine are mine,
All light of art or nature;—to my song
Victory and praise in its own right belong.
SHELLEY

One of the Seven Wonders of the ancient world, the famous Colossus of Rhodes, was a statue of Apollo, his head encircled with a halo of bright sunbeams, watching the vessels, with all their sails spread, passing in and out of the harbour, whose entrance he guarded for many a year.

CHAPTER VI

ARTEMIS

ARTEMIS (Diana, Phœbe, Selene, Cynthia), the fair twin sister of Apollo, was not only goddess of the moon, but also of the chase. In works of art this goddess is generally represented as a beautiful maiden, clad in a short hunting dress, armed with a bow, a quiver full of arrows at her side, and a crescent on her well-poised head.

Proud of her two children, Apollo and Artemis, Latona boasted far and wide that such as hers had never been, for they excelled all others in beauty, intelligence, and power.

THE STORY OF NIOBE

The daughter of Tantalus, Niobe, heard this boast, and laughed in scorn; for she was the mother of fourteen children—seven manly sons and seven beautiful daughters. In her pride she called aloud to Latona, and taunted her because her offspring numbered but two.

Shortly after Niobe even went so far as to forbid her people to worship Apollo and Artemis, and gave orders that all the statues representing them in her kingdom should be torn down from their pedestals and destroyed. Enraged at this insult, Latona called her children to her side, and bade them go forth and slay all her luckless rival's offspring.

Provided with well-stocked quivers, the twins set out to do her bidding; and Apollo, meeting the seven lads out hunting, cut their existence short with his unfailing arrows.

> Phœbus slew the sons
> With arrows from his silver bow, incensed
> At Niobe.
>
> HOMER (*Bryant's tr.*)

With all proverbial speed the tidings reached Niobe, whose heart failed when she heard that her seven sons, her pride and delight, had fallen under Apollo's shafts, and that they now lay dead in the forest, where they had eagerly hastened a few hours before to follow the deer to its cover.

As she mourned their untimely death she thought her cup of sorrow was full; but long ere her first passion of grief was over Artemis began to slay her daughters.

In vain the poor girls sought to escape the flying arrows. In vain Niobe sought to protect them, and called upon all the gods of Olympus. Her daughters fell one by one, never to rise again. The last clung convulsively to her mother's breast; but even in that fond mother's passionate embrace death found and claimed her. Then the gods, touched by the sight of woe so intense, changed Niobe into stone, just as she stood, with upturned face, streaming eyes, and quivering lips.

> One prayer remains
> For me to offer yet.
> Thy quiver holds
> More than nine arrows: bend thy bow; aim here!
> I see, I see it glimmering through a cloud.
> Artemis, thou at length art merciful:
> My children will not hear the fatal twang!
>
> W. S. LANDOR

The statue was placed on Mount Sipylus, close to a stream of running water; and it was said that tears continually flowed down the marble cheeks, for, though changed, Niobe still felt and wept for her great loss.

This story is an allegory, in which Niobe, the mother, represents winter, hard, cold, and proud; until Apollo's deadly arrows, the sunbeams, slay her children, the winter months. Her tears are emblems of the natural thaw which comes in spring, when winter's pride has melted.

As soon as the young goddess of the moon had been introduced into Olympus all the gods expressed a wish to marry her; but she refused to listen to their entreaties, begged her father's permission to remain single all her life, and pleaded her cause so ably that Zeus was forced to grant her request.

Every evening, as soon as the sun had finished his course, Artemis mounted her moon-car and drove her milk-white steeds across the heavens, watched over and loved by the countless stars, which shone their brightest to cheer her on her way; and as she drove she often bent down to view the sleeping earth, so shadowy and dreamlike, and to breathe the intoxicating perfume of the distant flowers. It seemed to her then as if Nature, so beautiful during the day, borrowed additional charms from the night.

THE STORY OF ENDYMION

One evening, as she was journeying over the land of Coria, she suddenly checked her steeds; for on the hillside she saw a handsome young shepherd asleep, his upturned face illumined by the moon's soft light. Artemis wonderingly gazed upon his beauty, and, descending gently from her chariot, she floated to his side, bent slowly, and dropped an airy kiss upon his slightly parted lips.

The youth Endymion, only partially awakened by this demonstration, half raised his fringed lids, and for a moment his sleep-dimmed eyes rested wonderingly upon the beautiful vision. He rose with a start, and rubbed his sleepy eyelids; but when he saw the moon, which he had fancied close beside him, sailing away across the deep blue sky, he felt sure that it must all have been a dream, but so sweet a dream that he cast himself down upon the grass, hoping to woo it to visit him once more.

According to Keats, the young shepherd set forth on a weary quest for the more-than-mortal lady of his vision, and sought her even in the depths of the sea:

> O love! how potent hast thou been to teach
> Strange journeyings! Wherever beauty dwells,
> In gulph or aerie, mountains or deep dells,
> In light, in gloom, in star or blazing sun,
> Thou pointest out the way, and straight 'tis won.
> Amid his toil thou gav'st Leander breath;
> Thou leddest Orpheus through the gleams of death;
> Thou madest Pluto bear thine element;
> And now, O winged Chieftain! thou hast sent
> A moon-beam to the deep, deep water-world,
> To find Endymion.

When the immortal gods learned of this love felt by one of their number for a mortal shepherd they were much surprised, for the Queen of the Night had been regarded as remote from romantic adventures. Zeus, however, offered Endymion his choice between instant death, in any form he pleased, or perpetual slumber in a cave on Mount Latmus. Endymion chose the latter, and there the ancients believed that he still lay, wrapped in dreamless sleep, and visited every night by the faithful goddess, who was also supposed to keep an eye upon the flocks which he had abandoned for her sake.

THE STORY OF ORION

Endymion was not, however, the only mortal loved by Artemis, for it is also related that her affections were bestowed upon a young hunter called Orion. All day long this youth scoured the forest, his faithful dog Sirius at his heels.

One day, in the dense shade of the forest, he met a group of nymphs, the seven Pleiades, daughters of Atlas.

Afraid lest he should never see them again were he now to lose sight of them, he pursued them eagerly; but the nymphs sped on, until, their strength failing, they called upon Artemis to help them. Their prayer was no sooner heard then answered, and Orion, panting and weary, came up just in time to see seven snow-white pigeons wing their way up into the azure sky.

There a second transformation overtook the Pleiades, who were changed into a constellation, composed of seven bright stars, and there they shone undimmed for ages; but when Troy fell into the enemy's hands all grew pale with grief, and one, more timid and impressionable than the rest, withdrew from sight to hide her anguish from the curious eyes of men.

Orion, like a fickle youth, was soon consoled for their disappearance, and loved Merope, daughter of Œnopion, King of Chios, whose kingdom he cleared of wild beasts. The King, however, kept on procrastinating when the young hunter asked to be allowed to marry Merope. Now, as Orion was anything but a patient man, the delay was very unwelcome indeed, and he made up his mind to abduct his bride instead of marrying her openly; but the plan was frustrated by Œnopion's watchfulness, and Orion was punished by the loss not only of his bride, but also of his eyesight.

Blind, helpless, and alone, he now wandered from place to place, hoping to find some one capable of restoring his sight. At last he reached the Cyclopes' cave, and one of them took pity on him, and led him to the sun, whose light cured him of his blindness.

Happy once more, he resumed his favourite sport, and hunted from morn till eve. Artemis met him in the forest, and they became close friends, but Apollo objected to this friendship, and resolved to end it. He therefore summoned her to his side. To divert her suspicions he began to talk of archery, and under the pretext of testing her skill as a markswoman bade her shoot at a dark speck rising and falling far out at sea.

Artemis seized her bow, and sent the arrow with such force and accurate aim that she touched the point, and saw it vanish beneath the waves, little suspecting that the dark head of Orion, who was refreshing himself by a sea bath, was given her as a target. When she discovered her error she mourned his loss with many tears, vowed never to forget him, and placed him and his faithful dog Sirius as constellations in the sky.

THE STORY OF ACTÆON

When Artemis had finished her nightly journey in her moon-car she seized her bow and arrows, and, attended by her nymphs, was wont to sally forth to hunt the wild beasts in the forest.

One summer afternoon, after an unusually long and exciting pursuit, she and her followers came to one of the still mountain pools where they often loved to bathe. The cool waters rippled so invitingly that the goddess and her attendants hastened to divest themselves of their short hunting garments and plunged in.

But unfortunately Artemis and her attendant nymphs had not been the only hunters out that day. Actæon the huntsman had risen at dawn to stalk the deer; and now, weary and parched with thirst, he too sought the well-known mountain spring.

As he drew near the accustomed spot Actæon fancied he heard bursts of laughter: so he crept on very cautiously, and soon, gently parting the thick branches, beheld Artemis and her nymphs bathing.

At the self-same moment the goddess turned to ascertain the cause of the rustle which had caught her practised ear, and met

Orpheus

J. M. Swan, R.A.

(*Page 48*)

By permission of Messrs E. J. van Wisselingh and Co.

Orpheus and Eurydice
G. F. Watts
(*Page 50*)
By permission of Mr Frederick Hollyer

the admiring gaze of the astonished young hunter. Speechless with indignation, she caught some water in her hollow palm and flung it in his face.

The glittering drops had no sooner touched the young man's eyes than he found himself transformed into a stag, with slender, sinewy limbs, tawny hide, and wide-branching antlers. As he stood there, motionless and dismayed, the distant baying of his hounds coming to join him fell upon his ear.

A thrill of fear shot through every vein, as, mindful of his new form, he bounded away through the forest. Alas! too late; for the pack had caught one glimpse of his sleek sides, and were after him in full cry.

In vain poor Actæon strained every muscle. His limbs refused their support, and as he sank exhausted to the ground the hounds sprang at his quivering throat and tore him to death as he lay.

Artemis was widely worshipped, and temples without number were dedicated to her service—among others the world-renowned sanctuary of Ephesus. The ancients also celebrated many festivals in honour of this fair goddess of the moon, who was ever ready to extend her protection over all deserving mortals.

> Queen and huntress, chaste and fair,
>   Now the Sun is laid to sleep;
> Seated in thy silver chair,
>   State in wonted manner keep:
> Hesperus entreats thy light,
> Goddess excellently bright.
>
> Earth, let not thy envious shade
>   Dare itself to interpose;
> Cynthia's shining orb was made
>   Heaven to clear, when day did close;
> Bless us then with wishèd sight,
> Goddess excellently bright.
>
> Lay thy bow of pearl apart,
>   And thy crystal-shining quiver;
> Give unto the flying hart
>   Space to breathe, how short soever:
> Thou that mak'st a day of night,
> Goddess excellently bright.
>
>   BEN JONSON

E

CHAPTER VII

APHRODITE

APHRODITE (Venus, Cytherea), goddess of love and beauty, is usually said to have sprung from the sea, whence her Greek name, Aphrodite—the ' foam-born.' She was the patroness of gardens and gardeners as well as of lovers : the rose, lily, hyacinth, crocus, and narcissus were sacred to her; so were the dove, the sparrow, the dolphin, and the swan.

Her first home was in the island of Cythera, whence she was wafted to Cyprus. That is why she is sometimes called Cytherea, or the ' Cyprian goddess.' The Hours and the Graces were her attendants; Flora, the goddess of flowers, and Zephyrus, the god of the west wind, obeyed her behest.

The Graces, daughters of Zeus and Eurynome, bore the names of Aglaia, Euphrosyne, and Thalia. Their duties are thus defined by Spenser :

> These three on men all gracious gifts bestow,
> Which decke the body or adorne the mynde,
> To make them lovely or well-favoured show;
> As comely carriage, entertainement kynde,
> Sweete semblaunt, friendly offices that bynde,
> And all the complements of curtesie :
> They teach us how to each degree and kynde
> We should our selves demeane, to low, to hie,
> To friends, to foes; which skill men call Civility.

Many artists have painted and many poets have tried to describe Aphrodite rising from the sea. She is usually represented poised lightly on a large rosy-tinted shell, with Flora and the Graces near her.

> Idalian Aphrodite beautiful,
> Fresh as the foam, new-bathed in Paphian wells,
> With rosy slender fingers backward drew
> From her warm brows and bosom her deep hair
> Ambrosial, golden round her lucid throat
> And shoulder : from the violets her light foot
> Shone rosy-white, and o'er her rounded form
> Between the shadows of the vine bunches
> Floated the glowing sunlights, as she moved.
>
> TENNYSON

The astonishing beauty of the foam-born goddess wrought a great havoc among the Olympian gods, to the no small indignation of some of the older goddesses.   She was proud and capricious, however, and Zeus, to punish her, decreed that she should become the wife of Hephæstus (Vulcan), the dark-browed blacksmith, the worst-favoured of all the gods.   This was rather hard on him.

ARES AND APHRODITE

The first person to win the fickle heart of Aphrodite was Ares (Mars), the fierce and comely god of war.   They used to meet at night, and to separate before Aurora unlocked the gates to let Apollo's golden chariot come forth.   In order to make sure that the sun-god should not see them together Ares placed a sentinel called Alectryon on guard.   One night the unfortunate Alectryon fell asleep, with the result that Apollo, having seen Ares and Aphrodite, hastened to tell Hephæstus what he had seen.   Furious, the blacksmith set off, bearing a huge net of steel chains, which he flung over the lovers, and there he kept them, like birds in a snare, until all the gods had laughed at them.   He then set them both free, and the first action of Ares was to punish the drowsy Alectryon by turning him into a cock.

> And, from out a neighbouring farmyard,
> Loud the cock Alectryon crowed.
>   LONGFELLOW

Several children were born to Ares and Aphrodite.   Hermione, or Harmonia, their daughter, married Cadmus, King of Thebes; and Cupid, their son, came to be regarded as the god of love. Cupid is often represented as a chubby, winged child, bearing the bow and arrows with which he gaily pierces the hearts of mortal men and women.   Sometimes he is shown blindfold, to typify the wildness of his shooting!   In other myths he appears as a beautiful youth.   Many poets have played fancifully with the idea of Cupid as a blind marksman.

> Cupid and my Campaspe played
> At cards for kisses; Cupid paid:
> He stakes his quiver, bow, and arrows,
> His mother's doves, and team of sparrows;

Loses them too; then down he throws
    The coral of his lip, the rose
Growing on's cheek (but none knows how);
    With these, the crystal of his brow,
    And then the dimple of his chin;
    All these did my Campaspe win:
At last he set [1] her with his eyes—
    She won, and Cupid blind did rise.

                    JOHN LYLY

THE STORY OF ADONIS

One day when Aphrodite was walking in a wood she noticed a beautiful tree beginning to crack asunder. As she paused to watch, the trunk parted, revealing a baby boy. The goddess took the child, put it in a casket, and confided it to Persephone, the Queen of the Shades.

Years passed. Aphrodite, being a goddess, remained as young as ever, but the baby grew up into a handsome youth, and became one of the most skilful hunters in the world. Aphrodite fell in love with him, but Persephone would not restore him to her, and the intervention of Zeus himself was necessary before the dispute could be settled. The All-Highest decreed that Adonis—as the young man was called—should spend four months of each year with Persephone, four months with Aphrodite, and four months wherever and however he pleased.

Adonis cared for nothing but the delights of the chase, and snubbed the Queen of Love unmercifully, which did not prevent her from mourning over him with frantic grief when he was slain by a wild boar.

Alas, poor world, what treasure hast thou lost!
    What face remains alive that's worth the viewing?
Whose tongue is music now?   What canst thou boast
    Of things long since, or any thing ensuing?
The flowers are sweet, their colours fresh and trim;
But true-sweet beauty lived and died with him.

. . . .

When he beheld his shadow in the brook,
    The fishes spread on it their golden gills;
When he was by, the birds such pleasure took,
    That some would sing, some other in their bills
    Would bring him mulberries and ripe-red cherries.

                    SHAKESPEARE

    [1] Staked or wagered.

Phœbus Apollo and the Hours
Guido Reni
(*Page 47*)

68

Artemis
From a statuette in bronze and enamel
Gilbert Bayes

THE STORY OF ANCHISES

Anchises, Prince of Troy, was yet another mortal whom Aphrodite loved. She bore him a son called Æneas, who, when the city of Troy was burned by the Greeks, rescued the aged Anchises and carried him to safety on his shoulders. After many wanderings Æneas landed at the mouth of the Tiber. Here he was kindly received by the King of Latium, whose daughter Lavinia he married, and here he ruled for several years, until an envious neighbouring prince, called Turnus, made war upon him. Turnus fell in battle, but his followers ultimately defeated Æneas, whose body was never found, and who was therefore believed to have been carried up to heaven. Julius Cæsar and all the Cæsars of his blood believed themselves to be descended from Æneas.

HERO AND LEANDER

Hero was a young priestess in the temple of Aphrodite at Sestos. One day, as she was making a sacrifice before the altar of the goddess, a youth called Leander saw and fell in love with her. His home was in the city of Abydos, on the opposite shore of the Hellespont, and it became his custom to swim across every night and visit Hero in the tower where she tended Aphrodite's sacred swans and sparrows.

To guide him through the dark waves the priestess used to hold a torch aloft on the top of the tower, but on a night of storm and high wind the beacon was extinguished. Leander, buffeting with the current, missed the easiest way to the shore, and died of exhaustion. His body was washed up at Sestos, and Hero, heartbroken, flung herself into the sea.

Shakespeare's friend Christopher Marlowe began, but did not live to finish, a long poem about these unfortunate lovers. This is the best-known passage, from which Shakespeare himself quotes a line in *As You Like It*:

> It lies not in our power to love or hate,
> For will in us is overrul'd by fate.
> When two are stript long ere the course begin,
> We wish that one should lose, the other win;

And one especially do we affect
Of two gold ingots like in each respect:
The reason no man knows; let it suffice,
What we behold is censur'd by our eyes:
Where both deliberate, the love is slight:
Who ever lov'd, that lov'd not at first sight?

PYRAMUS AND THISBE

Long ago in the city of Babylon there lived two lovers, a youth called Pyramus and a young girl whose name was Thisbe. Only a garden wall divided them, for they lived in adjacent houses, but as their parents had quarrelled they might as well have been divided by a wide sea.

Aphrodite, hearing their lamentations, made—or, at least, helped them to discover—a small chink in the wall, through which they were able to exchange their faithful vows. By this means they arranged to meet on a certain day beside a white mulberry-tree growing just outside the gates of the city.

Thisbe reached the place first, and as she paced to and fro, waiting eagerly for the coming of Pyramus, she heard a rustling among the bushes and turned to welcome him. But it was not Pyramus whose approach she had heard. A fierce, tawny lion stalked slowly towards her, licking its bloody jaws. Thisbe fled with a loud cry, dropping her veil in her flight. This the lion tore to shreds with its teeth before returning to its lair in the neighbouring forest.

Soon after Pyramus arrived, apologetic and out of breath, to find no Thisbe, only a bloodstained veil, which he recognized as hers, and the track of a lion's pads leading to the place—and away from it. In despair, believing that the beast had killed his lady-love, the unhappy youth drew his dagger and plunged it into his heart.

Thisbe, after a short interval, seeing that the lion had gone, went back to the trysting-place, and found Pyramus lying dead, with his dagger beside him stained with his own blood, and her veil pressed to his lifeless lips. This dagger she snatched from the ground, and a moment later she was lying dead beside her lover.

Till that day the fruit of the mulberry-tree had been pearly white; but ever since, according to the legend, the colour has been a deep red, in remembrance of the blood which flowed from the wounds of Pyramus and Thisbe.

This is the story which the Athenian artisans in Shakespeare's play *A Midsummer Night's Dream* enact before Theseus and Hippolyta, when one of the players carrying a lantern represented the moon, and another, bedaubed with plaster, was the best substitute they could find for a wall.

Pyramus is thus made to apostrophize the wall:

> And thou, O wall, O sweet, O lovely wall,
>   That stand'st between her father's ground and mine!
> Thou wall, O wall, O sweet and lovely wall,
>   Show me thy chink, to blink through with mine eyne!

The onlookers are very lenient in their criticisms and comments on the uncouth little play. "Well roared, Lion!" says one, when it is over; "Well run, Thisbe!" cries Theseus; "Well shone, Moon!" adds Hippolyta graciously.

ECHO AND NARCISSUS

Among the nymphs who followed Artemis the huntress through the woods was Echo. Her only fault seems to have been a tendency to chatter too much, but it was grave enough to bring upon her the wrath of Hera, who decreed that she should never speak again unless to repeat the last words said to her. For example, if some one said, "Do not go away!" she would involuntarily answer, "Go away!" This trick—or so it seemed —caused a great deal of misunderstanding, especially when she fell in love with young Narcissus, son of the river-god Cephissus. He imagined that she was mocking him, and poor Echo pined away until nothing remained of her but her voice.

Narcissus was absurdly vain of his own undoubted good looks, and another nymph whom he had slighted prayed to the gods in general, and Aphrodite in particular, that he might receive some punishment. The prayer was heard. Narcissus, bending over a glassy pool, beheld his own face, and was so enchanted with its beauty that he could not bear to leave the spot. There he remained until he died—according to some authorities, by falling into the water, though others hold that he simply wasted away with admiration for his own face.

All the nymphs mourned for Narcissus, Echo with the rest, and upon the reedy bank where he died the flower sprang up which bears his name to this day.

> Sweet Echo, sweetest Nymph, that liv'st unseen
>> Within thy aery shell,
> By slow Meander's margent green,
> And in the violet-embroidered vale,
>> Where the love-lorn nightingale
> Nightly to thee her sad song mourneth well.
>>> MILTON

PYGMALION AND GALATEA

Pygmalion, King of Cyprus, was a skilful sculptor. One day he determined to fashion the image of a very beautiful young girl. He gave it the name of Galatea, and, enchanted by the beauty of his own handiwork, prayed to the goddess of love to breathe the breath of life into the cold marble.

> O Aphrodite, kind and fair,
>> That what thou wilt canst give,
> Oh, listen to a sculptor's prayer,
>> And bid mine image live!
>>> ANDREW LANG

Aphrodite probably felt amused as well as triumphant at this change of opinion on the part of a mortal who had hitherto been proof against her influence. One day Pygmalion was moved to kiss the marble lips of the statue, and at that moment the goddess of love breathed the breath of life into the carven body.

Galatea proved to be even more delightful as a living being than she had been beautiful as a work of art, and in course of time Pygmalion and she became man and wife.

CUPID AND PSYCHE

Once upon a time there lived a king and queen who had three daughters. All were fair, but the very fairest was the youngest, whose name, Psyche, means ' the soul,' and also ' a butterfly.'

Aphrodite became jealous of the honour paid to Psyche, before whose feet people strewed garlands as if she had been the goddess of beauty herself, and told Cupid that he must inspire the girl with a sudden love for some unworthy creature.

In the garden of the goddess were two fountains, one sweet and the other bitter. Cupid took two amber vases, filled one from each fountain, and went to Psyche's chamber, where he found her sleeping. As he stooped and sprinkled her lips with drops of bitterness, touching her side with the tip of his fatal arrow, Psyche opened her eyes. He was invisible to her, but in his alarm he wounded himself, and immediately fell in love with her. His first step was to pour the waters of sweetness upon her hair, after which he flew away.

Time passed. The two elder daughters of the king and queen were sought in marriage by neighbouring princes, but Psyche, in spite of her loveliness, remained unwooed. Her parents began to fear that the gods were angry, and consulted the oracle of Apollo, by whom they were informed that the husband destined for their child was waiting for her on the summit of a neighbouring mountain, and, furthermore, that he was a monster whom neither gods nor men could resist.

Every one was in despair, but Psyche insisted that she must go forth and meet her fate. She was led, amid lamenting kinsfolk, to the mountain-top and there left, weeping and alone. Presently Zephyrus, the gentle west wind, lifted her in his arms and carried her to a flowery valley far away, where she fell asleep. When she woke she found herself in a grove of tall trees beyond which she saw a goodly palace, much more splendid than her father's house. She entered the wide-open door, and though she could see no one she heard voices humbly inviting her to bathe and to sup, while sweet music filled the air.

When she had bathed and eaten dusk fell, and with the darkness came her husband, whose very name she did not know and whose face she was not permitted to behold.

Psyche dwelt for some time in the palace, visited every night by Cupid, who came when darkness fell and departed before the first gleam of day. He sternly forbade her to light the lamp, to seek to look upon his face, or to ask his name. " If," he said, " you were to behold me haply you might adore, and haply fear. But I would rather you loved me as a mortal than that you should worship me as a god."

After some months Psyche began to pine for her kinsfolk, who were still ignorant of her fate, and with great difficulty she persuaded Cupid to allow her to invite her two sisters to come and visit her. They were much astonished when Zephyr brought them to the enchanted palace, and when they found themselves waited on by invisible spirits. Still greater was their surprise when they were told that their sister had never seen the face of her husband, and did not even know his name. Maliciously, they hinted to her that perhaps he was a fearsome monster, even as the oracle had foretold.

Sorely against her will, Psyche was persuaded to hide a lamp in her room, so that she might look upon her husband as he slept, and a dagger with which to slay him if he were indeed a monstrous being. When the light fell upon the face of the sleeping god she was ashamed of what she had done.

> And she began to sob, and tears fell fast
> Upon the bed.—But as she turned at last
> To quench the lamp, there happed a little thing
> That quenched her new delight, for flickering
> The treacherous flame cast on his shoulder fair
> A burning drop; he woke, and seeing her there
> The meaning of that sad sight knew full well.
>   WILLIAM MORRIS

Silently he spread his wings and departed through the wide casement. Psyche, trying to follow him, fell to the ground. The god paused for a moment in his flight and said, " I will punish you only by leaving you for ever. Love cannot live without faith." Then he rose into the air and was seen no more. When Psyche raised her head and looked round, the palace and its garden had vanished, and she was alone.

Cupid, heartbroken, sought the dwelling of his mother, Aphrodite, but she was absent, and he too had to grieve in solitude for his lost love.

A white sea-gull carried the news to the goddess of love, who was disporting herself in the blue depths of the sea, and, full of wrath and jealousy, she hastened to her son, whom she overwhelmed with reproaches. In vain Demeter and Hera interceded for him. Aphrodite was implacable.

Meanwhile poor Psyche was wandering hither and thither in search of her husband. Among those she met and questioned was Pan, who listened to her story and tried to comfort her. One day she reached a temple sacred to Demeter, the goddess of the harvest, where ears of corn, sickles and other implements were heaped wildly together. The goddess was pleased when she saw the sad-looking young worshipper trying to bring order into this confusion, and, taking pity on her, advised her to go to the temple of Aphrodite and beg for mercy.

Unfortunately the Queen of Beauty was not in a merciful mood. After bitterly upbraiding her suppliant she set her the almost impossible task of separating into distinct heaps all the wheat, barley, millet, and beans which were garnered in the temple granary for the benefit of the sacred pigeons.

Now Cupid, far away though he was, knew of the pitiful plight of Psyche, and at his behest a great horde of friendly ants came to her aid, so that the task was accomplished by the time Aphrodite returned to the temple some hours later.

Instead of being pacified, the goddess was angrier than before, guessing through whose aid Psyche had fulfilled her behest. The poor girl was given a morsel of black bread for her supper, and the next morning she was sent to gather wool from the golden-fleeced sheep grazing in a meadow not far away. Now these sheep were not of a mild and gentle breed, and the kindly god of the river beside their pasture warned Psyche, by the murmuring of his reeds, not to go near them, but to glean the shining wool from the sharp bushes instead.

Once more Aphrodite suspected—though this time not with reason—that Cupid had helped Psyche, and the next task she gave her was to go to the kingdom of shadows and take a box to Persephone, with a message begging her to put in it a little of her own beauty, since " while tending her sick son " Aphrodite had lost some of hers.

In despair, Psyche was about to fling herself from a high tower when a mysterious voice bade her take courage, and told her how, through a certain cave, she might find her way safely to the nether world, persuade Cerberus, the watchdog of Hades, to let her pass, and coax Charon, the ferryman of the dead, to take her across the dark river Styx in his boat. She was earnestly warned against eating anything but the plainest food during her journey, and also against meddling with the box, if Persephone should give it to her.

All these injunctions Psyche remembered, and all of them—except the last—she faithfully obeyed. If she had forgotten the command not to eat anything but simple fare in the land of shadows she would have been kept there, as Persephone was after eating the pomegranate given her by Pluto.

But the advice she found it hardest to follow was the advice not to peep inside Persephone's box. For she told herself that if ever she should find her lover again a touch of divine beauty upon her face might make him love her better and see new loveliness in his "Psyche purple-winged and pale." So with a trembling hand she raised the lid, only to fall into a strange waking trance.

> So that for fear and great distress
> She would have cried, but in her helplessness
> Could open not her mouth, or frame a word.
> WILLIAM MORRIS

Cupid, however, having now recovered from his wound, and knowing by his immortal power how things were with his beloved Psyche, flew to her side, and after restoring the spirit of sleep to the casket where Persephone had enshrined it he awakened the bewildered girl with a light touch from his arrow.

"Once more," he said, "curiosity has almost been fatal to thee, O foolish one! But now do my mother's bidding, and leave the rest to me."

While Psyche, grateful and penitent, was carrying the casket to the temple of Aphrodite Cupid winged his way to high Olympus, and there pleaded their cause so ardently before Zeus himself that the king of gods was touched. Hermes, the divine messenger, was sent to fetch Psyche, upon whom Zeus promised to bestow the gift of immortality if Aphrodite would agree to the marriage.

Cupid and Psyche were never parted again, and upon their daughter they bestowed the name of Delight.

One of the latest myths concerning Aphrodite is that of Berenice, who, fearing for her beloved husband's life, implored the goddess to protect him in battle, vowing to sacrifice her luxuriant hair if he returned home in safety. The prayer was granted, and Berenice's beautiful locks were laid upon Aphrodite's shrine, whence they, however, very mysteriously disappeared. An

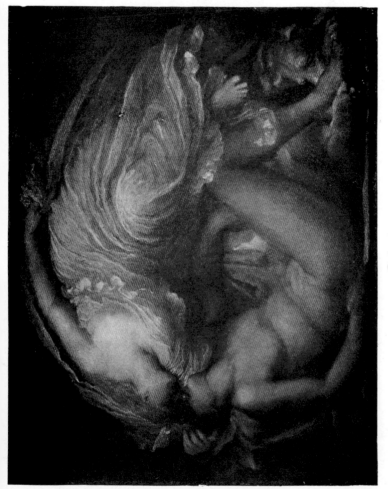

Endymion
G. F. Watts
(*Page* 62)
By permission of Mr Frederick Hollyer

76

Æneas and Anchises

Gilbert Bayes

(See Chapter XXVIII)

astrologer, consulted concerning the supposed theft, solemnly pointed to a comet rapidly coming into view, and declared that the gods had placed Berenice's hair among the stars, there to shine for ever in memory of her sacrifice.

APHRODITE IN ART AND LITERATURE

Aphrodite was always a favourite subject with sculptors and painters, who usually represented her standing on a shell, drawn by doves, or rising from the waves, or coming from her bath. As the most famous statue of her, the Venus of Milo (in the Louvre), has lost its arms, nobody knows exactly in what position the goddess was shown. Some authorities think she was holding a torch or a jar of ointment in one hand, while with the other she supported the heavy draperies which veil her lower limbs.

Venus Aphrodite plays an important part in epic, drama, and legend. She is usually represented as exacting and capricious, but capable of generous and compassionate impulses. Chaucer makes Cupid call her " Seynt Venus," which does not sound natural. Shakespeare imagines her saying to Adonis:

> Bid me discourse, I will enchant thine ear,
>   Or, like a fairy, trip upon the green,
> Or, like a nymph, with long dishevell'd hair,
>   Dance on the sands, and yet no footing seen.

In *Endymion*, Keats, speaking of the moon-goddess, makes one of the characters exclaim:

> Ah! see her hovering feet,
> More bluely vein'd, more soft, more whitely sweet
> Than those of sea-born Venus, when she rose
> From out her cradle shell.

The goddess found her way into medieval art, where we see her dressed like a lady of the period, but wafted through the air in a car drawn by doves, and into medieval legend, whence she proceeded to Wagnerian opera. Dryden, with the pomposity of his time, thus apostrophizes her:

> Beneath the sliding sun thou runn'st thy race,
> Dost fairest shine, and best become thy place.
> For thee the winds their eastern blasts forbear,
> Thy mouth reveals the spring, and opens all the year.
> Thee, goddess, thee the storms of winter fly.

CHAPTER VIII

HERMES

HERMES was the son of Zeus and a daughter of Atlas whose name was Maia. He was born in a cave on Mount Cyllene, in Arcadia. Among the Romans he was known as Mercury, and in both Greek and Roman art and legend he is represented wearing winged sandals and a winged cap, and carrying a winged wand twined with golden snakes. He was the messenger of the gods,

> The herald Mercury,
> New-lighted on a heaven-kissing hill.
> SHAKESPEARE

Among his inventions—or perhaps we should say his discoveries —were the lyre and the flute. The former is said to have originated in a tortoiseshell which he found lying empty on the ground. The young god stretched the dried fibres across the shell and struck them lightly with his fingers.

> There went
> Up from beneath his hand a tumult sweet
> Of mighty sounds, and from his lips he sent
> A strain of unpremeditated wit,
> Joyous and wild and wanton—such you may
> Hear among revellers on a holiday.
> SHELLEY

The wand of Hermes was a gift from Apollo in exchange for the lyre. His sandals were a gift from the gods, whose messenger he became, as was also the winged cap.

> Foot-feather'd Mercury appear'd sublime
> Beyond the tall tree tops; and in less time
> Than shoots the slanted hail-storm, down he dropt
> Towards the ground; but rested not, nor stopt
> One moment from his home; only the sward
> He with his wand light touch'd, and heavenward
> Swifter than sight was gone.
> KEATS

One of the quaintest fables about Hermes concerns his babyhood, when he stole the oxen grazing upon the Pierian Mountains.

78

These oxen belonged to his half-brother, Apollo, and the precocious infant drove them backward into a cave, so that their hoofmarks pointed in the direction opposite to the one they had really taken. Then he made a fire by rubbing laurel twigs together, and sacrificed two heifers to the gods, among whom he calmly included himself!

Apollo could hardly believe that the culprit was his baby brother, for Hermes loudly protested his innocence. " What *are* ' oxen '? " said the shameless child. " I never even heard the word until to-day! " Apollo hauled him before Zeus, who could not help being amused at the effrontery of the boy. Peace was made between them by the All-Highest, and it was on this occasion that Apollo and Hermes exchanged gifts.

We have already met Hermes in the story of Io and in that of Cupid and Psyche, and we shall meet him often again, for in his character as herald and messenger of Olympus he plays an important part in many myths and legends. He was the patron of travellers, merchants—and thieves. He escorted the souls of the departed to Hades, and in that character was called Psychopompus; under the name of Oneicopompus he was regarded as the lord of dreams and visions.

CHAPTER IX

ARES

ARES (Mars), son of Zeus and Hera, was the god of war, the personification of the angry clouded sky. He was more honoured among the Romans, under the name of Mars, than he was among the Greeks under his earlier name of Ares. He is said to have first seen the light in Thrace, a country noted for its fierce storms and war-loving people.

Never sated with strife and bloodshed, this god preferred the din of battle to all other music, and found delight in the toils and dangers of war. No gentle deeds of kindness were ever expected from him; no loving prayers were ever addressed to him; and the ancients felt no affection for him, but, on the contrary, shuddered with terror when his name was mentioned. We have already seen how he won the love of Aphrodite, and how their son was Cupid, the god of love.

Ares was generally represented in a brilliant suit of armour, a plumed helmet on his proud young head, a poised spear in one muscular hand, and a finely wrought shield in the other, showing him ever ready to cope with a foe. Shakespeare imagines the hand of Mars " beckoning with fiery truncheon."

His attendants, or some say his children, sympathized heartily with his quarrelsome tastes, and delighted in following his lead. They were Eris (Discord), Phobos (Alarm), Metus (Fear), Demios (Dread), and Pallor (Terror).

Enyo, or Bellona, goddess of war, also accompanied him, drove his chariot, parried dangerous thrusts, and watched over his general safety. By the Romans Mars and Bellona were therefore worshipped together in the self-same temple, and their altars were the only ones the Romans ever polluted by human sacrifices.

> And to the fire-ey'd maid of smoky war,
> All hot and bleeding, will we offer them:
> The mailèd Mars shall on his altar sit,
> Up to the ears in blood.
> SHAKESPEARE

OTUS AND EPHIALTES

As strife was his favourite element, Ares was very active indeed during the war between the gods and the giants, but in his martial ardour he frequently forgot all caution. On one occasion he was obliged to surrender to Otus and Ephialtes—two giants, who though but nine years of age were already of immense stature, since they increased in height at the rate of nine inches each month.

Proud of their victory over the god of war, these giants bore him off in triumph, and bound him fast with iron chains slipped through iron rings. Day and night they kept watch over him; and even when they slept the rattle of the chains, whenever any one of the gods attempted to set him free, woke them up, and frustrated all efforts to deliver him. During fifteen weary months poor Ares lingered there in durance vile, until Hermes, the prince of thieves, noiselessly and deftly slipped the chains out of the rings, and restored him to freedom.

In revenge for the cruel treatment inflicted by Otus and Ephialtes, Ares prevailed upon Apollo and Artemis to use their deadly arrows, and thus rid the world of these two ugly and useless giants.

Of a fiery disposition, Ares was never inclined to forgive an injury; and when Halirrhothius, Poseidon's son, dared to carry off his daughter Alcippe, Ares hotly pursued the abductor, and promptly slew him. Poseidon, angry at this act of summary justice, cited the god of war to appear before a tribunal held in the open air, on a hill near the newly founded city of Athens.

It was then customary for such cases to be tried at night, in utter darkness, so that the judges might not be influenced by the personal appearance of either plaintiff or defendant; and no rhetoric of any kind was allowed, that their minds might remain quite unbiased. Ares appeared before the judges, simply stated his case, and was acquitted. Since then the hill upon which his trial took place has been called the Areopagus (Ares' or Mars' Hill), and the judges of the principal court of justice at Athens received the name of Areopagitæ.

Ares, as we have seen, was the devout lover of Aphrodite, who

F

bore him three beautiful children—Hermione, Cupid, and Anteros. At a much later date Ares fell in love with a beautiful young Vestal named Ilia, a descendant of Æneas, who, in spite of the solemn pledge not to listen to a lover's pleadings until her time of service at the goddess Vesta's altar was accomplished, yielded to the god's impetuous wooing, and consented to a clandestine union.

ROMULUS AND REMUS

We now come to one of the most famous stories associated with the gentler side of the war-god's character, but it belongs to Roman and not to Greek mythology, and to a date much nearer our own times. Mars, as we should now call the Ares of Olympus, fell in love with a Vestal Virgin vowed to the sacred service of the goddess Vesta. Her name was Rhea Silvia, and she was the daughter of a certain king, Numitor of Alba, who had been driven from his throne by a younger brother called Amulius. Twin sons, Romulus and Remus, were born to Rhea Silvia, and their jealous great-uncle caused them to be thrown into the river Tiber. Some say that the babies were laid first in a wooden trough; other versions of the story say that their cradle was a wicker basket; but at all events it floated, and finally was washed ashore on marshy ground, near a fig-tree, afterwards regarded as holy on that account. As the helpless little beings lay crying a kindly she-wolf came by, and, taking pity on them, carried them back to her lair, where she tended them as if they had been her own cubs. A friendly woodpecker is also said to have helped to keep alive the two royal babes, who grew up tall and strong, and were adopted by a shepherd and his wife dwelling on what was afterwards known as the Palatine Hill. Born with a natural gift of leadership, they placed themselves at the head of a band of young shepherds, and after a time drove Amulius from the throne which he had usurped, and to which they restored their aged grandfather.

They then decided to found a city on the spot where they had spent their miraculous childhood, and a dispute arose between them which had a tragic end. Remus criticized the plans suggested by his elder brother and made fun of the wall which

Romulus had begun to build.   Indeed, to show how useless such a wall would be as a defence to the new city, he jumped mockingly over it.   Romulus became furious, and in his fury slew his younger brother.   (There is a curious resemblance here to the Biblical story of Cain and Abel.)

Romulus, having decided to call his new city Rome—after himself—now offered a place of refuge there to any outcasts or fugitives from justice who might care to join him.   As a result the earliest population of the future imperial city was of a very mixed and turbulent character.   They obtained wives for themselves by raiding the territory of a neighbouring tribe called the Sabines, and were altogether a very violent community.

After reigning over his city-state for many years Romulus vanished from the eyes of men during a fierce thunderstorm, and was regarded as having been caught up into heaven and numbered among the immortals.   The she-wolf who had nursed him was venerated by the later Romans, and a feast called the Lupercalia was held every year near the place where her den is said to have been.

CHAPTER X

HEPHÆSTUS

HEPHÆSTUS, or Vulcan, son of Zeus and Hera, god of fire and the forge, seldom joined the general council of the gods. His aversion to Olympus was of old standing. He had once been tenderly attached to his mother, and had even tried to console her when she was neglected by the All-Highest. On one occasion, intending to punish Hera for one of her usual fits of jealousy, Zeus hung her out of heaven, fast bound by a golden chain; and her son, perceiving her in this plight, tugged at the chain with all his might, drew her up, and was about to set her free, when Zeus returned, and, in anger at his son's interference, hurled him out of heaven.

The intervening space between heaven and earth was so great that his fall lasted during one whole day and night, ere he finally touched the summit of Mount Mosychlus, in the island of Lemnos.

> From morn
> To noon he fell, from noon to dewy eve,
> A summer's day; and with the setting sun
> Dropt from the zenith like a falling star,
> On Lemnos th' Ægean isle.
>   MILTON

Of course, to anyone but a god such a terrible fall would have proved fatal; and even Hephæstus did not escape entirely unharmed, for he injured one of his legs, which accident left him lame and somewhat deformed for the remainder of his life.

Now, although Hephæstus had risked so much and suffered so greatly in taking his mother's part, she never even made the slightest attempt to ascertain whether he had reached the earth in safety. Hurt by her indifference and ingratitude, he vowed never again to return to Olympus, and withdrew to the solitudes of Mount Ætna, where he established a great forge in the heart of the mountain, in partnership with the Cyclopes, who helped him to manufacture many cunning and useful objects from the metals found in great profusion in the depths of the earth.

Among these ingenious contrivances were two golden hand-maidens gifted with motion, who attended the god wherever he went, and supported his halting footsteps.

> Two golden statues, like in form and look
> To living maidens, aided with firm gait
> The monarch's steps.
>
> HOMER (*Bryant's tr.*)

Hephæstus also devised a golden throne with countless hidden springs, which, when unoccupied, did not present an extraordinary appearance; but as soon as anyone ventured to make use of it the springs moved, and, the chair closing around the person seated upon it, frustrated all attempts to rise and escape from its treacherous embrace.

Hephæstus dispatched this throne, when completed, to his mother, who, delighted with its beauty and delicate workmanship, proudly seated herself upon it, and found herself a prisoner. In vain she strove to escape; in vain the gods all gallantly came to her assistance. Their united strength and skill proved useless against the cunning springs.

Finally Hermes was sent to Hephæstus, primed with a most diplomatic request to honour high Olympus with his presence; but all the god's eloquence and persuasions failed to induce the god of the forge to leave his sooty abode, and the messenger was forced to return alone and report the failure of his attempt. Then the gods deliberated anew, and decided to send Bacchus, god of wine, hoping his powers of persuasion would prove more effective.

Armed with a flask of his choicest vintage, Bacchus presented himself before the immortal blacksmith, and offered him a refreshing draught. Hephæstus, predisposed to thirst, and incited to drink by the very nature of his labour, accepted the offered cup, and allowed himself to be beguiled into renewing his potations, until he was quite intoxicated. In this condition Bacchus led him passive to Olympus, made him release the Queen of Heaven, and urged him to embrace his father and crave forgiveness.

Although restored to favour, Hephæstus would not remain permanently in Olympus, but preferred to return to his forge and continue his labours. He undertook, however, the construction of magnificent golden palaces for each of the gods upon the

Olympian heights, fashioned their sumptuous furniture from precious metals, and further embellished his work by a rich ornamentation of precious stones.

> Then to their starry domes the gods depart,
> The shining monuments of Vulcan's art:
> Jove on his couch reclin'd his awful head,
> And Juno slumber'd on the golden bed.
>   HOMER (*Pope's tr.*)

Aided by the Cyclopes, Hephæstus manufactured weapons for Zeus, the dread thunderbolts, whose frightful power none could withstand, and Cupid's love-inspiring darts.

Hephæstus, in spite of his deformity, extreme ugliness, and well-known aversion to any home but his sooty forge, was none the less prone to fall in love with the various goddesses. He first wooed Athene, who, having sworn never to marry, contemptuously dismissed his suit. To console Hephæstus for this rebuff, and at the same time punish the goddess of beauty, who, according to some mythologists, had refused even *his* addresses, Zeus bestowed upon him the fair hand of Aphrodite, and sent her and her mischievous train of Loves and Graces to reside in the dark caves of Mount Ætna.

Amused by all the strange sights and sounds, the goddess at first seemed quite contented; but after a time this gloomy abode lost all its attractions: so she forsook her ill-favoured husband, and went in search of another, more congenial mate.

Some time after Hephæstus married one of the Graces, who, however, also seems to have soon wearied of his society, for she deserted him.

His children were mostly monsters, such as Cacus, Periphetes, Cercyon, etc., all of whom play an important part in heroic mythology. He is also the reputed father of Servius Tullius, sixth king of Rome, by a slave, Ocrisia, whom he was wont to visit in the guise of a bright flame, which played harmlessly about her.

Hephæstus was worshipped by all blacksmiths and artisans, who recognized him as their special patron, and venerated him accordingly.

> Those who labour
> The sweaty forge, who edge the crooked scythe,

Aphrodite
Capitol, Rome
(*See Chapter VII*)

Echo and Narcissus
Solomon J. Solomon, R.A.
(*Page 71*)
By arrangement with Messrs C. E. Clifford and Co.

Bend stubborn steel, and harden gleaming armour,
Acknowledge Vulcan's aid.

PRIOR

Great festivals, the Vulcanalia and the Hephæstia, were celebrated in honour of this god, who is generally represented as a
sturdy, muscular man, with one leg shorter than the other, and a
smith's tools in his hand.

CHAPTER XI

POSEIDON

WHEN Zeus assigned to each of his brothers a separate portion
of the universe he decreed that Poseidon, or Neptune, should
govern all the waters upon the face of the earth and be sole
monarch of the ocean.

> Neptune, the mighty marine god, I sing;
> Earth's mover, and the fruitless ocean's king,
> That Helicon and th' Ægean deeps dost hold.
> O thou earth-shaker; thy command, twofold
> The gods have sorted; making thee of horses
> The awful tamer, and of naval forces
> The sure preserver.   Hail, O Saturn's birth!
> Whose graceful green hair circles all the earth.
> Bear a benign mind; and thy helpful hand
> Lend all, submitted to thy dread command.
> HOMER (*Chapman's tr.*)

Before this new ruler made his appearance the Titan Oceanus
had wielded the sceptre of the sea; and regretfully he now resigned
it to his youthful supplanter, whom he nevertheless admired
sincerely, and described in glowing colours to his brothers.

> Have ye beheld the young God of the Seas,
> My dispossessor?   Have ye seen his face?
> Have ye beheld his chariot, foam'd along
> By noble winged creatures he hath made?
> I saw him on the calmed waters scud,
> With such a glow of beauty in his eyes,
> That it enforc'd me to bid sad farewell
> To all my empire.
> KEATS

LAOMEDON AND HESIONE

Poseidon, the personification as well as the god of the sea, was
of an exceedingly encroaching disposition.   Dissatisfied with the
portion allotted him, he once conspired to dethrone Zeus; but,
unfortunately for the success of his undertaking, his plot was discovered before he could put it into execution, and Zeus, in punish-

ment for his temerity, exiled him to earth. There he was condemned to build the walls of Troy for Laomedon, king of that
city, who in return promised a kingly recompense.

Apollo, also banished from heaven at that time, volunteered to
aid Poseidon by playing on his lyre and moving the stones by the
power of sweet sounds. The task satisfactorily ended, Laomedon,
an avaricious and dishonest king, refused the promised guerdon,
whereupon Poseidon created a terrible monster, which came upon
the shore, devoured the inhabitants, devastated everything within
his reach, and inspired all with great terror.

To save themselves from the awful death which threatened
them all the Trojans consulted an oracle, who advised the sacrifice
of a beautiful virgin, and promised the monster would disappear
as soon as he had devoured the appointed victim.

A young girl was therefore chosen by lot, led down to the seashore, and chained by the priest's own hands to a slimy rock. As
soon as her mourning friends had forsaken her the hideous serpent
came out of his lair in the waves and devoured her; then he
vanished, and nothing more was heard of him for a whole year, at
the end of which time he reappeared, and resumed his former
depredations, which were only checked by the sacrifice of a second
virgin.

Year after year, however, he returned, and year after year a fair
girl was doomed to perish, until finally the lot fell upon Hesione,
the king's only daughter. Laomedon could not bear the thought
of the terrible fate awaiting her, and tried every means in his
power to save her. As a last resort he sent heralds to publish far
and wide that the king would give a great reward to any man who
would dare attack and succeed in slaying the monster.

Herakles, on his return from the scene of one of his stupendous
labours, heard the proclamation, and, with no other weapon than
the oaken club he generally carried, slew the monster just as he
was about to drag poor Hesione down into his slimy cave. Laomedon was, of course, overjoyed at the monster's death, but, true
to his nature, again refused the promised reward, and by his dis-
honesty incurred the hatred and contempt of this hero also. Some
time after, having finished his time of servitude with Eurystheus,
Herakles, aided by a chosen band of adventurers, came to Troy
to punish him for his perfidy. The city was stormed and taken,

the king slain, and his wife and children carried to Greece as captives. There Hesione became the bride of Telamon; while her brother Podarces, later known as Priam, was redeemed by his people and made King of Troy.

Laomedon's failure to pay his just debts was the primary cause of the enmity which Poseidon displayed towards the Trojans during their famous war with the Greeks.

Their term of exile ended, the gods were reinstated in their exalted positions, and hastened to resume their former occupations; but in spite of the severe lesson just received Poseidon was not yet cured of his grasping tendencies. Not long after his return from Troy he quarrelled with Athene for the possession of the recently founded city, then nameless, but afterwards called Athens, and entered into the memorable contest in which he was signally defeated. He also disputed the sovereignty of Trœzen with Athene, and that of Corinth with Apollo. In the latter instance, the disputants having chosen Briareus as umpire, the prize was awarded to him as the most powerful of all the gods except Zeus.

As god of the sea Poseidon did not generally remain in Olympus, but dwelt in the coral caves of his kingdom, over which he ruled with resistless sway. By one word he could stir up or calm the wildest storm and cause the billows to roar with fury or subside into peaceful ripples.

> He spake, and round about him called the clouds
> And roused the ocean,—wielding in his hand
> The trident,—summoned all the hurricanes
> Of all the winds, and covered earth and sky
> At once with mists, while from above the night
> Fell suddenly.
>
> HOMER (*Bryant's tr.*)

The rivers, fountains, lakes, and seas were not only subject to his rule, but he could also cause terrible earthquakes at will, and, when he pleased, raise islands from the deep, as he did when Latona entreated him to shelter her from Hera's persecution.

Poseidon loved the Gorgon Medusa in the days of her youth and beauty, and when some drops of blood fell from her severed head into the salt sea foam he produced from them the graceful winged steeds Pegasus and Chrysaor.

Psyche and Zephyrus
Harry Bates
(*Page 73*)
By permission of Mr Frederick Hollyer

Pan and Psyche
Sir E. Burne-Jones
(*Page 75*)
By permission of Mr Frederick Hollyer

Poseidon is also said to be the father of the giants Otus and Ephiates, of Neleus, Pelias, and Polyphemus.

AMPHITRITE

The Queen of the Ocean, Poseidon's own true and lawful wife, was a Nereid, one of the fifty daughters of Doris and Nereus, the personification of the calm and sunlit aspect of the sea. Her name was Amphitrite, or Salacia. At first she was in great awe of her distinguished suitor, and in her fear fled at his approach, leaving him no chance to admire any of her charms except the grace and celerity with which she managed to flit, or rather glide, out of his sight.

> Along the deep,
> With beauteous ankles, Amphitrite glides.
> HESIOD (*Elton's tr.*)

This conduct grieved Poseidon so sorely that he sent a dolphin to plead his cause and persuade the fair nymph to share his throne. The messenger, carefully instructed beforehand, carried out the directions with such skill that Amphitrite formally consented to become Poseidon's wife.

The king of the deep was so overjoyed at these good tidings that he transferred the dolphin to the sky, where he forms a well-known constellation. Poseidon and Amphitrite in due time became the happy parents of several children, among whom the most celebrated is Triton, whose body was half man and half fish, and who gave his name to all his male descendants.

IDAS AND MARPESSA

Like all other gods, Poseidon took a lively interest in men's affairs, and sometimes interfered in their behalf. On one occasion, for instance, he even lent his beautiful chariot to a youth by the name of Idas, who, loving a maiden dearly, and unable to win her father's consent to their union, had resolved to carry her off. Marpessa, for such was the girl's name, submitted; and the lovers were blissfully speeding along in Poseidon's chariot, when her father, Evenus, perceiving their escape, started in pursuit of them. In spite of the most strenuous efforts, he could not over-take the fleeing pair, and in his anger plunged into a river, where he was drowned, and which from him received the name of Evenus.

Idas and Marpessa were just congratulating themselves upon their narrow escape, when suddenly Apollo appeared before them, and, checking their steeds, declared he loved the maiden too, and would not tamely yield her up to a rival.

This was equivalent to a challenge; and Idas, stepping down from the chariot, was about to engage in the fight, when suddenly out of a clear sky a thunderbolt came crashing down to earth, and an imperious voice was heard to declare that the quarrel could be settled by Marpessa only, and that she should freely choose the suitor she preferred as husband.

The maiden glanced at both her lovers. Remembering that Apollo, being immortal, would retain all his youthful bloom when her more ephemeral beauty had vanished, and that he would probably cease to love her, she held out her hand to Idas, de-claring she preferred to link her fate to that of a mortal, who would grow old when she did, and love her as long as they both lived. This choice was approved by Zeus; and the lovers, after reaching a place of safety, returned the wondrous chariot to Poseidon, with many thanks for his timely aid.

All the Nereides, Tritons, and lesser sea divinities formed a part of the sea-god's train, and followed closely when he rode forth to survey his kingdom.

Poseidon had, besides this, many subordinates, whose duty it was to look after the various seas, lakes, rivers, fountains, etc., confided to their special care. In harmony with their occupa-tions, these divinities were either hoary river-gods (such as Father Nile), slender youths, beautiful maidens, or little babbling chil-dren. They seldom left the cool waves of their appointed dwel-lings, and strove to win Poseidon's approbation mostly by the zeal they showed in the discharge of their various duties.

PROTEUS AND POSEIDON

Proteus, too, another inferior deity, had the care of the flocks of the deep, and he always attended Poseidon when it was safe to leave his great herds of sea-calves to bask on the sunny shores.

> In ages past old Proteus, with his droves
> Of sea calves, sought the mountains and the groves.
> COWPER

In common with all the other gods, Proteus enjoyed the gift of prophecy, and had the power to assume any shape he pleased. The former gift he was wont to exercise very reluctantly; and when mortals wished to consult him he would change his form with bewildering rapidity, and unless they clung to him through all his changes they could obtain no answer to their questions.

> Shouting [we] seize the god: our force t' evade,
> His various arts he soon resumes in aid:
> A lion now, he curls a surgy mane;
> Sudden our hands a spotted pard restrain;
> Then, arm'd with tusks, and lightning in his eyes,
> A boar's obscener shape the god belies:
> On spiry volumes, there, a dragon rides;
> Here, from our strict embrace a stream he glides;
> And last, sublime, his stately growth he rears,
> A tree, and well-dissembled foliage wears.
> HOMER (*Pope's tr.*)

But if these manifestations proved unavailing to drive his would-be hearers away the god answered every question circumstantially.

Amphitrite, Poseidon's wife—generally represented as a beautiful nymph, crowned with seaweed, and reclining in a pearl-shell chariot drawn by dolphins or sea-horses—was worshipped with her husband.

Poseidon, majestic and middle-aged, with long, flowing hair and beard, wearing a crown and brandishing a trident, or three-pronged fork, was widely worshipped throughout Greece and Italy, and had countless shrines. His principal votaries were the seamen and horse-trainers, who often bespoke his aid.

Many large temples were dedicated exclusively to the worship of Poseidon, and games were frequently celebrated in his honour.

The most noted of all were undoubtedly the Isthmian Games—
a national festival held every four years at Corinth, on the isthmus
of the same name.   Hither people came from all points of the
compass and all parts of the then known world, either to witness
or to take part in the noted wrestling, boxing, and racing matches,
or in the musical and poetical contests.

> King of the stormy sea!
> Brother of Jove, and co-inheritor
> Of elements!   Eternally before
> Thee the waves awful blow.   Fast, stubborn rock,
> At thy fear'd trident shrinking, doth unlock
> Its deep foundations, hissing into foam.
> All mountain-rivers, lost in the wide home
> Of thy capacious bosom, ever flow.
> Thou frownest, and old Æolus thy foe
> Skulks to his cavern, 'mid the gruff complaint
> Of all his rebel tempests.   Dark clouds faint
> When, from thy diadem, a silver gleam
> Slants over blue dominion.   Thy bright team
> Gulphs in the morning light, and scuds along
> To bring thee nearer to that golden song
> Apollo singeth, while his chariot
> Waits at the doors of heaven.   Thou art not
> For scenes like this: an empire stern hast thou;
> And it hath furrow'd that large front: yet now,
> As newly come of heaven, dost thou sit
> To blend and interknit
> Subduèd majesty with this glad time.
> O shell-borne king sublime!
> We lay our hearts before thee evermore—
> We sing, and we adore!
>   KEATS

CHAPTER XII

PLUTO

PLUTO [1] (Dis, Hades, Orcus, Aïdoneus), son of Cronus and Rhea, and, therefore, brother of Zeus, received as his share of the world the supervision of the Infernal Regions, situated beneath the earth, and was also appointed god of the dead and of riches, for all precious metals are buried deep in the bosom of the earth.

This god inspired all men with a great fear. They never spoke of him without trembling, and they were wont to sacrifice black sheep to him, averting their faces and beating the ground with their hands. Whenever the stern god set out on an expedition he donned a helmet of invisibility given to him by the Cyclopes, and climbed into his chariot drawn by four coal-black steeds; and if any obstacle presented itself to impede his progress he struck it with his two-pronged fork, the emblem of his power, and the obstacle was immediately removed. It was on one of these occasions that Pluto abducted Persephone, the fair goddess of vegetation (daughter of Demeter), whom he set on his throne in Hades and crowned as his queen.

Pluto is always represented as a stern, dark, bearded man, with tightly closed lips, a crown on his head, a sceptre and a key in hand, to show how carefully he guards those who enter his domains, and how vain are their hopes to effect their escape. No temples were dedicated to him, and statues of this god are very rare. Human sacrifices were sometimes offered on his altars; and at his festivals, held every hundred years, and thence called Secular Games, none but black animals were slain.

His kingdom, generally called Hades, was very difficult of access. According to Roman traditions, it could only be entered at Avernus, a volcanic lake not far from Cumæ, in Southern Italy, but the Greeks asserted that there was an entrance near the

---

[1] Besides this Pluto, god of the Infernal Regions, the ancients also worshipped Plutus, a son of Demeter and Jason, who was known exclusively as the god of wealth. Abandoned in infancy, he was brought up by Pax, the goddess of peace, who is often represented holding him in her lap. Because Plutus insisted upon bestowing his favours upon good and noble mortals only, Zeus soon deprived him of his sight. Since then the blind god's gifts have been distributed indiscriminately.

Promontory of Tænarum, in Laconia. Both nations believed, however, that it was an almost impossible feat to get out again if one were rash enough to venture in.

> Easy it is Avernus to descend;
> But to win back into the light of day,
> That is a toil, a labour.
>
> VIRGIL

To prevent all mortals from entering and all spirits from escaping Pluto placed a huge three-headed dog, called Cerberus, to guard the gate.

From thence a long subterranean passage, through which shadowy spirits glided incessantly, led to the throne-room, where Pluto and Persephone sat in state, clad in their sable robes. This sombre realm was watered by four rivers: the Styx, so sacred that by it the gods swore their most binding oaths; the Acheron, river of woe; the Phlegethon, river of fire; and the Cocytus, the river of wailing.

> Four infernal rivers, that disgorge
> Into the burning lake their baleful streams—
> Abhorrèd Styx, the flood of deadly hate;
> Sad Acheron of sorrow, black and deep;
> Cocytus, named of lamentation loud
> Heard on the rueful stream; fierce Phlegethon
> Whose waves of torrent fire inflame with rage.
> Far off from these, a slow and silent stream,
> Lethe, the river of oblivion, rolls
> Her watery labyrinth.
>
> MILTON

In Roman mythology the name of the lake was Avernus, and it was across the Acheron that the souls of the departed were borne in a small boat by Charon, the ferryman of the world of shades. Among the Greeks the general name of Tartarus was given to the gulf into which the four infernal rivers flowed, and it was across the Styx that Charon went to and fro. Each soul was expected to pay for its passage, and the ' legal fare ' was a small coin called an *obolus*. These coins were placed upon the tongues of dead people, otherwise it was believed that the ferryman might keep them waiting for a hundred years on the brink of the river. One of the most famous fragments in Latin literature is the passage in which Virgil describes the souls stretching out their arms lovingly towards the distant shore, the shore they are longing to reach as Charon's craft moves slowly across the dark waters.

Near Pluto's throne were seated the three judges of Hades, Minos, Rhadamanthus, and Æacus, whose duty it was to question all newly arrived souls, to sort out the confused mass of good and bad thoughts and actions, and to decide upon their ultimate doom. If the good outweighed the evil the spirit was led to the Elysian Fields; but if, on the contrary, the evil prevailed the spirit was condemned to suffer in the fires of Tartarus.

The guilty souls were always entrusted to the three snake-locked Furies (Diræ, Erinnyes, or Eumenides), who drove them with their stinging lashes to the gates of Tartarus. These deities, who were sisters, and children of Acheron and Nyx, were distinguished by the individual names of Alecto, Tisiphone, and Megæra, and with Nemesis, goddess of revenge, were noted for their hard hearts and the merciless manner in which they hurried the ghosts entrusted to their care over the fiery flood of the Phlegethon and through the brazen gates of their future place of incessant torment.

> On the left bank
> He sees a fortress girt with triple walls
> Washed by the flaming waves of Phlegethon,
> The stream of Tartarus, crashing on the rocks.
> The adamantine columns of its gate
> Might neither men nor gods cast down in war:
> Hard by an iron tower springs to the sky,
> And there, with blood-stained robe and wakeful eyes,
> Tisiphone keeps ward, by night and day.
>
> VIRGIL

THE STORY OF IBYCUS

The Furies also had an important part to play upon earth as the avengers of unfilial deeds, irreverence to age, inhospitality, murder, perjury, and certain minor crimes. They secured the punishment of those who had incurred their wrath in various ways, and the following story is told of the murder of Ibycus, a poet dear to Apollo.

While on his way to a musical contest at Corinth this poet was attacked and slain by two robbers, and in despair he called upon a flock of cranes which was passing overhead at the time to bear

G

witness to the foul deed. When his body was discovered there was great grief throughout Greece, and all men demanded vengeance upon the murderers.

Shortly after a play was being enacted in the great amphitheatre in which the Furies were very vividly represented, and the multitude of spectators sat in deep silence listening to the awful denunciations of the Furies upon the secret murderers.

Suddenly a flock of cranes was seen winging its flight above the arena, and a voice from the audience was heard: " See, comrade, the cranes of Ibycus! " Quick to grasp the meaning of this strange exclamation, the spectators shouted with one accord: " He is the murderer of Ibycus! " This was true, and the murderers—there were actually two of them—forthwith confessed, and were shortly afterwards executed for their crime.

The three Fates (Mœræ, Parcæ), sisters, also sat near Pluto's throne. Clotho, the youngest, spun the thread of life, in which the bright and dark lines were intermingled. Lachesis, the second, twisted it; and under her fingers it was now strong, now weak.

> Twist ye, twine ye! even so,
> Mingle shades of joy and woe,
> Hope, and fear, and peace, and strife,
> In the thread of human life.
>
> SCOTT

Atropos, the third sister, armed with a huge pair of shears, remorselessly cut short the thread of life—an intimation that another soul would ere long find its way down into the dark kingdom of Hades. It is she whom Milton calls " the Fury with the abhorrèd shears."

THE STORY OF THE DANAIDES

Among the culprits destined to suffer for untold ages beneath the knotted whips of the Furies were the fifty daughters of Danaus, King of Argos. Their father had promised them in marriage to the fifty sons of his brother Ægyptus. The marriage preparations were all completed, when Danaus suddenly remembered an ancient prophecy which foretold that he would perish by the hand of his son-in-law.

It was now too late to prevent the marriages, so, calling his daughters aside, he told them what the oracle had said, and, giving them each a sharp dagger, bade them slay their husbands on their wedding night. The marriages were celebrated, as was customary, with mirth, dance, and song; and the revelry continued until late at night, when, the guests having departed, the newly married couples retired. But as soon as Danaus's daughters were quite certain their husbands were fast asleep they produced their daggers and slew them. One of the brides only, Hypermnestra, loved her husband too dearly to obey her father's command, and when morning broke only forty-nine of Ægyptus's sons were found lifeless. The sole survivor, Lynceus, to avenge his brothers' death, slew Danaus, thus fulfilling the ominous prophecy; while the gods, incensed by the Danaides' heartlessness, sent them to Hades, where they were compelled to toil for ever attempting to fill with water a large cask with a hole in the bottom.

TANTALUS

Another of the famous sinners who suffered in Tartarus was Tantalus, King of Phrygia, one of the numerous semi-mortal sons of Zeus. Tantalus was permitted to sit at table with the Olympian gods, and he played a trick upon them which they could not forgive. Thinking to deceive them, and then laugh at their stupidity, he set before them the roasted flesh of his own son Pelops. But the gods were in no wise deceived. The young man was restored to life, and his impious father was condemned to stand for ever up to his neck in a pool of water without being able to satisfy his burning thirst. Hence comes our word ' tantalizing.' Above his head dangled delicious fruits, but these also he was not permitted to taste.

SISYPHUS

This tyrannous king of Corinth was punished for his many misdeeds by being forced to push a heavy stone to the summit of a steep hill and then see it crash down to the bottom again every time. You will remember that when Orpheus descended to

Hades his sweet music won a moment's respite for Sisyphus, as well as Tantalus.

IXION

Another victim of his own wrongdoing who felt the influence of Orpheus's music was Ixion, King of the Lapithæ. This king had slain his father-in-law, who was pressing him for the payment of a sum of money he had promised to give in exchange for his daughter's hand in marriage. Zeus, angered by the double sin of a broken promise and the murder of an old man, summoned Ixion to appear before him and answer for his crimes.

Most imprudently Ixion took advantage of the occasion to start a flirtation with Hera. His punishment was to be lashed to an ever-revolving wheel of fire.

THE ELYSIAN FIELDS

Very far from the flames and terrors of Tartarus were the Elysian Fields, the meadows of never-fading asphodel, where men and women who had lived righteously on earth enjoyed their eternal reward.

> Fortunate fields, and groves, and flowery vales;
> Thrice happy isles!
>
> MILTON

Resting Hermes
Greek bronze found at Herculaneum
(Page 78)
National Museum, Naples.   Photo Brogi

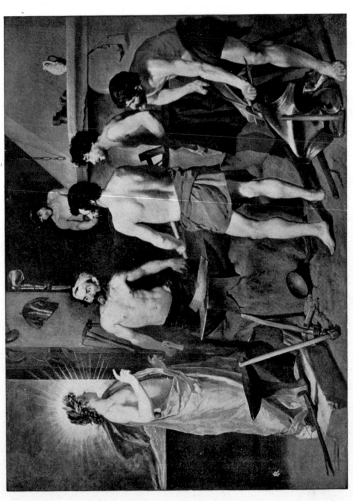

Bacchus at the Forge of Hephæstus
Velasquez
(*Page 86*)
Photo Anderson

CHAPTER XIII

BACCHUS (DIONYSUS)

YOU will remember Cadmus, King of Thebes, and his queen, Hermione. One of their daughters, Semele, was a maiden of such transcendent beauty that Zeus himself, the All-Highest, fell in love with her. Though he used to visit her in the guise of a simple mortal, he did not conceal his real name from her, and Semele felt duly flattered. Presently the rumour of Zeus's latest love-affair reached the ears of Hera, who promptly determined to bring it to an end. Disguising herself as Semele's aged nurse, Beroë, she hobbled into the young girl's room and, catching her in a confidential mood, induced her to talk of her divine lover.

"Zeus himself?" exclaimed the pretended nurse. "Why, child, what proof have you that it is Zeus himself?"

"He told me so," answered Semele trustfully.

"And you believed him! Well, well! I should not be too sure. Ask him to let you see him in all his godlike splendour. If he refuses you will know what to think."

Semele pondered long and anxiously upon these words, and finally resolved to act upon the supposed Beroë's hint. The next time Zeus came to see her she coaxed him to swear by the river Styx, the most solemn oath any god could swear, that he would grant her one solitary request. When he had sworn, and she had made her request, Zeus was appalled. He knew that even if he assumed what was known as his 'lesser panoply,' with mild lightnings and faint thunders, no mortal could look at him and yet live. He was bound, however, by his vow. And he had no choice but to appear before her dazzled eyes in the glory and splendour of his divine power. At the sight Semele fell swooning to the ground, and in a few moments both she and the house in which she lived were reduced to ashes by the flames which played round the head of the king of the gods. Zeus could neither save her nor restore her to life, but he was able to snatch from the fire their new-born son, Dionysus—often called Bacchus—destined to be the " monarch of the vine," the patron of the vine-growers and the wine-distillers and every one who makes or drinks wine. It was particularly among the Romans that he was a convivial god. Among the Greeks he bore a more solemn character as a god of fertility and vegetation.

BACCHUS AND HIS VOTARIES

The baby boy was by his divine father placed in the care of Semele's sister, Ino, Queen of Thebes, but Hera's jealous watchfulness and her desire to destroy the child caused Zeus to hand him over to Hermes to be carried to the far-off domain of certain nymphs known as the Nysiades. These nymphs tended the infant Bacchus with such care that Zeus, as a reward, changed them into the group of stars now called the Hyades.

When the boy was old enough to do lessons he was handed over to the satyr Silenus, son of the goat-footed god Pan. Silenus does not seem, according to our ideas, at all a suitable person for a tutor, being far too easygoing and genial, but he and his young charge seem to have got on very well.

When Bacchus was grown-up he made a discovery destined to have an important influence upon the lives of men. He discovered how to make wine from grape-juice. When the unresting enmity of Hera drove him forth and made him for many years a wanderer on the face of the earth he carried everywhere with him the cult of the vine, and many followers gathered round him wherever he went. Among the countries which he visited was India, where he remained some time before returning to his native city of Thebes, of which his cousin Pentheus was now king. Pentheus had heard of this new worship introduced by Bacchus, and accompanied by wild songs and dances by women votaries known as Bacchantes, and he did not desire that it should be introduced into his dominions. But his subjects had other views, and when the god, crowned with vine-leaves and standing in a chariot drawn by leopards, drew near great throngs of excited people rushed forth to greet him.

Keats, in his poem *Endymion*, thus describes the feelings of a young girl who saw the Bacchic procession drawing near:

And as I sat, over the light blue hills
There came a noise of revellers: the rills
Into the wide stream came of purple hue—
   'Twas Bacchus and his crew!
The earnest trumpet spake, and silver thrills
From kissing cymbals made a merry din—
   'Twas Bacchus and his kin!
Like to a moving vintage down they came,
Crown'd with green leaves, and faces all on flame;
All madly dancing through the pleasant valley.

The maiden joins the gay dance, which leads her through many strange lands and far, till she can say:

I saw Osirian Egypt kneel adown
   Before the vine-wreath crown!
I saw parch'd Abyssinia rouse and sing
   To the silver cymbals' ring!
I saw the whelming vintage hotly pierce
   Old Tartary the fierce!

Pentheus, determined that the new cult should not spread in Thebes, sent messengers to seize Bacchus, but the god eluded them, and they succeeded only in capturing one of his followers, who was brought before him, and, in reply to the King's questions, related the following story:

" My name is Acetes, and I was born in Mæonia. My parents were poor fisherfolk, and I followed their calling until, having grown skilful in the art of steering by the stars, I sailed my ship to more distant shores in quest of gain. It chanced one day that we grounded on the island of Dia, and certain of my men, having gone to fetch fresh water, brought back with them a beautiful youth whom they had found asleep on the shore. Him they proposed to hold captive for ransom, but I, aware that here was no ordinary mortal, prayed the stranger to pardon us all.

" Bacchus—for it was he—shook off his drowsiness and asked where we were taking him. ' Where,' asked the sailors, ' would you like to go? ' ' Naxos,' replied the young god, ' and if you land me there you will be well rewarded.'

" They agreed, but when I would have steered towards Naxos they overbore me, and turned the ship's prow towards Egypt, where they were minded to sell the youth as a slave. He wept, and I, seeing his tears, wept also, but the evil-minded seamen laughed at us both, and the wind filled the sails and bore us even farther from Naxos.

" Then, suddenly, the ship stopped short, as if fixed immovably to solid earth. In vain the seamen crowded on more sail, and tugged harder at the oars. With amazement we beheld long trails of dark ivy clinging to the prow and tangling among the oars, while a mighty vine, laden with purple grapes, drooped from the mainmast. At the same moment the sound of sweet flutes was heard. Then we beheld the god himself, crowned with vine-leaves, bearing in his hand a spear wreathed with ivy. At his feet lay brightly striped tigers, and round him gambolled the spotted panther and the keen-eyed lynx. Hardly had the crew time to gaze upon these wonders when they found themselves swimming in the sea, transformed into dolphins. Of twenty men I alone was left in the body of a man.

" ' Fear nothing,' said the god to me. ' Steer thou towards Naxos.' I obeyed him; and when we disembarked on the shore of that island we kindled sacred fires upon his altars and celebrated the Bacchic rites."

When Acetes had thus far told his story King Pentheus arose in wrath and gave orders that he should immediately be slain. But Bacchus did not desert his faithful follower, whom he made invisible and thus saved from death.

In the end it was the cruel King of Thebes who perished. He was slain in the confusion of the Bacchanalian festival by worshippers who, probably deluded by the god, mistook him for a wild boar. The worship of Bacchus, or Dionysus, as the god of corn and wine was thus established in the isles of Greece.

It must not be imagined that this god was the patron merely of revelry and of merriment induced by drinking wine. He was the god of fertility in general, whose flesh was changed into corn and his blood into wine every year, in order that men might eat, and drink, and live.

BACCHUS AND MIDAS

One day the old satyr Silenus was found lying asleep by some peasants, who carried him to the palace of their king. The name of this king was Midas, and he feasted Silenus royally before restoring him to his divine pupil, Bacchus. The god, grateful for this kindness shown to his tutor, told Midas to name his own reward. Very foolishly the King desired that everything he touched should turn to gold. At first it gave him great joy to see his wish granted, and chairs, tables, and vases suddenly changed into solid yellow metal. But when bread and apples underwent the same change into what Shakespeare calls " gaudy gold, hard food for Midas," the stupid man began to realize his blunder. Growing more and more hungry and thirsty, he finally prayed aloud to Bacchus to take back his uncomfortable gift.

" Go," said the god, " to the fountain-head of the river Pactolus, in Lydia, and bathe in the waters."

This Midas hastened to do, with the result that the divine gift was transferred from him to the river, of which the sands were ever after tinged with gold.

How Midas got into trouble through the decision he gave in a musical contest between Pan and Apollo has already been related.

BACCHUS AND ARIADNE

The island of Naxos, to which Bacchus had prayed the seamen of Acetes to carry him, was always a favourite resort of the god, and it was here that he found the beautiful Cretan princess Ariadne after she had been abandoned by Theseus. The early part of the story will be told later in this book, for Theseus was one of the most famous figures in Greek myth and legend.

When Bacchus saw Ariadne seated in tears on the seashore he drew near and gently asked the cause of her distress. When she told him his heart was touched with pity both by her beauty and by her sorrow, and he determined to use all his divine powers to console her. This he did so well that they fell in love with each other, and his most brilliant gift to her, a crown adorned with seven golden stars, afterwards became the constellation known as Ariadne's Crown. As she was a mortal and not a goddess, she died after some years, and her ashes were shrined in a rich vase in one of the temples of the people known as the Argives—men of Argos.

By the Romans also Bacchus was held in high honour as the

god of fertility and of the grape-harvest, and Virgil in his *Georgics* tells us some of the quaint ways in which the country folk were wont to celebrate his rites.

> Likewise the Ausonian folk, of Trojan breed,
> With rustic mirth and grinning masks of bark
> Invoke thee, Bacchus, and upon tall pines
> Hang fragile, wavering images of thee.
> Therefore the vineyards bring forth rich increase,
> The foison of the valleys overflows,
> Where'er the god reveals his kindly face.
> And therefore, as our fathers did, we sing
> In praise of Bacchus, bearing in our hands
> Broad platters and baked offerings, while a goat
> Is led unto the altar by its horn.

Bacchus is usually represented as a beautiful youth crowned with vine-leaves, holding in his hand a wand tipped by a fir-cone and twined with ivy.   But he was sometimes imagined as a baby, and at certain harvest festivals in Greece his image, in the likeness of a smiling infant, used to be carried in procession in a sort of cradle woven of rushes or willows.   Among birds the magpie was said to be his favourite.

The Greeks held festivals in his honour at which prizes were offered for the best tragedies and comedies, and in this way the cult of Dionysus came to be closely associated with the development of the Greek drama, which is said to have grown out of the mummings of the cultivators during the grape-harvest.

CHAPTER XIV

DEMETER AND PERSEPHONE

DEMETER (CERES), daughter of Cronus and Rhea, and one of Zeus's numerous consorts, was goddess of agriculture and civilization. Her manifold cares were shared by her daughter, Persephone (Kore, Proserpina), the goddess of vegetation. Whenever her duties permitted this fair young goddess hastened off to the island of Sicily, her favourite place of resort, where she wandered about all day long, attended by a train of laughing girls, gathering flowers on the green slopes of Mount Ætna, and dancing with the nymphs in the beautiful plain of Enna.

> Sacred Goddess, Mother Earth,
>   Thou from whose immortal bosom,
> Gods, and men, and beasts have birth,
>   Leaf and blade, and bud and blossom,
> Breathe thine influence most divine
> On thine own child, Proserpine.
>
> If with mists of evening dew
>   Thou dost nourish these young flowers
> Till they grow, in scent and hue,
>   Fairest children of the hours,
> Breathe thine influence most divine
> On thine own child, Proserpine.
>
>   SHELLEY

One day, weary of labour, Persephone called these fair playmates to join her and spend a day gathering flowers. The maidens sang merry lays as they wound their long garlands; and the joyous song of Persephone, mingled with ripples of silvery laughter, attracted the attention of Pluto, who happened to be driving past in his dark chariot drawn by four fiery coal-black steeds. The god stepped out of his car, and cautiously peeped through the thick foliage.

He saw Persephone sitting on a mossy bank, almost buried in many-hued blossoms, her laughing companions grouped around her. Pluto could not but think how her youth and beauty would relieve the gloom of his dark kingdom.

Long ere this he had tried to persuade one after another of the goddesses to share his throne; but one and all had refused the honour, and declined to accompany him to a land where the sun never shone, the birds never sang, and the flowers never bloomed. Hurt and disappointed by these rebuffs, Pluto had finally registered a solemn vow never to go wooing again; and so, instead of gently inviting Persephone to become his queen, he resolved to carry her away by main force.

Straight through the bushes he strode, direct to the spot where she was seated. The noise of crackling branches and hasty footsteps made the assembled maidens swiftly turn. One glance sufficed to identify the intruder, for none but he had such a dark, lowering countenance; and all exclaimed in mingled wonder and terror at his unwonted presence in those sunlit regions.

Frightened by his impetuous approach, the trembling nymphs first crowded around Persephone, who, in her terror, dropped all her pretty flowers and stood motionless among them. Her uncertainty as to his purpose was only momentary, for, catching her in his brawny arms ere she could make an attempt to escape, he bore her off to his chariot, in spite of prayers and struggles, and drove away as fast as his fleet steeds could carry him.

> O Proserpina,
> For the flowers now, that frighted thou let'st fall
> From Dis's waggon! daffodils,
> That come before the swallow dares, and take
> The winds of March with beauty; violets dim,
> But sweeter than the lids of Juno's eyes.
>
> SHAKESPEARE

He was soon out of hearing of the wild cries and lamentations of the nymphs, who vainly pursued him, and tried to overtake their beloved mistress. Afraid lest Demeter should come and force him to relinquish his new-won treasure, Pluto drove faster and faster, nor paused for an instant until he reached the banks of the Cyane river, whose waters, at his approach, began to seethe and roar in a menacing fashion and spread themselves as much as possible, to check him in his flight.

Pluto quickly perceived that to attempt to cross the river in his chariot would be madness, while by retracing his footsteps he ran the risk of meeting Demeter, and being forced to relinquish his

Poseidon
Adam, Louvre
(*Page* 93)
From a photograph by Levy et ses fils

The Fates
Michelangelo
(*Page* 98)
Photo Anderson

prize. He therefore decided to have recourse to other means, and, seizing his terrible two-pronged fork, struck the earth such a mighty blow that a crevice opened under his feet, through which horses and chariot plunged down into the darkness of the Lower World.

Persephone turned her weeping eyes to catch a parting glimpse of the fair earth she was leaving, and then, with a fond thought of her anxious mother, who when evening came would vainly seek her child in all her favourite haunts, she quickly flung her girdle into the Cyane, and called to the water-nymph to carry it to Demeter.

Meanwhile the sun had sunk below the Sicilian horizon; and Demeter, returning from the fields of fast-ripening grain to her own dwelling, sought for the missing Persephone, of whom no trace could be found except the scattered flowers. Hither and thither the mother wandered, calling her daughter, wondering where she could be and why she did not come to meet her. As time passed and still Persephone did not appear Demeter's heart beat fast with apprehension, and the tears coursed down her cheeks as she rushed about from place to place, calling her daughter.

Night came, and Demeter, kindling a torch at the volcanic fires of Mount Ætna, continued her search. Day dawned, and still the mother called, awakening the morning echoes with her longing cries for her child. Her daily duties were all neglected. The rain no longer refreshed the drooping flowers, the grain was parched by the ardent rays of the sun, and the grass all perished, while Demeter roamed over hill and dale in search of Persephone.

Weary at last of her hopeless quest, the goddess seated herself by the wayside, near the city of Eleusis, and gave way to her overwhelming grief.

> Long was thine anxious search
> For lovely Proserpine, nor didst thou break
> Thy mournful fast, till the far-fam'd Eleusis
> Received thee wandering.
>
> *Orphic Hymn*

DEMETER AND TRIPTOLEMUS

To avoid recognition the goddess had assumed the appearance of an aged crone; and as she sat there by the wayside in tears she attracted the attention of the daughters of Celeus, King of Attica. Having heard her bewail the loss of her child, they entreated her to come to the palace, and, knowing nothing was so likely to comfort her, offered her the charge of their infant brother Triptolemus.

Demeter, touched by their ready sympathy, accepted the offer; and when she arrived at the palace the royal heir, a feeble child, was entrusted to her care. At her touch he became rosy and well, to the unbounded astonishment of the royal family and all the court.

In the night, while Demeter sat alone with her charge, it occurred to her that she might confer a still greater blessing upon him, that of immortality: so she anointed his limbs with nectar, murmured a powerful charm, and placed him upon the red-hot coals, to consume all the perishable elements left in his body.

The Queen, Metaneira, who had thought it somewhat imprudent to leave the child thus alone with a stranger, now stole noiselessly into the apartment, and with a wild shriek rushed to the fire and snatched her child out of the flames, pressed him anxiously to her breast, and, after ascertaining that he was quite unharmed, turned to vent her indignation upon the careless nurse; but the aged beggar woman had vanished, and in her stead she confronted the radiant goddess.

> From her fragrant robes
> A lovely scent was scattered, and afar
> Shone light emitted from her skin divine,
> And yellow locks upon her shoulders waved;
> While as from lightning, all the house was filled
> With splendour.
>
> *Homeric Hymn*

With a gentle reproof to the Queen for her untimely interference, Demeter explained what she fain would have done. The spell was broken; she could not now make the boy immortal. But she still befriended him, as will be seen hereafter. Demeter finally returned to Sicily, and while she was wandering along the river-banks one day the waters suddenly cast a glittering object at her feet. She recognized the girdle her daughter had worn when she had parted from her—the girdle which Persephone had confided to the nymph Cyane at the very moment when Pluto's dark chariot was plunging down into the underworld.

Joyfully she embraced the token, and, thinking she must now be upon Persephone's track, hastened on until she came to a crystal fountain, by whose side she sat down to rest. Her eyes were heavy, and she was about to forget her trouble in sleep, when the murmur of the fountain increased, until she fancied it was talking—not as mortals do, but in its own silvery accents.

ARETHUSA AND ALPHEUS

The goddess was not mistaken; for a few minutes later she could distinguish words, and heard the fountain entreat her to listen, if she would hear what had befallen her child. The fountain then went on to tell how she had not always been a mere stream, but was once a nymph called Arethusa. Here is her story, in the lovely lyrical form given to it by Shelley:

> Arethusa arose
> From her couch of snows
> In the Acroceraunian mountains,—
> From cloud and from crag,
> With many a jag,
> Shepherding her bright fountains.
> She leapt down the rocks,
> With her rainbow locks
> Streaming among the streams;—
> Her steps paved with green
> The downward ravine
> Which slopes to the western gleams;
> And gliding and springing
> She went, ever singing
> In murmurs as soft as sleep;
> The Earth seemed to love her,
> And Heaven smiled above her,
> As she lingered towards the deep.

> Then Alpheus bold,
> On his glacier cold,
> With his trident the mountains strook;
> And opened a chasm
> In the rocks—with the spasm

All Erymanthus shook.
    And the black south wind
    It unsealed behind
The urns of the silent snow,
    And earthquake and thunder
    Did rend in sunder
The bars of the springs below.
    And the beard and the hair
    Of the River-god were
Seen through the torrent's sweep,
    As he followed the light
    Of the fleet nymph's flight
To the brink of the Dorian deep.

Oh, save me!   Oh, guide me!
    And bid the deep hide me,
For he grasps me now by the hair!
    The loud Ocean heard,
    To its blue depth stirred,
And divided at her prayer;
    And under the water
    The Earth's white daughter
Fled like a sunny beam;
    Behind her descended
    Her billows, unblended
With the brackish Dorian stream:—
    Like a gloomy stain
    On the emerald main
Alpheus rushed behind,—
    As an eagle pursuing
    A dove to its ruin
Down the streams of the cloudy wind.

    Under the bowers
    Where the Ocean Powers
Sit on their pearlèd thrones;
    Through the coral woods
    Of the weltering floods,
Over heaps of unvalued stones;
    Through the dim beams
    Which amid the streams
Weave a network of coloured light:
    And under the caves,
    Where the shadowy waves
Are as green as the forest's night;—
    Outspeeding the shark,
    And the sword-fish dark,
Under the Ocean's foam,
    And up through the rifts
    Of the mountain clifts
They passed to their Dorian home.

In her flight from the river-god Arethusa passed underground, through the realms of Pluto, and there she had beheld Persephone, sitting enthroned as the Queen of the Underworld. Coming to the light of day in the form of a fountain, she spoke with rippling murmurs to the sorrowful Demeter, who thus learned for the first time the fate of her lost child.

Demeter was not backward in importuning the All-Highest to intervene, and at last he agreed, provided that Persephone had eaten nothing during her sojourn in the underworld. Hermes, accompanied by Spring, was sent to tell Pluto that he must allow Persephone to return to her mother. Aware that the condition dictated by Zeus had not been fulfilled, the King of Hades expressed his willingness to obey. But at the critical moment a spirit of darkness called Ascalaphus declared that the queen had eaten part of a pomegranate containing six seeds. Therefore it was finally agreed that she should spend six months, one for each seed, in the realm of her husband, and six months on the surface of the earth. That is how the ancients explained the alternation of winter and summer.

Tennyson represents the two divine beings, Demeter, or Ceres, and Persephone, or Proserpina, at the moment of their joyful 'reunion,' and makes the mother goddess, even as she clasps her daughter in her arms, feel a thrill of terror lest the dark horses of Pluto's chariot-team should ascend from the depths beneath their feet,

> And all at once their arch'd necks, midnight-maned,
> Jet upward through the mid-day blossom. No!
> For, see, thy foot has touch'd it; all the space
> Of blank earth-baldness clothes itself afresh,
> And breaks into the crocus-purple hour
> That saw thee vanish.

When Persephone descended to Hades her joyful looks changed to pale sadness, and instead of dancing gaily through the flowery meadows she sat in mournful state beside her lord, the King of Hell. As she was a vegetation goddess, associated in men's minds with the return of spring, Persephone was an object of intense devotion in Greece and Italy, often sharing her temples and her altars with her mother, the golden-haired Queen of the Corn-fields. This is how Virgil addresses the husbandmen in his agricultural poems, the *Georgics*:

H

The yearly rites to Ceres shall you pay
Upon the joyful sward, when winter wanes
And spring is fair.   The lambs are fat and now
The wine is mellowest.   At such a time
Slumbers are sweet, and shadows throng the hills.

Let all the country lads give honours due
To Ceres, mixing honey, milk, and wine.
Thrice lead the chosen victim round the field,
Of springing crops, and with it all the choir
Of blithe companions, bidding Ceres grace
Their roof-trees.   Let no cultivator lay
His sickle to the ripened ears until,
With oaken leaves about his forehead bound,
He has for Ceres danced his artless dance
And sung his uncouth hymns.

After her long, sad quest had ended Demeter returned to
Eleusis, where her former nursling, Triptolemus, had grown to
man's estate.   The earth was still suffering from the blight and
barrenness which had resulted from her absence, and she chose
this young prince to be the messenger of her mercy to mankind
by teaching them the use of the plough, the sickle, and the spade.

Ceres first taught mankind to turn the soil
With iron, when even in Dodona's grove
Was dearth of acorns and of arbutus.
Even the corn was smitten at that time,
With cruel mildew feeding on its stalks,
Where barren thistles reared their spiky heads.
The crops died, and a shaggy wilderness
Usurped the smiling fields, where weeds and burrs,
Grim darnel and wild oats held sterile sway.

VIRGIL

So that he might spread the precious knowledge far and wide
Demeter lent to Triptolemus her own chariot drawn by two
dragons, and when in Scythia the king of the country would
treacherously have slain the stranger prince she changed the false
monarch into a lynx.

Eleusis was the chief centre of the religious rites sacred to
Demeter.

Bacchus and Ariadne
Titian
(*Page* 105)

Pluto and Proserpine
Ludovisi Museum

CHAPTER XV

HESTIA

HESTIA, or Vesta, daughter of Cronus (or, as some say, Saturn) and Rhea, was the goddess of fire, especially the fire kindled on the hearth of a human habitation, and thence the patron divinity of home. Both among the Greeks, under the name of Hestia, and among the Romans, under the name of Vesta, she was held in high honour. The hearth was a very holy spot to the pagan family, and might almost be called an altar, since the fire that burned upon it was regarded as sacred. When a Greek baby boy was five days old his father would lift him in his arms and run with him round the hearth—which was in the centre of the house, not, as now, against a wall. This was so that Hestia should take the child under her protection, especially while he was learning to toddle.

The temples of Vesta were circular, and they were served by virgin priestesses, whose lives were dedicated to her. Though wooed by both Apollo and Poseidon this goddess had remained aloof, even more aloof than Artemis, for there is no record of her having relented towards god or man.

The Romans believed that the cult of Vesta had been brought into their country—Latium—by the hero Æneas, whose adventures we shall soon relate. Numa Pompilius, one of the earliest kings of Rome, built a temple in her honour, where was preserved the famous Palladium of Troy. This temple stood in the very centre of the Roman Forum, and the welfare of the whole city and State was believed to depend upon the maintenance of the sacred flame which it enshrined, guarded by priestesses called the Vestal Virgins.

They were at first four and afterwards six in number, and were under the control of the Pontifex Maximus, the head of the priestly college which directed the religious affairs of Rome. It was he who by the drawing of lots elected a new Vestal when there was a vacancy in the priesthood. The candidate had to be between six and ten years of age, perfect in mind and body, and of

Italian birth.   Her training took ten years; then she spent another ten carrying out her sacred duties; then another ten instructing novices.   Finally, at the age of forty, she was free, if she so desired, to return to the busy world, and even to take a husband!

The Vestals, in addition to keeping the sacred flame alive, had to go every day and fetch water from the fountain of Egeria, on the outskirts of the city.   They were also the custodians of a mysterious and very sacred object brought by Æneas from Troy, called the Palladium, and supposed to be a very ancient and probably shapeless image of the goddess Athene.   Another legend declares that this object was a shield, which had fallen down from heaven.   They had privileges as well as duties.   At public games and festivals places of honour were set aside for them, and when they went abroad a lictor, carrying the *fasces*, the axe in the centre of a bundle of rods, went before them, as he was wont to go before the principal magistrates.   If a Vestal gave evidence in a court of law it was not necessary for her to swear to speak the truth—her simple word was enough.   If she met a criminal by pure chance, on the way to execution, she could, if she so pleased, give him a free pardon then and there.   The cult of Vesta was piously observed in Rome till well into the Christian era, when, in the year 380, the sacred fire was quenched and its virgin guardians were dispersed by the Emperor Theodosius, called ' the Great.'

THE STORY OF NUMA POMPILIUS AND EGERIA

We have just mentioned that one of the duties of the Vestal Virgins was to bring water from the fountain of Egeria.   This was the legend which belonged to that spring.

Numa Pompilius, who founded the temple of Vesta, was a Sabine philosopher of great virtue and wisdom whom the Romans, after the mysterious death of Romulus, chose to be their second king.   He was a peace-loving man, who encouraged arts and crafts and taught, or tried to teach, his subjects to worship the gods without the intervention of graven images or superstitious rites.   During his reign of forty-three years he raised the Roman people from comparative barbarism to a state of peaceful and pious activity never known before in that land.   Through all his difficulties he was helped and guided by a nymph called Egeria.   Ovid says she was his wife, but other ancient poets think she was merely his more-than-mortal counsellor and friend.

It must have been very convenient for Numa to be able to tell his people that all the laws he wished to institute and all the customs he wished them to adopt had the full approval of the divine nymph whom he was wont to visit from time to time. When, after a long reign, the wise old King died, the disconsolate Egeria wept until she turned into a fountain.

CHAPTER XVI

CEYX AND HALCYONE

THERE was a certain King Ceyx of Trachin, in Thessaly, who had a beautiful and devoted wife called Halcyone, a daughter of Æolus, the king of the winds. Now Ceyx had occasion—the wherefore is too long a tale to tell now—to go and consult the famous oracle at Delphi. In vain his Queen implored him to let her share the hardships and perils of the journey. All the comfort he could give her was a solemn oath to return before the moon should twice have been at the full. She watched him from the shore when his galley put to sea, and saw him standing on the high poop, waving his hand to her, as long as he was within sight of land; then when the mast had vanished beyond the horizon she returned to the lonely palace to weep and to pray for her lord's safety.

When night fell the sea began to grow rough, and the wind was so strong that the captain of the ship gave orders to lower the yard and reef the sail, while the rowers drew in their now useless oars.

The storm grew more fierce, and amid the crash of waves, wind, and thunder men could not hear each other speak. Ceyx was thinking of Halcyone, while with the hand that once was wont to hold the royal sceptre he clung fast to a breaking spar. After the goodly ship had filled with water and had sunk he still kept himself a little while afloat, praying to the waves to bear his body to his native shore, so that he might receive the rites of burial from the dear hands of his Queen. Then as the dim dawn broke over the sea a dark billow crashed over his head, and he was overwhelmed.

Meanwhile Halcyone was counting the days till his return and busily weaving fair new robes for herself and for him. She burned incense to all the gods, but more especially to the Queen of Heaven, praying that her husband might return, and that he might never love any woman more than herself—which last prayer was granted. At last Hera, who knew that Ceyx was dead, said to Iris, the rainbow messenger, " Go, Iris, most faithful handmaiden, to the abode of Sleep, and bid him send to Halcyone a dream telling her of the death of her lord."

So Iris donned her many-hued mantle, and sought the darkling hollow, washed by the slow waters of Lethe, where Hypnos, the god of sleep, had his abode. (Hypnos was called by the Romans Somnus.)

Round the entrance to the cavern where the god dwelt grew masses of poppies and of those herbs whose juices bring oblivion; and inside, upon an ebony couch, Hypnos lay dreaming, surrounded by empty masks and images of a thousand shapes and colours. Iris delivered her message, and flew away in haste lest she too should lapse into slumber. And then Hypnos summoned Morpheus, one of his numerous children, a spirit skilful in mimicking the looks and the voices of mortal men. In order to fulfil the behest of Hera this spirit put on the outward form of Ceyx, and went and stood, with a pale face and water dripping from his hair, beside the couch of Halcyone, to whom he spoke in her husband's own well-remembered voice. " Look on me, unhappy wife! Do you recognize your Ceyx? Alas, your prayers availed nothing! I am dead. Even as I uttered your name the salt waves filled my mouth."

With bitter tears Halcyone started up, crying aloud, " Wait for me! Whither do you go so fast? We will go together! "

Her attendants, hearing her cries, came to her bearing a lamp, and she told them what had befallen, and sought for the wet footprints of Ceyx upon the floor. When morning came she went down to the seashore, and lingered at the spot where he had kissed her farewell. And presently, as she gazed over the moving waters, she saw something like a man's body, borne shoreward by the tide.

" Alas, poor man," said she, " whoever you may be, and alas for your wife, if such you have! " But now the dead form of Ceyx was so near that she could see that it was he; and with a loud cry, lifting her trembling hands above her head, she would have flung herself into the water. Then, in an instant, her arms changed to wings, and in the likeness of a sea-bird she fluttered over the crests of the waves. The gods saw her, and as she tried to fold her wings round the lifeless head of her lord they changed them both into birds.

Thus came into existence the azure-plumed birds called halcyons, who, as men said, nested and reared their brood upon the face of the waters.   Seven days before the shortest day of the year and seven days after, even in the heart of winter, the waves of the sea are hushed.   This Æolus does, for the love of his daughter Halcyone.   So ran the story.

It is of this charming legend that Milton was thinking when he wrote in his *Ode on the Morning of Christ's Nativity*:

Birds of calm sit brooding on the charmèd wave.

CHAPTER XVII

ÆOLUS

NOT very far from the drowsy realm of Hypnos, but on the surface of the world, were the Æolian Islands, now known as the Lipari Islands, where the god Æolus (sometimes called Hippotades), king of the winds, held sway.

He is said to have received his royal dignity from the hands of Hera, and was therefore regarded as especially devoted to her service. Mythologists differ as to the name of his wife and the number of their children, but it seems clear that among his blustering sons were Eurus and Boreas, the east and north winds, while the gentler side of the family was represented by Zephyrus (whom the Romans called Favonius), the west wind, and Notus (or Auster), the south.

Not unnaturally poets and seafarers, farmers and travellers, at all times much preferred the milder winds to their more strenuous brethren.

This is how the greatest of Roman poets describes the abode of the father of all the winds:

> Here Æolus, within his cavern vast,
> Curbing the violent blasts and thundering storms,
> Holds them enchained. They chafe and fret the while
> Against their bars, the mountains make deep moan.
> He sits upon his throne, with sceptred hand
> Calming their fury; wherein did he fail
> They would drive sea, and land, and arching sky
> Whirling before them through the gusty air.
>
> **VIRGIL**

Æolus, king of the winds, shared with Dædalus the honour of inventing the sails which bear the ships so swiftly over the tide. It was he, too, who, according to Homer, bound all his children but one in a leather bag, which he gave to Odysseus (Ulysses) when the latter visited Æolia. Thanks to this gift, Odysseus reached the shores of Ithaca, and would have landed in safety had not his men, in view of port, untied the sack to see what was in it, and thus set free the angry winds, who stirred up the most terrible tempest in legendary history.

The people of the antique world, especially those engaged in trading by sea, paid great respect to the winds.   In Athens a temple was erected in their honour, which still stands.   It dates from the first century before Christ, and on it the winds are represented in human forms.   The Greeks of Homer's time imagined Boreas and Zephyrus as dwelling in a cavern in Thrace, whence Iris would summon them at the behest of Hera or of other Olympian beings.   After the battle of Thermopylæ, Boreas, whom the Athenians had anxiously invoked, rose in his might and scattered the Persian fleet lying at anchor off Cape Sepias. White animals were sacrificed to the south and west winds, black animals to those of the north and east.

CHAPTER XVIII

HERAKLES

MANY of the unseen beings in whom the ancients believed, and to whom they offered worship, were natural forces, such as the sun and the moon, the winds and waters, the flowers and the vines, and the vegetation returning every spring. But there were other divine, or semi-divine, personifications who were probably once real mortal men and women who by some remarkable gift of body or mind raised themselves above their fellows while they lived, and were, by the common consent of later generations, venerated as gods after death.

Among these was the hero Herakles (Hercules, Alcides), the pagan ' opposite number ' of Samson in the Bible. His mother was Alcmene, a granddaughter of Perseus and Andromeda, whose history we shall soon relate, and his father was none other than Zeus, the All-Highest. He was born in Thebes, and from his birth he was the object of Hera's unrelenting hatred. She sent two large, scaly serpents to kill him as he lay in his cradle, but the amazing infant strangled them with his already powerful hands, thereby adding to the annoyance of the ox-eyed Queen of Heaven.

To mankind at large Herakles passed as the son of his stepfather, Amphitryon, King of Thebes, son of Alcæus—hence his surname (as we should now call it) Alcides. He was entrusted to the care of Rhadamanthus, who was supposed to teach him wisdom and virtue, Chiron, the learned Centaur, who was his instructor in athletics and manly sports, and Linus, who taught him music. One day his music-master attempted to punish Herakles for some fault, and the young man, unaware as yet of his more than mortal strength, smote him so hard with his lute that he fell dead. To punish him for this evil deed Herakles was sent away to the mountains, where he grew taller and stronger than ever, and distinguished himself by slaying a lion which had been destroying flocks and herds near the town of Thespiæ, in Bœotia.

During his time of exile he is said to have encountered two women, Kakia, or Vice, and Arete, or Virtue. Each offered to be his friend and guide, one promising him riches and delights, while the other offered struggles and hardships. It may have been a sudden recollection of the good advice of Rhadamanthus which moved the youth to prefer Arete, and she certainly kept her word to him, for his career on earth was laborious and painful to the last. This is the incident usually described as ' The Choice of Herakles.'

THE HATRED OF HERA

Unlike some muscular men, Herakles had a taste for the finer arts, especially music. He competed against Apollo at Delphi, rather to the annoyance of the sun-god, but after the other gods had intervened the two became and remained excellent friends.

The city of Thebes was at that time much harassed by the neighbouring city of Orchomenus, and King Amphitryon, together with his son, Iphicles, resolved to end this oppression. In this he was so valiantly aided by Herakles that he gave him as a reward the hand in marriage of the Princess Megara. They lived very happily for some years with their children, and then the implacable hatred of Hera once more made itself felt, and she bewitched Herakles, so that, not knowing what he did, he slew his own children. He would have slain Amphitryon also, but Athene smote him on the head with a stone and stunned him. When he recovered consciousness he was himself again, distressed and bewildered at what he had unwittingly done, and ready to expiate the sin of murder by whatever means the high gods should decree. Zeus, prompted by his wife, ruled that Herakles should enter the service of his cousin, Eurystheus, King of Argos and Mycenæ, and perform whatever hard tasks that king should dictate.

THE LABOURS OF HERAKLES

Eurystheus, a spiteful and jealous person, set himself with enthusiasm to find a series of twelve thoroughly difficult and dangerous undertakings—the same which are usually known as the Twelve Labours of Herakles. The gods, pitying the culprit whose crime had been forced upon him by the Queen of Heaven, armed him with certain weapons which were of great service to him in his long-drawn-out ordeal. Athene gave him a helmet, Hermes a sword, Zeus a shield, Apollo a bow and arrows. Poseidon provided a horse, but as the Labours were performed upon dry land we may assume that it was not one of the sea-god's blue-maned and scaly-tailed steeds.

(1) THE NEMEAN LION

The first Labour of Herakles was to slay a terrible lion which was laying waste the country round about the city of Nemea. It was a much more alarming beast than the lion he had slain at Thespiæ, for neither sword nor arrow could pierce its hide, and blows from the massy club which the hero also carried were equally ineffectual. Finally Herakles pursued the creature into its den, and strangled it, just as he had strangled the two serpents when he was a baby. He stripped off the lion's skin and, flinging it round him like a cloak, hastened off to Mycenæ to inform Eurystheus that the first of his behests had been duly carried out. So alarmed was the King at the sight of Herakles clad in the lion's skin that he hastily issued an order that henceforth his cousin should come to the gates of the city to give an account of his exploits, but without venturing inside!

(2) THE HYDRA

In a swamp near the well of Amymone there dwelt a horrible water-serpent called the Hydra. Pagan authorities differ as to the number of its heads, some saying that it had nine, others that it had fifty, or even a hundred. Whatever the number may have been when the Hydra was hatched out, it was liable to be multiplied by two, for whenever one of its ugly heads was cut off a couple at once sprang up in its place, unless the severed stump was seared with fire.

The Second Labour of Herakles was to destroy this monster. He had the advantage on this occasion of a helping hand from his young kinsman Iolaus, son of Iphicles, now King of Thessaly, who, as fast as the hero lopped off the Hydra's heads, thrust a red-hot iron against the stump. During the struggle Hera, annoyed to see that the hated Herakles was getting the best of it, sent a sea-crab to bite his foot, but it was crushed by a hasty blow from the already famous club, and all that the Queen of Heaven could do was to install the creature among the stars as the constellation still known as Cancer, which in Latin means a crab. When finally the Hydra was disposed of Herakles dipped his arrows in its venomous blood, an action which before long he had cause to regret.

(3) THE STAG OF CERYNEA

Between Arcadia and Achaia, among the hills of Cerynea, there roved a marvellous stag, with antlers of gold and hoofs of bronze; and this stag Herakles was bidden to bring alive into the presence of Eurystheus. (This does not tally with the story that the timorous King forbade the hero even to enter the gates of his city of Mycenæ; but perhaps Eurystheus proposed on that occasion to lock himself up in the brazen urn which he had had made as a sort of ' funk-hole.')

Herakles spent a whole year hunting the marvellous stag, and when finally he succeeded in catching it Artemis snatched it from him, demanding with anger how he had dared to lay hands on a creature sacred to herself. The goddess relented, however, when the hard-worked hero explained that he was merely carrying out one of the Labours divinely imposed upon him in expiation of his sin.

(4) THE ERYMANTHEAN BOAR

Mount Erymanthus, in Arcadia, was haunted by a peculiarly fierce boar, and the next Labour of Herakles was to catch it. Unfortunately this mountain was also frequented by the Centaurs, those strange beings, half man, half horse, to whose care various famous people, including Æsculapius and Herakles himself, had been confided in their youth. One of them, called Pholus, entertained the hero hospitably, but refused to give him any wine, pleading that what he had was not his personal property, but belonged to the Centaur tribe in general. Herakles, with a surprising lack of good manners, broke the cask and drank the wine. When the other Centaurs hurried to the spot, and would have burst into the dwelling-place of Pholus, excited by the smell of the

The Return of Persephone
Lord Leighton
(Page 113)
By permission of the Fine Art Society, Ltd.

126

Herakles' Struggle with Death for the Life of Alcestis

Lord Leighton

(Page 43)

By permission of the Fine Art Society, Ltd.

liquor, the guest began to shoot at them with his poisoned arrows, and was so unlucky as to wound his old tutor, Chiron, in the knee. The pain was unendurable, and Chiron implored the gods to let him die like a mortal man, taking away his gift of immortality. This they did, transferring him to the heavens in the form of the constellation Sagittarius (the Archer).

Pholus too suffered from having entertained Herakles. In endeavouring to extract one of the poisoned barbs from a fellow-Centaur he gave himself a mortal wound. Unlike Chiron, he was not immortal. Herakles paid him all the rites due to the dead, and buried him on the side of a mountain afterwards called Pholæ.

The hero then went ahead with his task of catching the boar, which he pursued for many miles through deep snow. When at last he succeeded in catching it he bore it back in triumph to Mycenæ—and Eurystheus was so much appalled at the sight that he hid himself in his brazen shelter for several days!

(5) THE AUGEAN STABLES

Augeas, King of Elis, was a very negligent man. He had an immense number of oxen, also goats, but the huge stables in which they were kept remained without being cleaned from one year's end to another. To clean these indescribable stables was the fifth, and, one would imagine, the most disagreeable, Labour of Herakles.

When he arrived at Elis the hero struck a bargain with the King, according to which, in return for cleaning the stables, he should receive a certain number of the beasts in them. But after he had accomplished the task by turning the rivers Alpheus and Peneus out of their natural courses and making them wash away the foul mire, the King refused to abide by his word, claiming that the rivers, and not the hero, had actually done the work. When Phyleus, the King's young son, sided with Herakles, he was driven from the kingdom. Herakles thereupon invaded and conquered Elis, put Augeas to death, and established Phyleus on the vacant throne. Few of the Labours have produced more metaphorical allusions than the Fifth, and many people speak of cleansing the Augean stables who have very vague ideas as to who cleansed them first or why they were so named.

(6) THE STYMPHALIAN BIRDS

The inhabitants of the valley of Stymphalus were much afflicted by flocks of large and fierce birds, who were wont to devour men as well as animals. The Sixth Labour of Herakles was to destroy these horrible creatures.

(7) THE CRETAN BULL

In the island of Crete there was at this time a beautiful but very dreadful bull, a gift from Poseidon to Minos, the King of Crete. Because Minos, struck by the beauty of the animal, hesitated to sacrifice it as the sea-god had intended that he should, Poseidon drove the bull mad, and the Seventh Labour of Herakles was to catch and tame the beast. It must have been a pleasant change after so much killing.

(8) THE HORSES OF DIOMEDES

Diomedes, King of Thrace, a cruel and eccentric prince, was wont to feed his horses upon human flesh. The Eighth Labour of Herakles was to obtain and bring to Eurystheus these famous though fierce animals. This he accomplished by killing Diomedes when he offered resistance and flinging his body to the horses, which he afterwards succeeded in driving before him to Mycenæ. We are not told how long Eurystheus remained in his brazen jar on *that* occasion, and there are conflicting stories as to the fate of the horses. According to one version they were driven —or escaped—to the hills of Arcadia, where Apollo sent even wilder beasts to destroy them; the other legend is that they were dedicated to Zeus, became tame, and that the breed was still in existence in the days of Alexander the Great.

(9) THE GIRDLE OF HIPPOLYTA

The daughter of Eurystheus greatly desired a beautiful girdle in the possession of Hippolyta, the Queen of the warlike race of women known as the Amazons. The Ninth Labour of Herakles was to obtain this girdle. He journeyed to the land of the Amazons, where all the arts of war and peace were practised exclusively by strenuous and man-hating women, and did actually succeed in winning the goodwill of their Queen, and in persuading her to give him the girdle. But Hera, disguising herself as an Amazon, spread a false rumour that the stranger was carrying off their Queen by main force. The Amazons sprang to arms, and Herakles, imagining that Hippolyta had played him false, killed her on the spot. After which he set sail, bearing the girdle with him. (There is a less cruel version of the tale according to which the hero, instead of slaying the Queen of the Amazons, handed her over to his friend Theseus, who married her.)

(10) THE OXEN OF GERYON

Geryon was a queer monster with three bodies who ruled over the island Erythea—the Red Island, so called because it lay under the rays of the setting sun. He had a celebrated herd of oxen, and these Herakles now had to bring to Mycenæ. This time his travels took him very far afield—some say as far as Spain. It was on this journey that he brought into existence the Pillars of Hercules, on either side of the Strait of Gibraltar, now called Ceuta and Gibraltar, but then Calpe and Abyla. Some writers declare that he did this by splitting one peak asunder, thus making it into two, and letting the sea flow between; others maintain that by his great strength he bent the two summits together and formed a temporary bridge. He slew the giant and the double-headed dog guarding the oxen, and then, probably with considerable difficulty, transported them from Erythea to the realm of Eurystheus.

(11) THE APPLES OF THE HESPERIDES

Far away in the golden realm of the sunset lay the lovely gardens of the Hesperides, where, guarded by a dragon which never slept, hung the golden apples given to Zeus by Hera on the day of their marriage.

The Hesperides were three beautiful nymphs, but whether the

I

daughters of Hesperus or of Atlas, his brother, is a little uncertain.   They helped the dragon to watch over the apples, and to obtain some of these was the eleventh task imposed upon Herakles.

After many wanderings in quest of the blissful gardens the hero, aided by sage counsels from the sea-god Nereus, reached that part of Africa where the giant Atlas was holding the whole heavens (some say the whole globe of the earth as well) upon his shoulders.   To him, as the father (or perhaps the uncle) of the Hesperides, the wanderer addressed an earnest prayer for help. The giant, after some demur, finally agreed to try to obtain three of the golden apples, on condition that while he went in quest of them Herakles should stand in his place and hold up the heavens. After an interval, which seemed very long to his deputy, Atlas returned, bearing the apples, but feeling a strong reluctance to resume his burden.   Why should not *he*, instead of Herakles, take the apples to Eurystheus?

" Why not, indeed? " assented the hero ; adding only a modest request that the giant should shoulder the heavens again for just a moment, to enable him to get a pad to put between his back and its immense load.   This Atlas agreed to do, but no sooner was the great mass of stars once more resting upon its former support than Herakles snatched up the apples and set off in much haste for Mycenæ.

(12) THE DOG CERBERUS

The gates of the nether world were guarded by a particularly fierce three-headed dog called Cerberus—a dog whom we met when we followed Orpheus down among the shades.

The Twelfth Labour of Herakles was to fetch Cerberus—a task which even *he* had not the courage to attempt without more than mortal aid.   He persuaded Athene and Hermes to go with him, and they all three descended through a dark chasm in the flank of Mount Tænarus, in Laconia.   Pluto happened to be in a more or less obliging humour.   He not only agreed to the temporary absence of his watch-dog—provided that Herakles could carry him off without using any weapon to stun or injure him—but also consented to release from bondage two famous men, Theseus and Pirithous, whom his visitor counted among his friends.

Cerberus was duly overpowered, carried to Mycenæ, and subsequently restored to his master.

One version of the story says that Pirithous was not released with Theseus.

Herakles, having completed his Twelve Labours, returned to Thebes, but instead of settling down quietly to rest after his years of toil he almost at once set off in quest of new adventures. First of all he formally renounced his wife Megara, having reached the conclusion that their marriage had been displeasing to the gods. About this time he is said to have accompanied Jason and the Argonauts—whose story will soon be related—on their voyage to Colchis. Another version places this enterprise later in his eventful career. It will also be remembered that he released Prometheus and restored Alcestis to life.

HERAKLES AND ANTÆUS

Poseidon and Gæa were the parents of a gigantic son called Antæus, whom no man might conquer or kill as long as he could touch with some part of his huge body the earth from which he had been born. It was the unpleasant habit of Antæus to challenge any stranger to a wrestling match, with the stipulation that if they were defeated the penalty would be death. Never by any chance had one of them escaped.

Herakles crossed the path of this giant, and when, during the wrestling match which followed, he perceived that Antæus could not be beaten unless he were cut off from all contact with the earth, he lifted his adversary in his mighty arms and strangled him aloft in the air.

A much later tradition relates that as the hero lay sleeping after this exploit an army of tiny people, the Pygmies, arrived, and set to work to besiege him as if he had been some large city. He awoke, roared with laughter, picked up some of the little fellows, packed them in his lion's skin, and then bore his captives off to Mycenæ.

(For a long time mythologists and other learned men regarded this tale of a race of very small creatures as a mere fable, without any element of truth; but during the last century explorers found in Central Africa a tribe of which the average ' grown-up ' stature was only about four feet.)

THE LATER ADVENTURES OF HERAKLES

Hera, the unforgetting goddess, still pursued the far-travelled adventurer with her hatred. Once more she bewitched him so that in a fit of passion he killed some one dear to him—this time it was his friend Iphitus—and once more he had to expiate a crime of blood. He was condemned to spend three years in abject servitude to a queen of Lydia called Omphale, who, to humiliate him, insisted that he should wear a woman's dress while she flaunted in his famous lion's skin.

At the end of the three years his trials began again. In the world of the shades he had met Meleager, son of Œneus, King of Ætolia, who urged him to seek the hand of his sister Deianeira. This Herakles now resolved to do, so he betook himself to Ætolia, only to find that other suitors were already contending for the beautiful princess, among them the river-god Achelous. The struggle narrowed itself to a duel between those two, in the course of which the god assumed the form of a bull, only to have one of his horns torn off. Herakles proved the victor, and the Naiades, or river-nymphs, of the place retrieved the severed horn, filled it with fruits and grain, and gave it to the goddess of plenty, called by the Romans Fortuna. This was the Cornucopia, or Horn of Abundance.

HERAKLES AND DEIANEIRA

After their marriage Herakles and Deianeira lived happily for several years, and three children were born to them. One day, when they were on a journey, they came to a stream called the Evenus, which was so swollen that it could not be crossed on foot. Bridges had not yet been invented, and there was no boat in sight, not even the trunk of a tree, to help them. Suddenly a Centaur, whose name was Nessus, came up and offered to carry the princess on his back if her husband would swim after them. This was agreed upon, but no sooner had Nessus reached the farther bank

Herakles and the Hydra
B. Picart

Atlas
B. Picart

than he made off as fast as his four hoofs could gallop, with his passenger still on his back. Furious, Herakles struggled ashore, bent his famous bow, sent one of his envenomed arrows speeding after the Centaur, and wounded him mortally at the first attempt. Before he died Nessus hypocritically professed great regret, and spoke these words to Deianeira:

>   Take
> This white robe.   It is costly.   See, my blood
> Has stained it but a little.   I did wrong:
> I know it, and repent me.   If there come
> A time when he grows cold—for all the race
> Of heroes wander, nor can any love
> Fix theirs for long—take it and wrap him in it,
> And he shall love again.
>
>   LEWIS MORRIS

THE ROBE OF NESSUS

Now, at an earlier stage in his career Herakles had been deeply in love with Iole, daughter of Eurytus, King of Œchalia.   After promising to give Iole to her heroic wooer the King broke his word, and the memory of this perfidy never faded from the mind of Herakles, who now determined to make war upon the faithless sovereign.   This he did with such vigour that in the end he slew not only Eurytus but three of his sons.   Then after many years of separation Herakles and Iole came once more face to face—and found that they were as much in love as ever they had been. Rather than part from her again, the victor determined to take her with him, and to let her share with him the triumph and splendour of his return.

These things came to the knowledge of his wife, who was waiting for him at home, and she remembered the magic robe of Nessus.   At the critical moment a messenger called Lichas arrived from Herakles, bidding her send him a goodly garment, as he was about to raise an altar to Zeus on Mount Œta, and had with him nothing fit for so solemn an occasion.   Deianeira gave to the messenger the Centaur's robe.

Standing before the newly erected altar, Herakles donned the magic garment, which, as the vindictive Nessus had foreseen, immediately scorched and seared his whole body with terrible poison. In vain he tried to tear it off—it clung all the closer, enfolding his limbs in a mesh of pain.

Then the ill-fated hero realized that his hour had come to die. He caused a funeral pyre, formed of gigantic tree-trunks torn up by the roots, to be built on the summit of the mountain, and upon this pyre he spread his lion's skin before he laid himself down, and ordered his friend Philoctetes to set a torch to the base. This Philoctetes at first refused to do, but Herakles promised that if he would obey he should inherit his bow and arrows. Almost as he spoke flames sprang up all round him, kindled, as some suppose, by no mortal hand. Zeus, looking down from Olympus, held that Herakles had now suffered enough on earth, and, having destroyed so many evil beings during his life, deserved to be numbered among the immortal gods.

When the flames sank down the friends of the dead hero could find no trace of his body, not so much as a handful of ashes. He had been caught up into heaven.

The wrath of Hera was at last appeased, and to seal her reconciliation with Herakles she gave him the hand of her daughter Hebe in marriage. Poor Deianeira meanwhile had died of sorrow. Iole had married another, and the children of Herakles had taken refuge from the fury of Eurystheus with Ceyx, King of Trachin.

HERAKLES AND THE POETS

No mythological character has been a greater favourite among poets than the son of Zeus and Alcmene. More commonly under the Latin form of his name—Hercules—he appears and reappears in every variety of verse, epic and lyric, grave and gay.

In Shakespeare's comedy *Love's Labour's Lost* a company of oddly assorted people give a performance before the King of Navarre, and the most diminutive of the band is chosen for the part of Hercules. As the boy enters the village schoolmaster, who is also the pageant-master, declaims:

> Great Hercules is presented by this imp,
> Whose club kill'd Cerberus, that three-headed Canis;
> And when he was a babe, a child, a shrimp,
> Thus did he strangle serpents in his manus.

Coriolanus, in the play of that name, says to his energetic mother, Volumnia:

> If you had been the wife of Hercules,
> Six of his labours you'd have done, and saved
> Your husband so much sweat.

From an allusion in *Hamlet* we know that the sign of the Globe Theatre was Herakles—and not, as might have been expected, Atlas—carrying the world upon his shoulders. Elsewhere we find the hero's strength and valour mentioned. Hippolyta, in *A Midsummer Night's Dream*, remarks:

> I was with Hercules and Cadmus once,
> When in a wood of Crete they bay'd the bear.

In *Antony and Cleopatra* we find Antony thinking of the story of the revengeful Centaur:

> The shirt of Nessus is upon me; teach me,
> Alcides, thou my ancestor, thy rage.

Spenser, in the *Faerie Queene*, when he wishes to indicate the severity of the struggle between his Red Cross Knight and the " dreadful Beast," says:

> Not that great Champion of the antique world,
> Whom famous Poetes verse so much doth vaunt,
> And hath for twelve huge labours high extold,
> So many furies and sharp pits did haunt,
> When him the poysoned garment did enchaunt,
> When Centaures blood and bloodie verses charmd;
> As did this knight twelve thousand dolours daunt.

And elsewhere he speaks of the hero as

> Hercules, that did advance
> To vanquish all the world.

The Roman tragic poet Seneca devoted a whole tragedy to *Hercules Furens* (*Hercules Insane*) and another to *Hercules Œtæus*. So conscious were the Romans of the gigantic stature of Hercules that they had a proverb, *Ex pede Herculem*, which means that you can recognize Hercules—or a statue of Hercules—from the size of the foot.

Sophocles, one of the greatest of Greek dramatists, wrote a

play called the *Trachiniæ*, of which the scene is laid in Trachis, and wherein the episode of the robe of Nessus is graphically portrayed.   According to this version, Deianeira discovered after she had dispatched Lichas with the robe, but too late to stop him, that it was a deadly gift.   She has rubbed the fabric with a weft of white wool to clean it, and she sees the wool crumble away upon the table, as if it were consuming itself with inward fire.

Ovid gives a painfully vivid description of the sufferings of Hercules when the poisoned robe clings to his powerful limbs, and describes how the terrified Lichas concealed himself in a hollow rock, whence he is hauled by the dying man.

> " Didst thou, O Lichas, bring this deadly gift,
> And shalt thou be the reason of my death? "
> Trembling, with pallid cheeks and stumbling tongue
> Lichas would fain have uttered some excuse,
> But even as he spoke, and tried to clasp
> Alcides by the knees, he was caught up,
> Whirled thrice, or more than thrice, round in the air,
> And then, with greater force than from a sling,
> Hurled headlong into the Eubœan sea.

In the tragedy of *Hippolytus* by Euripides, one of the most romantic of classical poets, there comes a moment when the chorus, conscious of evil and doom impending, utter a passionate wish that they might go

> To the strand of the Daughters of the Sunset,
>   The Apple-tree, the singing and the gold;
> Where the mariner must stay him from his onset,
>   And the red wave is tranquil as of old.
>   MURRAY'S *tr.*

Poets of later ages in many lands have also been haunted by the thought of the sunset gardens, the apples of gold, and the three deathless daughters of Hesperus guarding their divine treasure. The Hydra too, the Nemean lion, the robe of Nessus, the stables of Augeas, and other images and incidents associated with the life-story of the son of Zeus and Alcmene have passed into what is called the ' language of allusion ' in every civilized country of the world.

CHAPTER XIX

PERSEUS

ACRISIUS, King of Argos, had a very beautiful daughter called Danaë, whom he looked forward to seeing happily wedded to some neighbouring prince. But one day an oracle uttered the strange and perturbing prophecy that the King would be put to death by the son of Danaë, and from that day it became the main interest of Acrisius to make certain that his daughter should never have a son. He set artisans to work to build a massive tower of brass, and when it soared glittering towards the sky he imprisoned the princess in the top storey, and posted armed guards all round to prevent her from escaping.

Zeus, looking down from heaven, saw Danaë sitting solitary on her tower-top, and, changing himself into a shower of gold, he descended to visit her. And then once again Hera had reason to be jealous of a mortal maiden, for the daughter of Acrisius was added to the long list of the unofficial consorts of the All-Highest, in whom King Solomon would have found a dangerous rival in any contest as to who possessed the greater number.

For a time King Acrisius fondly believed that his plan was, and would remain, completely successful; but to his horror the news reached him one fine morning that a baby boy had been born in the brazen tower. It now seemed as if the words of the oracle might possibly come true, but even in his distress of mind the King hesitated to stain his hands with innocent blood. He accordingly gave orders that Danaë and her baby should be put in a large wooden cask and set adrift in the sea.

The winds and waves, more merciful than man, bore the cask and its living burden safely to the island of Seriphus, where it was washed up on the beach. A fisherman, seeing it there, drew near, and, not without some difficulty, wrenched up the planks. Instead of the wealth he had hoped to find he found a beautiful young girl, speaking a strange tongue, and clasping in her arms a young baby. Much surprised, the man took them both to the palace of the king of the island, Polydectes, by whom they were kindly received.

The boy Perseus grew up at the court of this king, and was trained in all the manly exercises suitable to his age and rank; but when he reached man's estate he was placed in a difficult and even dangerous position by the desire of Polydectes to marry Danaë, who was determined never to be his wife.

The King, seeing that he would never gain his end while the youth was at hand to act as his mother's champion and defender, appealed to the love of adventure natural to a spirited young man and persuaded Perseus to set forth upon a most perilous undertaking—nothing less than the destruction of the Gorgon Medusa, whose glance turned everything to stone.

PERSEUS AND MEDUSA

The Gorgons were three terrible sisters of whom the third alone was mortal. Snakes grew on their heads instead of hair, and they were more dreadful to behold than words can describe. They had three equally unattractive sisters known as the Græaæ, who had only one eye between them. William Morris thus depicts them in *The Doom of King Acrisius*:

> There sat the crones that had the single eye,
> Clad in blue sweeping cloak and snow-white gown;
> While o'er their backs the straight white hair hung down . . .
> And singing, still they rocked their bodies bent,
> And ever each to each the eye they sent.

It was to these most unattractive old dames that Perseus first directed his steps when he set forth on his great adventure. He managed, by quickness and audacity, to get possession of their one precious eye, and refused to yield it up until they had told him how he might obtain the famous Helmet of Hades, which makes the wearer invisible. The Græaæ, thus taken by surprise, gave him the information he desired, and also full instructions as to how he should reach the abode of the Gorgons.

The immortal gods, perhaps at the request of Zeus himself, were well disposed towards their courageous young kinsman. Pluto readily lent Perseus the helmet, Hermes added his winged sandals, and Athene her highly polished shield, in which he could see the face of the Gorgon reflected, and thus avoid the doom of being turned suddenly into stone. (Another story has it that Perseus received the helmet and sandals, together with a magic pouch in which to carry the head of Medusa, from the Hesperides, and this version was chosen by Sir Edward Burne-Jones as the subject of one of his pictures.)

Thus armed, the youth rose into the air unseen by any mortal eye, and sped towards the dwelling of the three terrible sisters, Stheno, Euryale, and Medusa. So tilting his glittering shield that the distorted features and snaky locks of the youngest were clearly visible on its surface, Perseus drew his sword and cut off Medusa's head at one blow, as she lay asleep.

Shelley wrote some lines on the marble mask of the dead Medusa by Leonardo da Vinci, in which he says:

> Its horror and its beauty are divine.
> Upon its lips and eyelids seems to lie
> Loveliness like a shadow.

Carrying the head in one hand, Perseus rose again into the air, and drops of the Gorgon's blood fell to the earth far beneath. Some drops of this blood, falling on the sands of Libya, turned into serpents, but from others sprang the winged horse Pegasus, which we shall meet later in the story of Bellerophon, and another similar animal called Chrysaor. Meanwhile Perseus floated on,

> Borne by the winds like to some vagrant cloud,
> Through space he veers, now eastward and now west.
> Thrice he beheld the Bear, and thrice the Crab; [1]
> And then at last, when day began to wane,
> Far in the west, fearing to trust the night,
> He came to earth where Atlas ruled as lord,
> Seeking a resting-place till Lucifer
> Should usher forth Aurora's fiery car.
> There Atlas was, the son of Iapetus,
> Greater in bulk than any mortal man.
>
> .   .   .   .   .   .
>
> Upon his pastures fed a thousand flocks,
> And herds as many, in a peaceful land,
> The trees were golden, branches, leaves, and fruit.
> To him spake Perseus: "Friend, if high descent
> Have value in thine eyes I am Zeus's son.
> If valiant enterprise thou dost admire
> Thou wilt praise mine. Shelter I crave of thee;
> Some place where I may rest." But Atlas mused
> Upon the words an oracle once spoke;

[1] The constellations Ursa Major and Cancer.

For the Parnassian Themis had foretold,
" A day shall come, O Atlas, when thy trees
Shall be bereft of gold, and that rich prize
Shall be the portion of some son of Zeus."

OVID

Not unnaturally alarmed at the claim of the mysterious stranger to be the son of the All-Highest, the giant peremptorily ordered Perseus to depart.   When the young man hesitated to obey Atlas would have used violent measures, but he was speedily punished, and the oracle as speedily fulfilled.

" Since," said Perseus, " you care so little for my goodwill, take this gift from me! "   And therewith, bending his own face aside, he held up the Gorgon's head.   In a moment the giant turned into a mountain, his beard and his hair into woods, his bones into rocks.   So lofty was the summit, which had been his head, that certain of the stars now rested on it.

PERSEUS AND ANDROMEDA

The scene now shifts to the land of Ethiopia, where ruled a king and queen called Cepheus and Cassiopeia.   The Queen very foolishly boasted that she was more lovely than the Nereides, and for this boast she was punished in more ways than one.   She was turned later into a constellation, but so near the pole-star that for half the year she must hang head-downward ; and Poseidon imme-diately sent a sea-monster to ravage her husband's realm.   This is why Milton, in *Il Penseroso*, describes her as

That starrèd Ethiop queen that strove
To set her beauty's praise above
The Sea-Nymphs, and their powers offended.

Cepheus, as was the wont of people in those days who found themselves in difficulties, consulted an oracle, which told him that the only way to get rid of the sea-monster would be to sacri-fice to it his young daughter Andromeda.   She was betrothed to a prince called Phineus, but he does not seem to have made any effort to rescue her from this horrible fate.

With many tears the father and mother took their child to a rock jutting out into the sea, and bound her there with heavy chains to await her doom.

Perseus
Canova   140

Danaë and the Tower of Brass
Sir E. Burne-Jones
By permission of Mr Frederick Hollyer 141

Meanwhile Perseus was winging his flight in that direction, and from afar he caught sight of Andromeda, clinging like a marble image to the sharp crag, her hair waving in the sea-breeze, and her eyes running with tears. He was so struck by her beauty that he almost forgot for the moment to keep in motion the wings upon his helmet and sandals. Dropping lightly on to the rock beside her, he begged her to tell him her name and the reason why she was thus fettered. At first Andromeda was too abashed and too frightened to speak; but when he urged her again she told him of her mother's boast and the punishment it had brought, and she also told him her name. Almost before she had finished her story a wild commotion in the waves and a distant roaring sound announced the approach of the hungry sea-monster.

The King and Queen had now drawn near, and were rending the air with their cries. To them spoke Perseus: " There will be time for weeping hereafter, but short is the time for giving aid. What if I demand your daughter in marriage? I am Perseus, the son of Zeus, and of that Danaë to whom he came in the guise of a golden shower; I am he who slew the serpent-locked Gorgon, he who has dared to move on wings through the vast air. All I ask is that if I save her from the monster she may be mine."

Eagerly the King and Queen gave the required promise, implored his help, and offered their kingdom by way of a dowry. And now the sea-monster was cleaving the waves like some mighty and swift galley, the seething foam making a white track behind it. Perseus leaped into the air and hovered for a moment, while the great beast, mistaking his shadow on the sea for himself, flung its whole weight upon the insubstantial form. Meanwhile the youth swooped down like an eagle and drove his sword up to the hilt into its shoulder.

Maddened with pain, the monster reared itself on its tapering tail, leaving its scaly back uncovered, and clutching at the nimble Perseus, while all the waves were stained purple with its blood. The youth now became aware that the wings upon his sandals were heavy with water, and so instead of trusting himself to their support he clung with one hand to a half-submerged rock, while with the other he gave the beast no less than four mortal wounds. With tears and exclamations of joy the King and Queen hailed him as their son-in-law, the deliverer and the chosen husband of their daughter.

The first care of Perseus was to dispose of the Gorgon's head in some way which should prevent it from turning more living creatures into stone. He strewed seaweed and water-plants upon a hollow in the sand, and laid Medusa's head face downward upon them, and instantly they were turned to stone. When the sea-nymphs saw what had happened they amused themselves by bringing more weed to that place, and seeing it change from spongy fibre into hard stone. "Even to this day coral has this character, for what in the sea was a plant, removed from the sea becomes stone," [1] according to Ovid, who tells the story of Perseus in the fourth book of his *Metamorphoses*.

The next care of Perseus was to erect three altars of turf, that in the centre to Zeus, and those on the right and the left to Hermes and Athene. The wedding feast then began, amid fluttering garlands, and cheered by the sweet music of the lyre and the flute.

Medusa's head was not fated, however, to rest undisturbed in its bed of coral. Phineus, the former betrothed of Andromeda, came suddenly on the scene, and, with a band of well-armed adherents, tried to take the bride by force from her bridegroom. A fierce battle followed. Javelins hurtled through the banquet-hall, the clash of bronze blades drowned the music, and the polished pavement was stained with blood. But Athene stood unseen beside Perseus in the fray, and with her shield turned aside the sharp weapons from his head. Even so the young man was sorely beset. Then he bethought him of the Gorgon's head, which he had not left lying in its bed of coral. Crying aloud that every man who was on his side must either shut his eyes or turn his face away, he held up the staring mask of the dead Medusa.

In a moment two hundred men became as many images of stone. Some were petrified in the act of hurling a javelin, others with upraised sword, others warding off a blow.

Phineus, however, had had the presence of mind to look the opposite way, and he now pleaded with Perseus for his life. But

---

[1] The ancients were, of course, ignorant of the real nature and origin of coral.

his rival relentlessly forced him to meet the fatal eyes of the Gorgon, and he too was stiffened into grey stone.

Meanwhile, in the distant island of Seriphus, Polydectes was still wooing the reluctant Danaë, who, having no longer a son to defend her, fled for sanctuary to the temple of Athene. Her only friend was the fisherman Dictys, who had saved her from the sea many years before. (Some people say that though only a fisherman this Dictys was of royal race.)

At this juncture Perseus suddenly appeared, still carrying Medusa's head, and still armed with the helmet, shield, and sandals lent to him by the immortal gods. In spite of these visible evidences of the truth of the young man's story, Polydectes affected to doubt it, and was promptly punished for his scepticism by being turned into stone. Perseus then established the loyal-hearted Dictys on the vacant throne, and gave back to his divine protectors the magic objects they had bestowed upon him. Upon the shield of Athene he placed the Gorgon's mask, where it is often to be seen in statues of the goddess.

During all these eventful years King Acrisius had probably lived quite tranquilly in the belief that he had succeeded in averting the doom foretold by the oracle. But news came to him one day that his daughter and her son still lived, and that they were journeying towards Argos with the son's wife Andromeda. Full of fears, the aged King fled for shelter to the court of his friend Teutanias, King of Larissa.

Now it befell that Teutanias was holding funeral games in honour of his father, and at such games any stranger was welcome to try his skill. Perseus, having heard of the celebrations at Larissa, resolved to interrupt his journey to Argos in order to take part. He was anxious to prove his expertness in throwing quoits, but by some evil chance the quoit which he threw flew aside and mortally injured one of the spectators. As anyone will at once guess who knows the unfailing accuracy of these ancient oracles, that spectator was none other than King Acrisius, the grandfather of the quoit-thrower. (One version of the story says that Acrisius had come to Larissa not to hide from Perseus, but to seek a reconciliation.)

The death of his grandfather made Perseus the heir to the throne of Argos, but he could not bear to enter upon a heritage which had come to him in so tragic a manner. He exchanged his kingdom for another, called Tiryns, on the sea-coast of Argolis, where he built a new capital city to which he gave the name of Mycenæ. It is said that he gave it this name because the pommel of his sword, which in Greek is called *mykes*, had fallen on the place where he resolved to build it.

After his death Perseus received divine honours, and became a constellation in the heavens. He was honoured especially by the Egyptians and the Athenians, and so appreciative were the latter of the merciful conduct of Dictys that they dedicated a temple to him in Athens.

Andromeda also was changed into a group of stars which still bears her name.

PERSEUS AND THE POETS

The story of Perseus being one of the most picturesque in ancient legend, it is hardly surprising that poets have often turned to it for metaphors and images. Spenser speaks of people who "stand astonished like to those who read Medusa's mazeful head," and Milton alludes to "Medusa with Gorgonian terror" guarding the Lethean ford. The latter poet has also an interesting theory concerning the shield of the virgin goddess of wisdom:

> What was that snaky-headed Gorgon shield
> That wise Minerva wore, unconquered virgin,
> Wherewith she freezed her foes to congealed stone,
> But rigid looks of chaste austerity,
> And noble grace that dashed brute violence
> With sudden adoration and blank awe?

Elsewhere he refers to the constellation Andromeda, when he describes Satan standing high above "the circling canopy of Night's extended shade":

> From eastern point
> Of Libra to the fleecy star that bears
> Andromeda far off Atlantic seas
> Beyond the horizon.

(The "fleecy star" is the sign of the Zodiac Aries, or the Ram, which is just beneath Andromeda, so that she seems to be resting on its back.)

Nearer our own time Thomas Gray, Dante Gabriel Rossetti, Tennyson, Lewis Morris, and other poets, great, less great, and comparatively small, have remembered one part or another of the legend, and Charles Kingsley wrote a poem in hexameter measure on Andromeda, where he tells how the sea-monster approached,

Lazily coasting along, as the fish fled leaping before it.

CHAPTER XX

THESEUS

ÆGEUS, King of Athens, had no son to inherit his throne, but as he had fifty nephews, known as the Pallantides, it did not seem as if an heir would be lacking. The King, however, greatly desired to have a son of his own, and adopted the obvious plan of going to consult an oracle. On his way home from this expedition he paused at the court of the King of Trœzen, with whose daughter Æthra he promptly fell in love. They were married, but Ægeus hesitated to take his bride back to Athens with him, lest the Pallantides should be jealous, and should destroy any boy baby born of their marriage. He accordingly left Æthra in her father's house, with instructions that if a son were born to her he should be brought up at Trœzen and should come to Athens only when he was a grown man. He also gave her a sword, and told her to bury it under a large stone. When their son was strong enough to lift the stone he would be old enough to journey to Athens, with the sword girt about him, there to make himself known to his father. Æthra promised to obey, and some time after the departure of Ægeus a beautiful son was born to her, whom she named Theseus. The general belief was that Poseidon was the father of the child, who grew up strong and handsome, and was trained in all princely and manly lore at his grandfather's court. At last his mother thought that he was of an age to try to lift the stone under which the sword was concealed, and this he did with so little difficulty that she had no choice but to let him set off for Athens.

The youth decided that to make the journey by sea, though the quickest and the easiest way, would be the least exciting. So he took the land route, which led through districts infested by robbers and other disagreeable beings. One of these robbers, whose name was Procrustes, had invented a peculiarly cruel and grim method of torturing his victims. This was to lay them on a certain bed, and if they were too short for it to stretch their limbs to the necessary length, whereas if they were too tall he would cut off their feet. Theseus put this ruffian to death, as he did also another bad character, Sciron, whose dead body neither the earth nor the sea was willing to receive, and who therefore floated in mid-air until he was changed into a group of rocks which bore his name.

An even more horrible adversary was the giant sow, Phæa, which killed and ate solitary travellers. Her also Theseus slew. According to some reports the Calydonian boar, of whom we shall hear more later on, was the offspring of this animal.

When Theseus reached Athens he found that his father had taken to wife the sorceress Medea, who by her arts divined that the stranger was none other than the son of Ægeus. She succeeded in making the King believe that this youth had come to his court for no good purpose, and at the banquet in the palace that night she so contrived that Ægeus should hand a cup of poisoned wine to his guest. Regardless of the laws of hospitality, and believing what Medea had told him, the King was about to watch the effects of the deadly draught when suddenly he dashed the cup from the young man's grasp, for, hanging on his side, he recognized the sword he had left with Æthra at Trœzen. Joyfully he proclaimed before the whole of Athens that this was his son, and the people were glad to think that the doughty destroyer of Procrustes, Phæa, and other dangerous creatures would one day be their king.

The fifty rivals, the Pallantides, were not unnaturally annoyed, and they organized a mass attack upon their unwelcome kinsman, who, however, succeeded in slaying them to the last man. A taste for killing seems to have grown upon Theseus, for his next exploit was to capture and sacrifice a famous wild bull which ravaged the plain of Marathon, ten miles from Athens. Then came an exploit even more perilous. It was nothing less than an expedition against the horrible Cretan monster the Minotaur, which every year devoured seven youths and seven maidens, chosen by lot from among the young people of Athens. This terrible tribute was exacted by Minos, King of Crete, in whose mysterious labyrinth the horror lived.

DÆDALUS AND ICARUS

Before describing the adventures of Theseus in Crete we must go back some years, and relate the curious story of Dædalus and Icarus.

Dædalus, an Athenian of royal birth, was a remarkable craftsman and also an inventor. He could make statues which moved like living creatures. He is said to have invented the wedge, the sail, the saw, the auger, and many other useful things. He had a nephew called Talus,[1] and a son, Icarus, whom he instructed in his marvellous arts, but it was with surprise and resentment that he realized that not only was Talus the more apt pupil, but also that he bid fair to surpass his teacher. In a fit of jealous rage Dædalus flung his too-clever nephew out of the window, and then, in order to escape from the just punishment of his crime, fled to Crete, taking his son with him.

Minos, King of Crete, received the fugitives with alacrity, glad to avail himself of their skill. Among the tasks which he confided to Dædalus was that of constructing a labyrinth in which to confine the Minotaur, the dreadful creature which for some years had preyed upon the people of the kingdom. With great patience and ingenuity Dædalus planned and built a maze of masonry so intricate that nobody who had reached the centre could hope ever to find their way out again, and in the centre was the abode of the man-eating monster.

After a little while Minos no longer regarded the brilliant artificer with favour, and he chose a grim method of showing his displeasure. This was to shut up Dædalus, with his son Icarus, in the very labyrinth which the elder man had made. They soon grew very weary of their prison, and the inventiveness of Dædalus proved equal to the occasion. He made two pairs of large, plumy wings, to be attached with wax to the shoulders of the wearer, and with the aid of these wings he and Icarus escaped from the labyrinth and flew up into the blue sky.

The youth had been solemnly warned not to fly too high, lest the warmth of the sun should melt the waxen fastenings of his

---

[1] According to some authorities, the name of the too-clever nephew of Dædalus was Perdix, and it was he who invented the saw. Athene, pitying his fate, changed him into the partridge, which still bears his name.

Perseus and the Grææ
Sir E. Burne-Jones
By permission of Mr Frederick Hollyer

148

Perseus and the Hesperides
Sir E. Burne-Jones
By permission of Mr Frederick Hollyer

149

pinions, but the exhilaration of the flight excited him so much that he forgot everything else, and rose higher and higher, till suddenly the wax loosed its hold, and that which Dædalus had dreaded came to pass :

> With melting wax and loosened strings
> Sank hapless Icarus on unfaithful wings;
> Headlong he rushed through the affrighted air,
> With limbs distorted and dishevelled hair;
> His scattered plumage danced upon the wave,
> And sorrowing Nereids decked his watery grave;
> O'er his pale corse their pearly sea-flowers shed,
> And strewed with crimson moss his marble bed.
>   ERASMUS DARWIN

The grief-stricken Dædalus continued his flight alone, and finally reached Sicily, where he was graciously received by King Cocalus, and proceeded to build a temple to Apollo, in which he hung up his wings as a votive offering.

When Minos heard where the fugitive had found sanctuary he set sail for Sicily with a large fleet, but one of the daughters of Cocalus contrived that the King of Crete should bathe in a bath full of boiling water, and so brought about his unlamented death.

THESEUS AND THE MINOTAUR

Let us now return to Athens, where the whole city was plunged into mourning as the day approached for the annual tribute of youths and maidens to set sail for Crete. Theseus determined to go with them, and, by slaying the Minotaur, to put an end to this cruel sacrifice. Ægeus was reluctant to give his consent, and when finally it was given he made the condition that if his son were successful the black sails on his ship should be replaced by white ones, so that watchers on the shore could see from afar off, as the vessel winged homeward, what the result of the adventure had been. Theseus gladly promised, and set off, followed by the anxious prayers of the Athenians, and accompanied by six youths and seven maidens. When they reached Crete Minos had them all brought before him, so that he could make sure that the due number of victims had been sent. At his side stood his fair young daughter Ariadne, through whose heart Cupid immediately shot one of his golden arrows. The princess at once resolved that the heroic Athenian must somehow be saved from what seemed to be his inevitable doom. Skilfully she contrived to slip into his hand a ball of silken twine, and to whisper in his ear that if he unrolled it as he advanced into the labyrinth, and kept a firm hold upon it, he would by that means be able to find his way out again after slaying the Minotaur.

The beast was waiting hungrily in its lair for its terrible banquet, but Theseus, aided by the prayers which Ariadne offered on his behalf to the high gods, drove his sword, not once, but many times, through its dusky hide. Like a huge oak-tree the Minotaur crashed to the ground, and, leaving it lying dead, the conqueror, holding fast to the silken clue, made his way out of the mysterious maze and into the light of day.

Not unnaturally Theseus was eager to set sail for Athens, but Ariadne would not be prevailed upon to let him depart without her. Indeed, the only possible excuse for the subsequent behaviour of Theseus was the fact that it was she who wooed him, and not he who wooed her. There has always been a tendency to think that when a hero rescues a maiden it is the right and obvious thing that they should fall in love and ' live happy ever after,' but this story is a famous exception to the rule.

The ship bearing the returning travellers and their royal companions from Crete to Athens was driven by the winds to the island of Naxos, and there, while she was sleeping on the seashore, Theseus basely abandoned Ariadne. As we have already related, she was found and rescued by one greater than he.

In the haste and excitement of departure the young man had forgotten to give orders that the black sails on his ship should be replaced by white ones as a signal to those watching on the Athenian shore that all was well. Ægeus, standing on a lofty rock and gazing out to sea, beheld the dark sails moving across the waters, and with a cry of despair flung himself into what is still called the Ægean Sea in memory of him.

Theseus now succeeded to his father's throne, and reigned over Athens for some years with justice and wisdom.

THESEUS AND THE AMAZONS

When he had been established some little time Theseus went on a warlike expedition against the Amazons, and carried off their Queen, Hippolyta. (Some authorities say that her name was not Hippolyta, but Antiope.) The indignant women-warriors marched to her rescue, and were decisively defeated in a battle which unfortunately ended in the death of their Queen, slain by a chance arrow. Her son, Hippolytus, grew up to be an ardent hunter and a pious votary of Artemis. After her death Theseus made a curious choice of a second wife—none other than Phædra, daughter of Minos, King of Crete, and a younger sister of the abandoned Ariadne.

PIRITHOUS OF THESSALY

The next threat of war came from one of the numerous sons of Zeus, Pirithous of Thessaly, King of the Lapithæ, who invaded the plain of Marathon. Theseus led an army to repel him, but when the two came face to face Pirithous was so much struck by the gallant mien of Theseus that he exclaimed, " Be thou the judge—what dost thou demand? " " Thy friendship," replied the other, and they became fast friends from that hour.

Theseus was present at the wedding-feast of the King of the Lapithæ with the Princess Hippodamia, when a great many Centaurs who were among the wedding-guests became first tipsy and then violent: he aided the Lapithæ to overcome these unmannerly creatures in a battle which has frequently been represented by artists of a much later period who desired a fine subject. It is said that Herakles also was ' among those present,' and, if so, the Lapithæ were indeed fortunate in their allies.

Both these royal friends, when they became widowers, desired to wed daughters of Zeus. Theseus aspired to take as his wife Helen, the youthful daughter of Leda, destined afterwards to be the cause of the Trojan war, but she was rescued by her twin brothers, Castor and Polydeuces (Pollux). Pirithous turned his thoughts towards Persephone, already enthroned in Hades as the wife of Pluto. As he had helped Theseus to carry off Helen, he now asked, not in vain, that his friend should accompany him on his perilous journey to the underworld. Unfortunately Pluto recognized the intruders, and fixed them immovably upon a rock by the portals of his palace until Herakles delivered them. (One version of the story says that only Theseus was set free, the King of the Lapithæ being left to his hard fate.)

Another adventure of Theseus was his expedition against Creon, King of Thebes, who had refused to give the rites of burial to the warriors slain in the battle between him and Adrastus, King of Argos. This king, aided by Theseus, overcame Creon, and buried the warriors with all the ceremony demanded by the religion of the time.

After a while Theseus lost his popularity with his Athenian subjects, and at last was fain to seek refuge on the island of Skyros, where he either died a natural death or was treacherously slain. Cimon, a real historical character who lived and ruled in Athens in the fifth century before Christ, brought from Skyros a gigantic skeleton, which was believed to be that of Theseus, and was laid with great solemnity in a specially built shrine called the Theseum.

PHÆDRA AND HIPPOLYTUS

We have already mentioned Hippolytus, the son of Theseus and Hippolyta, who grew up to be a keen hunter and an ardent votary of Artemis. Upon his return from the chase it was his wont to deck the altar of the " fair, silver-shafted Queen " with fresh blossoms, but upon the altar of Aphrodite he would lay not a solitary bloom. This negligence annoyed the goddess of love, and she determined to be swiftly and amply avenged.

Theseus being absent from home, his young wife Phædra was left almost alone with her aged nurse, who noticed with anxiety that her beloved nursling was growing ever more melancholy and moody. One day a chance allusion to Hippolytus brought such a sudden rush of colour to the girl's pale face that the nurse guessed her secret—she had fallen in love with her stepson, Hippolytus. The old woman, thinking only of Phædra's unhappiness, prayed fervently to Aphrodite, and then sought out the young prince, to whom she revealed what she had discovered.

There were two excellent reasons why Hippolytus should thrust her angrily from him—one, his loyalty to his father, and the other, his devotion to Artemis. But the nurse had had the forethought to exact from him a most binding and terrible oath never to tell any man what she had told him, and his fidelity to that oath brought about his death.

Aphrodite, delighted that things were looking so dark for the disdainful youth, watched, or, perhaps, directed, the swift course of events. When Phædra realized that Hippolytus both knew of her love for him and rejected it she was overwhelmed with shame and fury, and she took a terrible way of punishing her stepson. Before hanging herself from the roof-beam of her chamber she wrote upon a tablet a false and cruel lie, and tied the tablet to her wrist, so that some one should find it there after her death.

It chanced that Theseus, who arrived upon the scene immediately after, was the person to discover and read the fatal message, which declared that Phædra had killed herself for very shame because during his father's absence Hippolytus had made love to her. In his blind rage Theseus accused his son, who, bound by the oath he had sworn to the nurse, could not prove his innocence, and could only appeal to his father to seek the truth from some oracle.

Now many years before Poseidon had promised Theseus that he would grant him one boon, whatever he might choose to ask, one only, but of any imaginable kind. In his despair the King of Athens now invoked the sea-god to his aid, and implored him to slay Hippolytus.

Poseidon, as firmly bound by his oath as the unfortunate young prince had been by his, had no choice but to obey. As Hippolytus, sad at heart, was driving his chariot with its four mettlesome horses away from his father's palace a horrible monster rose suddenly out of the sea, roaring like thunder, and half-hidden in swirling surges of foam. Terror-stricken, the horses took the bits between their teeth and bolted, heedless of the voice and hand of the master whom they had once been so ready to obey. The chariot was broken asunder upon a rocky crag, and lamenting bondsmen bore the dying prince into the presence of his father.

Meanwhile Artemis, aware of the tragic fate which had overtaken her votary, could do nothing to help him, for there was an unwritten law that no god or goddess should interfere with the actions of another, more especially when such actions involved mortal men. One thing, however, she could do. Descending in the form of a shining cloud, she spoke to Theseus, telling him that his son was innocent, and that all the evil that had been wrought was the doing of Aphrodite.

By the time that Hippolytus was carried into the palace his father knew the truth, and with vain and bitter words of sorrow obeyed the bidding of Artemis, who, speaking from the cloud, said:

> O seed of ancient Ægeus, bend thee now
> And clasp thy son. Aye, hold and fear not thou!
> Not knowingly hast thou slain him; and man's way,
> When gods send error, needs must fall astray.
> And thou, Hippolytus, shrink not from the King,
> Thy father. Thou wast born to bear this thing.
> Farewell!
>
> EURIPIDES (*Murray's tr.*)

Chaucer's Knight has a great deal to say about Theseus in the story of Palamon and Arcite, borrowed by him from the works of the contemporary Florentine poet Boccaccio. Of course all three, Boccaccio, Chaucer, and Chaucer's Knight, imagine Athens as a many-towered medieval town and Theseus as a knight in the armour of the age of chivalry. They also agree in endowing Hippolyta with a sister called Emelye, who is the heroine of the story in the *Canterbury Tales* which begins thus:

> Whilom, as oldė stories tellen us,
> Ther was a duc that hightė [1] Theseus;
> Of Atthenes he was lord and governour,
> And in his tymė suich a conquerour,
> That gretter was ther noon under the sonne.
> Ful many a richė contree hadde he wonne;
> That with his wysdom and his chivalrie
> He conquered al the regne of Femenye,[2]
> That whilom was y-clepėd [3] Scithia;
> And weddedė the queene Ypolita,
> And broghte hire hoom with hym in his contree,
> With muchel glorie and great solempnytee,
> And eke hir fairė suster Emelye.

In Chaucer's version of the story of Theseus and Ariadne (whom he calls Adriane) in the *Legende of Good Women* we are

[1] was called.
[2] The feminine realm—*i.e.* that of the Amazons.
[3] was called.

told that this princess and her sister Phædra heard the young stranger complaining loudly of his lot as they stood on the palace wall gazing at the " bryghte mone." Another unexpected detail is the plan made by the two sisters to help Theseus by giving him not only a " clewe of twyne " to find his way out of the maze, but also some balls of wax and tow to throw into the mouth of the Minotaur, " To sleke his hunger, and encombre his teeth."

The English poet is more severe than any of the classical poets on the action of Theseus in abandoning Ariadne. He calls the hero the " grete untrewe of love," and sternly bids him " be rede for shame! "

As we have already mentioned in telling the story of Pyramus and Thisbe, Shakespeare devotes a great part of the *Midsummer Night's Dream* to the festivals held in honour of the wedding of Theseus and Hippolyta.

CHAPTER XXI

JASON AND THE GOLDEN FLEECE

IN this story we meet many characters familiar in fairy-tales—the cruel stepmother, the wicked uncle, the long-lost prince, to say nothing of the dragon and the witch: and it begins quite in the proper style.

Once there was a king, who had a son and daughter, and the queen, their stepmother, hated them both. The king's name was Athamas, and his kingdom was the city-state of Thebes in Bœotia. The queen was Ino, daughter of Cadmus and Hermione, and the children were called Phryxus and Helle. Sent by Poseidon, a marvellous winged ram with a fleece of shining gold rescued the boy and girl from their cruel stepmother, and flew away with them over the sea. Unfortunately Helle lost her balance and tumbled into what has ever since been called the Hellespont, but Phryxus held on firmly to his strange steed, which deposited him in the realm of Æetes, King of Colchis. The King received the youth kindly, and sacrificed the ram to Zeus, hanging up its marvellous fleece, which he placed in the charge of a fierce dragon. A little later he gave Phryxus his daughter Chalciope as his wife, but he envied his son-in-law the possession of the Golden Fleece, and after a time he basely murdered him in order to get hold of it.

Now Athamas had two nephews, Æson, King of Iolcos, and Pelias, not yet king of anywhere. Pelias was very envious of his brother, and made war upon him, and finally overthrew him, but the King's son Jason was saved, and handed to the wise Centaur Chiron to be brought up as befitted a prince.

(According to one version of this story, Æson entered into a compact with Pelias that he should reign only until Jason was of an age to mount the throne.)

Pelias exercised royal power for some years, troubled only by the prophecy of an oracle that he would one day be in danger through a man wearing a single sandal. Meanwhile Jason was growing up into a stalwart youth, and when Chiron considered

The Minotaur

G. F. Watts

By permission of Mr Frederick Hollyer

The Lament for Icarus
Herbert J. Draper
National Gallery of British Art
(*Page* 148)

that he was old enough he revealed to him the story of his birth, and counselled him to go and claim his birthright.

JASON AND HERA

Jason accordingly set out, and presently he came to a deep stream. At a point where there was a ford he saw an aged woman sitting leaning on a staff and looking timidly at the swift water. Chiron had had the forethought to impress upon his pupil that alone of all the human race Pelias had done him an injustice, and that towards other men and women he must be friendly and helpful. He promptly offered to carry the old woman across the stream on his back, if she would lend him her staff, to which she gratefully agreed. As he struggled through the water Jason realized with astonishment that the seemingly meagre and withered crone was extremely heavy. It was only with considerable difficulty that he was able to reach the farther bank, and during the transit he lost one of his sandals. When at last he deposited his burden safely on dry land he saw that she had mysteriously changed into a tall, handsome being, of more than mortal stature and majesty, with a gorgeous peacock standing at her side.

Rightly identifying her as Hera, the Queen of Heaven, he fell on his knees and invoked her powerful aid. This she promised him before she vanished from his sight.

Jason, not troubling to supply himself with a second sandal, continued his way, and at last reached Iolcos, where his uncle was engaged in holding a public festival. Pelias soon became aware of the presence of a stranger wearing only one sandal, and ordered his guards to seize the young man. Jason thereupon revealed his identity, and claimed his heritage.

The King was far too wily to reject this claim openly. Instead he received his nephew with fair words, and set a banquet before him. Presently a minstrel was summoned to amuse the guests, and, instigated by Pelias, he sang the story of the Golden Fleece, and of the perfidy of Æetes in slaying the young Phryxus. Jason listened intently, and he could not but agree with Pelias that to avenge Phryxus and recover the treasure would be an exploit worthy of a hero.

THE QUEST OF THE FLEECE

Pelias thereupon suggested that Jason himself should make the attempt, and promised that upon his return he should ascend the throne of Iolcos.   Jason, fired with enthusiasm, set about gathering together a band of stout companions and also building a ship large enough to carry them across the " wine-dark sea."   The Greeks had not at that time attained any great skill in shipbuilding, but, after many difficulties, Jason found a man called Argus who consented to tackle the task, and with some help from Hera and Athene the first great ship ever built by man came into being, the *Argo*, with her fifty oars, her planks made of pine-trees from Mount Pelion, and her figure-head hewn, at Athene's command, from a branch of the Talking Oak in the sacred grove of Dodona. This figure-head also could talk, and on occasion gave good advice to the Argonauts.

This beautiful galley may have been called the *Argo* because that word in Greek means ' swift,' or it may have been called after Argus, the craftsman who made it.

Jason gathered together a band of the most famous heroes in the Isles of Greece, chiefly from his own land of Thessaly. Among them were some whom we have met already, such as Herakles, Theseus, Æsculapius, and Orpheus, and others whom we shall meet again, such as Meleager, Nestor, Castor, and Polydeuces.   Two useful members of the crew were the sons of Boreas, Zetes and Calaïs, who had wings on their shoulders.   It is said that Hera arranged with their grandfather, Æolus, that the winds should favour the good ship *Argo* from the time that she put forth from the port of Pagasæ, at the foot of Mount Pelion. Tiphys acted as pilot, and Æsculapius as ship's doctor.

Many adventures befell the heroes before they sighted Colchis. They spent some time at Lemnos, and then passed through the Hellespont and reached the country of the Doliones, by whose King, Cyzicus, they were cordially received.   Unfortunately Æolus neglected the instructions of Hera, and after the *Argo* had left this land the winds arose and drove her back again upon the shore.   In the darkness Cyzicus did not recognize the seafarers, and, mistaking them for enemies, led his people in a hasty attack upon them.   Jason slew him in this blind fray, and afterwards, with the other Argonauts, mourned for him, and performed the customary rites of burial.

Their next anchorage was off the coast of Mysia, where they had to obtain a fresh oar to replace a broken one, and where the hero's young page, Hylas, was sent to fetch fresh water.

HYLAS AND THE NYMPHS

The youth, carrying a bronze jar, came to a hollow fringed with rushes and maidenhair fern, and in the midst was a pool of clear water. As he bent to dip his jar the nymphs who dwelt in the pool seized his hands and clung to them, for they had never seen any mortal as fair as he. And, clinging fast, they dragged him down into the depths, where they held him in their arms, seeking with gentle words to comfort him.

Meanwhile one of the seafarers on the *Argo* shouted that the wind was good and that it was time to be away; but Herakles would not depart without Hylas, and went off to look for him, carrying his bow and his club. In the end he had to make his way to Colchis on foot, as the Argonauts could wait for him no longer.

FURTHER ADVENTURES OF THE ARGONAUTS

After a little time the Argonauts were again in need of fresh water, and as they were off the coast of a land inhabited by people called the Bebryces they decided to send some of their number ashore. The King of the Bebryces (Bithynians) challenged them to match him in a boxing bout, and was handsomely beaten by Polydeuces. They next cast anchor at the entrance to the Euxine, at Salmydessus, where they met with an aged and sightless king called Phineus, who was being cruelly persecuted by winged monsters, the Harpies. He knew the best course to Colchis, and also how they might steer between the clashing rocks known as the Symplegades, and these things he offered to reveal if only they would rid him of the Harpies. This the two sons of Boreas, Zetes and Calaïs, were soon able to do, and after they had received the promised instructions the Argonauts hoisted sail and bent to their oars again. They got through the Symplegades by sending a dove ahead of their ship, and rowing swiftly after her before the rocks, which had separated to let her pass, had time to clash again. Their last landfall before reaching Æa, the capital of Colchis, was the island of Arecia, where they encountered the children of Phryxus, whom Æetes had sent to claim the kingdom of their grandfather, Athamas.

When, after a voyage which, however exhausting, was certainly not monotonous, the Argonauts disembarked at their destination their leader boldly announced to King Æetes the quest upon which they had come to his kingdom. The King declared his willingness to deliver up the Fleece provided Jason would, in the space of one day, perform all the following feats:

(1) He was to tame two wild bulls, whose hoofs and horns were of brass, and who breathed flame.

(2) He was to harness these bulls to a plough made of the hardest stone, and plough a field which had never been cultivated before.

(3) He was to sow in this field the teeth of a dragon and then destroy the armed men who would immediately spring up.

(4) He was to kill the ever-wakeful dragon which kept watch at the foot of the tree from which the Golden Fleece was hung.

Such feats were manifestly beyond the powers of any common mortal to accomplish; but Jason was unexpectedly and super-naturally aided by the King's daughter, Medea, who was a sorceress of renown, and who had fallen in love with him in the impetuous fashion in which the daughters of mythological monarchs seem to have been disposed to fall in love with handsome strangers. On receiving his promise, sworn in the temple of Hecate, that if she succeeded in getting the Fleece for him he would make her his wife and take her with him on the *Argo*, this witch-princess put him in possession of the spells, herbs, and enchantments necessary to tame the bulls and to lull the dragon-guardian of the tree to sleep. She also counselled him to throw a stone into the midst of the armed men, so that they should turn and destroy one another.

All her instructions were carefully followed by Jason, and it is said that the other Argonauts, as well as King Æetes, were struck with terror and surprise at the ease with which he performed all these apparently impossible deeds. Even Medea turned pale.

Faithful to his oath, Jason took Medea with him when the *Argo* put forth to sea. They carried with them not only the Golden

Fleece, but also Absyrtus, the young son of King Æetes. Soon the Argonauts became aware of a ship in pursuit, and realized that Æetes, having discovered his loss, was on his way to recover his treasure and his daughter. In order to delay him, the ruthless Medea killed Absyrtus, and, having hewn his body in pieces, scattered these on the water, knowing that religion would compel the King to pause and gather them up, and give them due rites of burial.

Bending stoutly to their oars, the seafarers reached the island of the enchantress Circe, who warned Jason that he would yet suffer for the cruel murder of Absyrtus. Next they passed through the Pillars of Hercules, and, with the aid of the sea-nymph Tethys, who had a friendly feeling towards one of their number called Peleus, they escaped the two perilous rocks Scylla and Charybdis, whose names have always been synonymous for a terrible alternative. Their next danger was from the sweet songs of the Sirens, those sinister sea-maidens who were wont to lure unfortunate seafarers on to the cruel crags. Orpheus, however, proved himself an even sweeter singer than they, and the *Argo* escaped the fate which had overtaken many poor sailors in smaller and less famous ships than she.

Next they reached the island of the Phæacians, where they had a painful surprise, for the fleet of Æetes, which had continued the pursuit by a different course, was lying at anchor in the harbour. The queen of the island was appointed judge between the Colchians and the Argonauts, and, after hearing the evidence, decided that as Medea was now Jason's wife Æetes had no further claim either to his daughter or to the Golden Fleece, which was evidently regarded as her dowry.

After a stormy and troublesome voyage the *Argo* cast anchor off the promontory of Malea, in the Peloponnesus, where he was at last purified of the murder of the prince Absyrtus. Some say it was the talking figurehead which informed Jason that he would never reach home until the purification had taken place, and it was Circe who performed the appointed rites.

JASON AND MEDEA

And so at last Jason reached his native land, and Pelias was compelled to descend from the throne he had usurped so many

L

years before. Æson, the deposed king, was now very old and feeble, but Jason begged Medea to restore his father's lost youth and this she did by the means of her magic art. For nine nights she gathered strange herbs by moonlight, seeking them in far places to which she was carried by a chariot drawn by dragons. Then she set up two altars of turf, one to Hebe and one to Hecate; she hung them with green branches and sprays of vervain; she sacrificed a black ram, and poured forth libations of wine and milk. The actual rejuvenation she performed by cutting the old man's throat, letting all his blood drain out, and then filling his veins with the magic liquor from her cauldron—a liquor so potent that wherever a few drops fell the earth became green, and flowers sprang up. But when the daughters of Pelias besought her to do for their father what she had done for Æson she put no magic herbs in the cauldron, and the dead man did not come to life again. The people of Colchis were so indignant at this ruthless and cruel deed that Jason and Medea were forced to flee to Corinth, Medea possessing a great advantage in her dragon-chariot. At Corinth Jason and Medea are said to have lived very happily together for ten years, but at the end of that time Jason grew weary of his witch-wife, and his heart turned towards one of the daughters of Creon, the king of that land. (Mythologists disagree as to whether her name was Creüsa or Glauce.)

When Medea realized that she had been abandoned she planned a terrible revenge. Some poets say that she sent an envenomed robe to her rival, others that she gave her a crown which seared her temples; but there is pretty general agreement that she set Creon's palace on fire, and that the King and his hapless daughter perished in the flames. Upon Jason she wreaked a yet more dreadful punishment, for she killed before his eyes the two children she had borne him. Taunting him with fierce words, she then mounted her dragon-car, rose into the air, and flew to Athens, where, as we have already seen, she found a protector in King Ægeus.

Jason, broken-hearted, continued to live at Corinth, haunting the seashore, where the hulk of the *Argo* lay rotting. As he sat one day in the shadow of the old ship a mouldering beam broke off and fell upon his head, killing him instantly.

JASON AND MEDEA IN POETRY

Poets have always been attracted by every chapter in the story of the Fleece, and allusions to Jason, Medea, and the Argonauts abound in literature. Euripides, Ovid, Chaucer, and his contemporary John Gower are among those who felt the charm of this particular myth. This is how Gower describes Medea going to gather herbs by night:

> With open hed and fot al bare
> Hir her tosprad,[1] sche 'gan to fare;
> Upon hir clothés girt sche was,
> Al spechèles, and on the gras
> Sche glod[2] forth as an addre doth,
> Non otherwisè sche ne goth,
> Til sche came to the freisshè flod,
> And ther a whilè sche withstod.[3]
> Thriès sche torned hir aboute,
> And thriès eke sche 'gan doun lout;[4]
> And in the flod sche wette hir her,
> And thriès in the water ther
> Sche gaspeth with a drecching onde,[5]
> And tho[6] sche tok hir speche in hond,
> Ferst sche began to clepe[7] and call
> Upward unto the sterrès all,
> To wynd, to air, to see, to lond,
> Sche preide, and ek hield up hir hond
> To Echates,[8] and gon to cry
> Which is goddésse of sorcerie;
> Sche seidè, " Helpeth at this nede
> And as ye maden me to spede
> Whan Jason cam the Flees to seche,
> So helpe me now, I you beseche."

Shakespeare, who seems to have been re-reading Ovid when writing the *Merchant of Venice*, makes Bassanio say, speaking of Portia:

> Her sunny locks
> Hang on her temples like a golden fleece;
> Which makes her seat of Belmont Colchis' strand,
> And many Jasons come in quest of her.

Medea also figures in this play, for Jessica says to Lorenzo in the moonlit garden at Belmont:

> In such a night
> Medea gather'd the enchanted herbs
> That did renew old Æson.

---

[1] Her hair spread out.   [2] glided.   [3] paused.   [4] to bend down.
[5] a dreary sigh.   [6] then.   [7] cry.   [8] Hecate.

CHAPTER XXII

THE CALYDONIAN HUNT

ONE of the heroes who took part in Jason's expedition to Colchis was Meleager, the son of King Œneus and Queen Althæa of Calydon, in Ætolia. His sister was that Deianeira who afterwards became the wife of Herakles, and his aunt was Leda, from which it followed that Castor and Polydeuces (Pollux), Clytemnestra, and Helen were his cousins. All these family relationships are very complicated, but they are worth remembering, as they often have some influence on the course of one of the stories.

When Meleager was a baby the Fates foretold that his life would last only as long as a certain brand on the hearth should remain unconsumed. It seemed as if this meant that he would die within a few hours, but his mother, with great presence of mind, snatched the brand from the flames, plunged it into an earthen vessel, and resolved that it should be carefully kept there for ever.

The boy grew up strong and comely, and skilful in all manly sports, and his parents fondly hoped that by preserving the fatal brand they had frustrated the harsh decree of the Fates. While he was absent with Jason on the famous voyage to Colchis his father, King Œneus, unfortunately, when offering solemn sacrifices to the gods, omitted to pay to Artemis the honour due to the moon-goddess, who was deeply offended by this neglect. As an emphatic demonstration of her wrath she sent a terrible wild boar to lay waste the whole unhappy land of Calydon. The creature was larger than the bulls which grazed in the rich pastures of Sicily; its fierce eyes were flecked with blood; its bristles stood up like a palisade about a camp; its tusks were larger than the tusks of the Indian elephant. To the dismay of the farmers it ravaged their fields before the corn was ripe, trampled down the vines, and harassed the frightened flocks. The countryfolk fled to the shelter of the city, nor did they dare to come forth until Meleager, on his return from Colchis, gathered together a band of heroes and went forth to hunt the boar. This was the Calydonian Hunt, famous in legend, on which Swinburne based his magnificent poetic drama *Atalanta in Calydon*.

THE HUNTING OF THE BOAR

The returned Argonauts were, apparently, not yet weary of adventures, for many of them responded to the appeal of Meleager that they should help him to rid the land of Calydon of this living plague. Among the hunters were Castor and Polydeuces, Theseus and Pirithous, Telamon, father of Ajax the Greater, Phyleus, the son of Augeas whose stables Herakles had cleaned, Nestor, wisest of the Greeks, Laertes, father of Odysseus, who was afterwards the husband of Penelope, Peleus, and many other heroes of renown, and last, but not least, the only woman of the company, Atalanta, the fleet-footed huntress, daughter of Iasos of Arcadia, and famed throughout the Isles of Greece for her beauty and for her skill in the lore of the chase. She came to the hunt wearing garments much like those of a boy. Her hair was gathered into a simple knot; a plain polished buckle held the top of her tunic in place; over her left shoulder hung her ivory quiver, and in her right hand she held her bow.

Meleager, looking upon Atalanta, loved her. " Oh," he said to himself, " happy will that man be whom she shall vouchsafe to take for her husband! " But at the moment he could say no more.

As soon as all the hunters had met, on a wide plain in the shelter of a densely wooded slope, some of them spread nets, and others unleashed hounds, while others sought for the track of the boar's hoofs. Presently there was a loud crashing in the undergrowth, and down the dried channel of a winter watercourse edged with reeds and willows charged the terrible beast. As he came he scattered the hounds with fierce sidelong thrusts from his huge teeth.

The hunters raised a shout, and made ready to hurl their javelins. The first spear missed its mark and grazed the trunk of a maple-tree; the next was flung with too much force and went beyond its mark. Then Mopsus the soothsayer prayed to Apollo to grant that *his* weapon might be aimed aright. The god heard the prayer, but Artemis broke off the spear-head as it flew through the air, and only the wooden shaft hit the tough hide of the boar. And now the monstrous beast began to grow angrier yet, and it charged among the hunters like a stone flung from a war-sling. If Nestor had not vaulted, with the aid of his long spear, into the branches of a tree he would not have lived to fight in the Trojan war. The Great Twin Brethren, Castor and Polydeuces, pursued the boar on their milk-white horses, but, seeing itself hard pressed, it took cover for a while in a dense thicket. Telamon, following fast, tripped over a tree-trunk. Even as Peleus paused to help him to his feet Atalanta let fly an arrow from her bow which grazed the beast just below the ear and drew a little blood.

Meleager rejoiced even more than she. It is said that he was the first to point out that it was Atalanta who had shot the well-aimed arrow, and that he then promised her that she should receive her due reward. One hunter, however, was angry, and, swinging his battle-axe, cried aloud to the others to learn by how much the weapons of men excelled those of women. Even as he stood on tiptoe, with his arms above his head, the boar rushed at him and gored him to death.

With every moment the tumult and confusion grew more wild. Jason hurled a spear which glanced aside and wounded an in-offensive hound. Theseus was hardly more fortunate, for his weapon stuck in a beech-tree. But Meleager fared better, for a spear aimed by him pierced the back of the snorting beast.

Now the boar is plunging madly, blood streaming from its body, and foam from its jaws; now Meleager steps forward and thrusts another spear deep into the powerful shoulder. All the huntsmen shout, and though they still hesitate to draw too near the dying monster they all dip their weapons in his blood.

It was then that Meleager set his foot upon the boar's head and, turning to Atalanta, exclaimed, "Receive, O nymph, the spoil that is rightly mine, and let me share my glory with thee!" Both the head, with its huge tusks, and the hide, stiff with bristles, he bestowed upon her, amid envious murmurs from the bystanders. Among these were the two uncles of Meleager, his mother's brethren, Plexippus and Toxeus, who protested loudly against such honour being paid to a woman.

Hylas and the Water Nymphs
J. W. Waterhouse, R.A.
From the painting in the Manchester Art Gallery

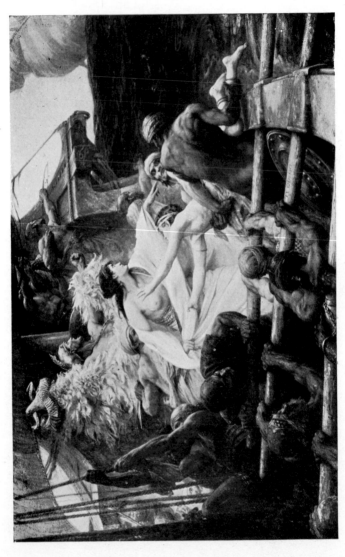

Medea and Absyrtus

Herbert J. Draper

By permission of the Corporation Art Gallery of Bradford

" Come," they said to Atalanta, " lay down these spoils—they are none of thine—and think not that thy beauty will anything avail thee." And they seized her with rough hands, bidding Meleager stand aside. Then their nephew, furious at the insult to the huntress, rushed to her aid; with his sword he pierced the heart of Plexippus, and clove the head of Toxeus from jaw to jaw.

News of the death of the boar soon reached the city, and Althæa, the Queen, came forth with great joy, bearing gifts for the gods. But the first thing she saw was a group of men bearing her two dead brothers in their midst. Her joy was turned to mourning; she put off her golden robe and clad herself in black; and then she asked in what wise her brothers had met their death. In her agony, when she heard that her own son had slain them, she hastened to the inner chamber where the fatal brand was preserved, snatched it forth, and laid it on a heap of dry logs, to which she set lighted torches. Four times the flames sprang up and died down, but they gained strength, and began to consume the brand.

" With death must death be requited," said the weeping Queen. " Shall Œneus rejoice in the triumph of his son while my father Thestius is childless? O ye ghosts of my brothers, accept this, my funeral offering to you both! "

It seemed to her that as the brand glowed it uttered a moan of pain; far off Meleager felt a sudden pang, and strove vainly to shake off the deadly influence stealing over him. Even as the flames rose and fell his agony increased or diminished; but at last the charred wood fell into ashes, and at that moment the soul of Meleager left his body.

So bitterly did his sisters lament their loss that Artemis, sated of revenge, changed them into birds, which flew up into the clouds, uttering sad cries.

ATALANTA AND THE GOLDEN APPLES

According to another story, which probably concerns the same fleet-footed huntress who took part in the Calydonian Hunt, Atalanta had declared that she would never marry unless some suitor came forward who could beat her in a foot-race. Several athletes tried, and failed, and paid the penalty of failure, which was death.

Ovid imagines these races to have been run in the Roman fashion, seven rounds of the long, low wall in the centre of the circus, at either end of which stood three wooden cylinders—the goals. Upon the wall were two columns supporting seven egg-shaped balls, their number corresponding to the number of rounds in each race. There is a little uncertainty as to the exact method of scoring, but one of these balls was either put up or taken down at the conclusion of each lap.

One day, when Atalanta was racing against yet another daring suitor, a youth called Hippomenes was among the onlookers, and as she flashed past him, with her hair streaming on the wind and her cheeks brightly flushed, he suddenly became conscious of a violent hope that none of the competitors might win. From this hope it was but a single step to the desire to enter the perilous contest himself. So he rose up and spoke these words to her: "Why dost thou seek an easy triumph by conquering feeble folk? Come, now, race against *me*. If I win thou shalt think it no shame to be beaten by the son of Megareus, who was the grandson of Poseidon. And if I lose all the greater will thy glory be."

Atalanta looked at him, and knew not whether to say yes or no, for she feared that some jealous god had chosen this means of sending to his death a youth of almost god-like beauty. But now the rest of the people were raising a clamour and asking when the race would begin.

It was at this critical moment that Hippomenes raised his eyes and his hands to Aphrodite and implored her to come to his aid. The goddess heard, and it chanced that she had been walking in a flowery field of Cyprus, sacred to herself, and that she was still carrying in her hand three golden apples plucked from a fair tree in the midst thereof. Unseen of everybody except Hippomenes, she drew near the youth, gave him the apples, and whispered wise counsels in his ear.

The trumpets sounded the signal for the race to begin, and both runners were swiftly on their way, seeming scarcely to touch the ground as they ran. For once the good wishes of the on-lookers were against Atalanta. They urged Hippomenes on with loud cries. Yet Atalanta could have passed him if she would.

When, with a great effort, he had got ahead of her he let fall one of the apples from the Cyprian tree. With a curiosity almost equal to that of Pandora, Atalanta swerved aside and paused just long enough to snatch the fruit from the ground. It was a brief pause, but it enabled Hippomenes to get well ahead, and the benches of the spectators rang with applause. Now on her mettle, the swift-footed huntress put forth all her strength, but a second time the descendant of Poseidon let an apple fall, and a second time she could not resist its lure. One apple remained, and, gasping forth a prayer to the Cyprian goddess, Hippomenes threw it down, not at the side of the track, but a little way off, so that in order to get it Atalanta would have to swerve farther aside than before.

Aphrodite, anxious that her man should win, intervened by making the apple very heavy, so that a great effort was needed to lift it from the ground. So was Atalanta outrun, and so did Hippomenes win her for his bride.

Their happiness, however, was of short duration, for owing to a lack of reverent service to the goddess Cybele, at whose temple they failed to make due offerings, Hippomenes and Atalanta were changed into a lion and a lioness.

(Apollodorus tells this story in a slightly different manner. He gives Melanion as the name of the successful suitor, and tells a picturesque tale of how Atalanta, as a baby, was left in a wilderness to die by her father, who had desired to have sons only, and, after being nursed by a she-bear, was adopted by some hunters, and led a care-free life in the forest until she was recognized and claimed by her parents. Some poets say that in the famous contests the suitor was always allowed to have the start, and according to one version the golden apples were from the garden of the Hesperides.)

Walter Savage Landor, in his poem called *Hippomenes and Atalanta*, makes the huntress turn aside only when the third apple was flung down.

> From his hand now dropt
> A golden apple; she lookt down and saw
> A glitter on the grass, yet on she ran.
> He dropt a second; now she seem'd to stoop:
> He dropt a third, and now she stoopt indeed:
> Yet swifter than a wren picks up a grain
> Of millet, raised her head: it was too late,
> Only one step, only one breath too late.

CASTOR AND POLYDEUCES (POLLUX)

The name of the first of the Great Twin Brethren is the same in Greek and in Latin, but the second brother is better known to English readers by his Latin name of Pollux. They were also known as the Dioscuri, the ' sons of the god '—*the* god being Zeus. Their mother was Leda, wife of Tyndareus, King of Sparta, and Zeus used to visit her disguised as a beautiful swan. Their sisters Clytemnestra and Helen were also famous in myth and legend.

As we have already seen, they took part in the quest of the Golden Fleece, and Polydeuces proved his skill as a boxer against the Bithynian king. They were also among the huntsmen who aided Meleager in the hunt of the Calydonian boar. Castor was a skilful tamer of horses, but, unlike his brother, he was not immortal, and he met his death in a quarrel which resulted from an exploit shared with Polydeuces. The two brothers had resolved to seize and carry off two maidens, Hilæira and Phœbe, the daughters of a certain Leucippus, and the two young men, Idas and Lynceus, who were betrothed to them, not unnaturally rushed to their rescue. In the fight which followed Castor was slain. Broken-hearted, Polydeuces implored Zeus to let him give his own life instead, and the All-Highest so far relented as to suffer the brothers to spend alternate days in the realm of shades and in the land of the living. But they cannot have been very happy, as this meant that neither could enjoy the company of the other. Finally they were placed among the stars, and form the constellation called Gemini (the Twins). They were patrons of seamen, who, when electrical storms flickered round the masthead, fancied that they could catch glimpses of two horsemen in glittering white armour.

Among the Romans the Dioscuri enjoyed great honour, especially Castor.

At the battle of Lake Regillus between the republican Romans and the people of Latium, who were fighting to replace the dynasty of Tarquin on the throne, the Great Twin Brethren appear in the thick of the strife, recognizable by their white armour and their white horses, and when Rome had won the day

Œdipus at Colonos

From the statue by Hugues in the
Luxembourg

Bellerophon and Anteia

Gertrude Demain Hammond, R.I.

(Page 183)

it was they who appeared to the citizens as heralds of victory.
Through the city they rode, to the temple of Vesta, in the Forum.

> When they drew nigh to Vesta,
>   They vaulted down amain,
> And washed their horses in the well
>   That springs by Vesta's fane.
> And straight again they mounted,
>   And rode to Vesta's door;
> Then, like a blast, away they passed,
>   And no man saw them more.
>
> .   .   .   .   .
>
> And Sergius the High Pontiff
>   Alone found voice to speak:
> " The gods who live for ever
>   Have fought for Rome to-day!
> These be the Great Twin Brethren
>   To whom the Dorians pray.
> Back comes the Chief in triumph
>   Who, in the hour of fight,
> Hath seen the Great Twin Brethren
>   In harness on his right.
> Safe comes the ship to haven,
>   Through billows and through gales,
> If once the Great Twin Brethren
>   Sit shining on the sails.
>
> .   .   .   .   .
>
> Here, hard by Vesta's Temple,
>   Build we a stately dome
> Unto the Great Twin Brethren
>   That fought so well for Rome."
>
>   MACAULAY

The temple was rebuilt by Tiberius about the year 6 B.C., and
its ruins are still to be seen.   It was the place where weights and
measures were officially tested, and inscriptions bearing the
names of Castor and Pollux are often found on these.

CHAPTER XXIII

ŒDIPUS, KING OF THEBES

THERE was a curse upon the family of Laius, King of Thebes, and the story of his unhappy son Œdipus is the story of the fulfilling of that curse. Laius, driven from his kingdom by Amphion and Zethus, took refuge with Pelops, son of Tantalus, whom we met in Hades, and then most ungratefully kidnapped the boy Chrysippus, son of his protector. In course of time Laius recovered his kingdom, and married a princess called Jocasta, but Apollo warned him that owing to his graceless conduct towards Pelops there was a dark curse on him and his, and that his own son would slay him.

When a boy was born to Jocasta the King called an aged shepherd to him and bade him carry the babe to a lonely hill-top called Mount Cithæron, first piercing his feet so that he should die. But the forlorn little creature was found and carried to the palace of King Polybus of Corinth, whose Queen, Merope, having no child of her own, resolved to adopt the foundling, to whom she gave the name of Œdipus—' swollen-footed.'

The boy grew up believing himself to be the true-born son of the royal pair, and all went well until one day a drunken reveller taunted him with being nothing of the sort. In order to learn the truth the young prince consulted the famous oracle at Delphi, which, without giving him a definite answer to his question, told him that it was his destiny to slay his father, marry his mother, and bring sorrow on his native city.

Thinking that this terrible decree referred to Polybus and Merope, Œdipus fled from Corinth, resolved never to return. It happened that his lonely journey took him to a point where two roads met, and there he encountered another traveller, an old man in a chariot, escorted by servants and preceded by a herald. Œdipus, who was accustomed to being treated with great deference, refused to pull his own chariot aside when curtly ordered to do so by the herald, who thereupon killed one of his horses. Furious, Œdipus leaped forth, and in the struggle which followed he slew the old man and all the attendants except one.

Nobody who is acquainted with the dreary infallibility of Greek oracles will need to be told that the old man was Laius, King of Thebes.

ŒDIPUS AND THE SPHINX

Œdipus, little recking that one part of the curse had been fulfilled, pursued his journey and at last reached the city of Thebes, his own native city, though he knew it not. There he found great dismay and confusion on all sides. The realm was being ravaged by a dread Sphinx, a monster with the head and shoulders of a woman and the body of a lioness, who crouched on a rock, and asked riddles of every traveller who passed. Nobody guessed the right answer, and everybody who failed to do so became the Sphinx's prey. Œdipus, careless of a life which he had ceased to prize, approached the monster, and expressed his willingness to try his fortune. " What animal is it," asked the Sphinx, " which in the morning goes on four feet, at noon on two, and in the evening on three? " " That animal," answered Œdipus promptly, " is a man. As a child he crawls, as a man he walks erect, in his old age he supports himself on a staff." This was the correct answer; and the Sphinx, furious at having found some one who could guess it, flung herself from the rock and died.

News meanwhile had reached the Thebans of the mysterious death of their absent King, but there was nothing to connect that event with the coming of the youth who had freed them from the horror at their gates. Creon, Queen Jocasta's brother, who was acting as regent, offered the crown, together with Jocasta's hand in marriage, to the astonished Œdipus, who accepted both, and who reigned in peace and prosperity for some years.

ŒDIPUS REX

Four children were born to Œdipus the King and his Queen— two sons, Eteocles and Polynices, and two daughters, Ismene and Antigone. It seemed as if all was well with the royal line of Thebes. And then plague and famine descended upon the land, and the people gathered in great multitudes outside the palace doors, imploring their King to intercede for them with the gods who were apparently wroth. Creon, the Queen's brother, was sent to Delphi to find what might be done to lift this blight from Thebes, and he returned with the puzzling message that an unclean thing, dwelling in that realm, must be cast out, and that the murderer of the dead King Laius must be tracked and punished.

It is certainly rather curious that Œdipus should not have made close inquiry into the circumstances surrounding the death of his predecessor, but he now threw himself eagerly into the task. Where, he asked, had the old King died? Did no one bring some tidings of the manner of his murder? Creon answered that Laius had been set upon by robbers and slain when he was on the road to Delphi, and that only one of those who went with him had returned, bemused with terror. In the confusion caused by the Sphinx and her ravages no man had at that time taken thought to avenge the King. " Then," said Œdipus, " be it my charge so to do. And solemnly I curse the murderer of Laius."

In those days lived a blind seer called Tiresias, and of him Œdipus resolved to seek counsel. To his surprise the old man was strangely reluctant to speak what was in his mind, though the King knelt before him, with upraised hands, saying, " Lo! We all bow down, imploring thine aid." Finding that prayers were of no avail, Œdipus grew angry, and it was then that Tiresias turned upon him with the terrible words, " Thou art thyself this unclean thing that must be driven forth." In his astonishment the King imagined that his brother-in-law, Creon, was plotting against him with the aid of the sightless seer, but Tiresias rebuked him sternly for the thought, and asked him how it befell that he knew nothing of his own birth. When Œdipus, stung by fear, grew angry again the old man sobered him with the words, " The two who gave thee birth held me in honour."

" You speak in dark riddles," said the King, and Tiresias answered tauntingly, " Aye, you too were a reader of riddles once. But now I tell you that the man you seek, the unclean murderer, is here."

Still obsessed by the unjust thought that all this was part of a dark scheme of Creon to drive him from the throne, Œdipus uttered the doom of death against his brother-in-law. But Jocasta, the Queen, came forth from the brazen doors of the palace, and demanded to know the cause of the clash between the two men. "Creon says," declared Œdipus, "that I am the murderer of Laius." Of course Creon had said no such thing, and when he denied it the King retorted, "This evil seer of thine says it was thus."

Jocasta, convinced of her brother's innocence, and anxious to soothe the King's fury, then said, "What talk is this of seers? No mortal man may read the purposes of the high gods. Hearken unto me. An oracle once said that my husband Laius should be slain by a son of mine, but when I bore my lord a son the babe was laid upon Mount Cithæron to die. And so the oracle was proved false. For Laius was killed by robbers, not by the hand of my child, long since dead."

Terror-smitten, the unhappy Œdipus poured forth stammering questions, scarcely daring to listen to the replies. Where exactly was Laius slain? At the cross-roads, in the land of Phocis, where one road comes from Daulia and one from Delphi. How long ago? As many years and months ago as the coming of Œdipus to Thebes. What manner of man was the old King? Tall, with white hair; in figure much like Œdipus himself. How many men went with him? Four, of whom one was a herald. Where is the one man who escaped alive? "On the day that you were crowned king," answered the Queen, "that man prayed that he might be sent to some place in the mountains, to tend his sheep, far from Thebes."

Then, the terrible truth breaking on him only by degrees, Œdipus realized that the curses he had uttered upon the slayer of Laius had been called down upon his own head. But he clung to one shred of hope. He must speak with the herdsman. If the fellow stuck to his tale of a band of robbers having assailed the King all would be well. But if instead he confessed that the slayer was one solitary man there could be no further doubt or uncertainty. So messengers were sent to fetch the herdsman, and in the interval a herald came from Corinth saying that Polybus was dead, and that the Corinthians called Œdipus to come and be their King. Again Jocasta spoke tauntingly of oracles. "Look," she said to Œdipus, "you have lived in exile all these years because Apollo foretold that you would kill your father—and the old man has died in peace, not by your hand."

" May be," returned the King, " but Merope still lives, and while she lives I cannot return to Corinth."

The herald, hearing these words, could not conceal his bewilderment, and Œdipus had no choice but to tell him the story of the oracle, and of his flight from Corinth and his exile in Thebes. " Hearken, my lord the king," said the herald then, " I can free you from this fear. You were no son of Polybus and Merope. None was born to them. It was I who carried you to the palace in my arms." " Am I then *your* son? " asked the King. " No more than you were his. I was tending sheep on Mount Cithæron one day, and another shepherd drew near with a weeping child in his arms—a child with a cruel iron spike driven through its feet. This man bade me take the babe and bear it to some far place to die. But I had pity on it, and, thinking there might be some mystery about its birth, I bore it to the palace of my King."

" Who was this shepherd? " asked Œdipus.

" One of those," returned the messenger, " who tended the flocks of Laius, King of Thebes."

His heart cold within him, Œdipus gave orders that the man should be sought, and very soon it became clear that it was the same who had escaped from the struggle at the crossroads, and who had asked to be sent to some far place on the day that Œdipus had been crowned.

When the old shepherd was found and brought before the King all doubt was soon at an end. He and the herald recognized each other. And, timidly and reluctantly answering the breathless questions of Œdipus, he acknowledged that it was from Jocasta's own arms that he had received the child whom afterwards, thinking maybe to save its life, he had given to another herdsman met by chance on Mount Cithæron.

The King fled into the palace with a cry of anguish:

> Oh, on these eyes
> Shed light no more, ye everlasting skies
> That know my sin. I have sinned in birth and breath.
> I have sinned with Woman. I have sinned with Death.
> SOPHOCLES (*Murray's tr.*)

The unhappy man's cup of sorrow was not yet full. In the inner room he found Jocasta lying dead, slain by her own hand.

From her mantle he snatched the broad brooch of gold, and with it he wounded his own eyes, so that never more should he behold the light of day.

The doom spoken by the oracle had now been fulfilled. It remained only to release the people of Thebes from plague and famine by driving forth from their midst the unwitting murderer and criminal whom they had honoured for many years as a just and goodly king. Œdipus pronounced the sentence on himself, and declared that he would make his way to the wild and solitary hill of Cithæron, the place where his father and mother had willed that he should die.

First he commended to the care of Creon his two young daughters, Antigone and Ismene, and it is at this tragic moment that the *Œdipus Rex* of Sophocles ends. But the story of Œdipus does not end there, and its attraction for Greek tragic poets died out only with the death of the ill-starred King in the *Œdipus at Colonos* of Sophocles.

Both Æschylus (in *Seven against Thebes*) and Euripides (in the *Phœnissæ*) handled the legend of Œdipus in its later stages, leading up to the tragedy of his daughter Antigone, where again Sophocles is the dramatic narrator. Among the lost plays of Æschylus, which scholars piously hope may yet come to light, are three the very titles of which show their connexion with this most terrible and tragic of all ancient stories—*Laius*, *Œdipus*, and *The Sphinx*.

Creon, now in command of the situation, decreed that Polynices and Eteocles, the two sons of Œdipus, should hold the throne of Thebes during alternate years—an arrangement bound to lead to trouble. He also desired to see Antigone married to his own son Haimon, but she resolved to follow her father into exile.

Here there is divergence between the versions dramatized by Euripides and Sophocles. In the *Phœnissæ* Euripides shows the two princes quarrelling and finally slaying each other, and Creon declaring, in the first place, that Polynices, as the attacker of his native city, shall not receive the rites of burial, and in the second place that Œdipus must be banished, and depart alone from Thebes. Antigone, though only a young girl, determines to bring all Creon's desires to naught. She will not marry Haimon; she will give rites of burial to her brother; she will not let her blind father go alone into exile.

M

The tale may be traced from that point in the *Œdipus Coloneus* of Sophocles, who differs from Euripides in making the exile of Œdipus precede instead of follow the fatal fight between his two sons.

THE DEATH OF ŒDIPUS

Œdipus, accompanied by Antigone, at last reached the place where the gods had foretold that he should die, a place one mile from Athens called Colonos, where there was a grove sacred to the Eumenides. The elders of the neighbourhood, knowing the identity of the blind wayfarer, would have driven him forth, but Theseus, King of Athens, took him under his protection, and promised him due rites of burial in the earth of Attica.

Soon after Ismene arrived, with the news that Eteocles and Polynices had come to blows; and hard on her heels came Creon, who, but for the intervention of Theseus himself, would have dragged the two girls from their father's arms. The next arrival from Thebes was Polynices in person, praying his father's blessing in his struggle to drive his usurping brother off the throne.

This blessing Œdipus would not give, and Antigone implored her brother in vain not to destroy both his native city and himself.

A sullen rumble of thunder warned the blind king that his death was near, and, after taking leave of his weeping daughters, he departed to a lonely spot, where only Theseus, his last friend, was with him when he died.

THE SEVEN AGAINST THEBES

Eteocles, being the elder son of Œdipus, had enjoyed the first spell of kingship after his father's tragic downfall, and during what we may call his ' year of office ' the younger son, Polynices, sojourned at the court of Adrastus, King of Argos, whose daughter he married. When, however, the year was up Eteocles stubbornly refused to make way for his brother, and Adrastus accordingly placed an Argive army under the command of Polynices, led by seven chieftains, of whom he himself was one. The names of the seven are variously given, but the list usually accepted is as follows: Polynices; Adrastus, King of Argos; Tydeus of Calydon,

half-brother of Meleager; Parthenopæus of Arcadia, son of
Atalanta; Capaneus and Hippomedon, both of Argos; Amphiaraus, husband of Eriphyle, sister of Adrastus.

THE SOOTHSAYERS

When Polynices fled from Thebes he took with him the marvellous necklace which Hephæstus had given to Hermione on her
marriage to Cadmus, and this necklace was now to play an important part in the story of the Seven against Thebes. Amphiaraus, being a soothsayer, foresaw that of the seven only
Adrastus would live to return, and therefore lifted up his voice
against the enterprise. He had promised, however, that if any
disagreement should arise between his wife and himself the final
decision should rest with her. In order to persuade Eriphyle to
give her vote against her husband's wish Polynices gave her
Hermione's necklace.

There was also a soothsayer in the ranks of the defenders of
Thebes—Tiresias, the blind seer, whom Creon and Eteocles consulted when they heard that an Argive army was marching against
the city. Tiresias declared that the defenders would triumph
only if Menœceus, Creon's son, voluntarily sacrificed himself in
the battle. This the heroic youth did not fail to do.

THE SIEGE

Thebes had seven gates, and to each of these Eteocles assigned
a special guardian, while Polynices, on his side, chose one of his
followers to assail each gate, himself being the attacker of the
gate defended by his brother.

The siege was fierce and long-drawn-out, and Zeus seems to
have given it his personal attention on more than one occasion.
Pursued by the Thebans, Amphiaraus was fleeing in his chariot
along the river bank, when the All-Highest hurled a thunderbolt
which made such a large hole in the ground that the soothsayer,
his chariot, and his charioteer were all completely engulfed.
Capaneus, who was inclined to brag, vowed that in spite of Zeus
himself he would force his way into Thebes; but even as he

climbed a ladder to scale the city wall a well-aimed and well-timed thunderbolt punished his arrogance. The wife of Capaneus, whose name was Evadne, cast herself in anguish on to his funeral pyre when the last rites were celebrated.

THE DEATH OF THE SONS OF ŒDIPUS

For some time the fortunes of war swayed to and fro, though usually in favour of the defenders. Finally it was decided, against the counsels of some of the elders, that a single combat between the brothers should decide the fate of Thebes. In this bitter duel Polynices slew Eteocles, and was slain by him. Their death made their uncle Creon King of Thebes, and he then issued the cruel decree that as Polynices had attacked his native city he must not receive the funeral rites which alone would give his spirit rest. The sequel to this decree we shall hear when we listen to the story of Antigone.

THE DOOM OF THEBES

Amphiaraus had been right when he foretold that of the seven attackers of Thebes only Adrastus would return. Before he departed on the fatal expedition he solemnly charged his son Alcmæon to avenge his death. There was none of the seven who did not leave at least one son to lament him, and in due course, led by the aged Adrastus, the Epigoni (those who come after) obeyed the behest of the Delphic oracle, which had bidden Alcmæon to march against Thebes. The Epigoni were Aigialeus, son of Adrastus; Thersandros, son of Polynices; Alcmæon, son of Amphiaraus; Diomed (Diomedes), son of Tydeus; Polydorus, son of Hippomedon; Sthenelos, son of Capaneus; Promachos, son of Parthenopæus. They captured and sacked the sinister, bloodstained city, and, by a curious irony, the only one of their number to perish was the only one whose father had not fallen in the previous siege—Aigialeus, son of Adrastus.

The old King of Argos, who on the earlier occasion had escaped

owing to the fleetness of his horse, Arion, died on the way home
simply of grief for the death of his son.

Alcmæon had still another part of his oath to his father to fulfil,
and that was to punish his mother, Eriphyle, who had been
tempted by the gift of Hermione's necklace to send Amphiaraus
to his doom.   He killed her, and in consequence was pursued for
many years by the Furies, until finally purified of his sin.

The necklace continued to bring so much evil and misfortune
upon every one who touched it that at last it was hung up as a
votive offering in the shrine of Apollo at Delphi.

ANTIGONE

When Creon pronounced the decree that Polynices should not
receive the rites of burial he—and every one else—believed that
he was dooming the spirit of the dead man to eternal wretched-
ness.   If the body were not duly buried the soul could not go
down into the world of shades, and was forced to wander, an
unquiet and lonely ghost, finding no resting-place either among
the living or the dead.

Antigone and Ismene, the sisters of Polynices, knew very well
that it was their duty to defy Creon's decree, and they also knew
that defiance would mean their own death.   Ismene faltered, but
in the steadfast mind of Antigone there was no faltering.   Guards
were posted near the spot where Polynices lay, but Antigone
managed to elude their notice long enough to strew dust upon the
body, which was thus, in a sense, duly buried; but they caught
sight of her in the very act of pouring libations of wine from a
bronze urn.   She was dragged before Creon, and this is how
Sophocles imagines that she answered the tyrant when he asked
if she had dared to disobey him:

> Yea! for not Zeus I ween proclaimed this thing;
> Nor Justice, co-mate with the nether gods,
> Not she ordained men such unnatural laws.
>
> .   .   .   .   .
>
> I knew that I must die—how should I not?—
> Though thou hadst ne'er proclaimed this.   If I die
> Before mine hour, I count it for my gain,
> For whoso lives as I, beset with sorrows
> Manifold, how should death be but his gain?

Even so for me to light upon this doom
Is no grief.   But had I endured that he,
My mother's son, should lie a tombless corpse,
That were mine anguish: not for this I grieve.[1]

ANTIGONE (*Way's tr.*)

Creon ordered his guards to take Antigone to a lonely cavern and leave her there to die; but after these orders had been obeyed Tiresias, the old blind seer, came to him and said that it was the will of the gods that Polynices should no longer be denied the rites of burial.

Creon, one hopes not reluctantly, set out to fulfil these behests. In order to reach the cave he had to pass the place where Polynices lay, and he paused to pour forth libations and raise and kindle a funeral pyre.   That pause meant death to Antigone, for when her uncle reached her lonely prison he found her dead, " throat-tangled in her girdle's fine-spun noose."

It has been said of Antigone that she " is, perhaps, the noblest of the young girls in Greek tragedy, a grave, sorrowful, resolute figure, from which neither much suffering nor stern resolve can quite abstract the grace of youth." [2]

[1] By permission of the literary executors of the late Arthur S. Way.
[2] *The Girl through the Ages*, by Dorothy Margaret Stuart.

CHAPTER XXIV

BELLEROPHON

BELLEROPHON was a grandson of Sisyphus, whom we met in Hades pushing a heavy stone up a hill. His father, Glaucus, King of Corinth, was famous for his love of horses and of chariot-racing.

In his youth the prince spent some years at the court of King Prœtus of Argos, and while he was there the wife of the King, whose name was Anteia, fell in love with him. When Prœtus perceived that the Queen was taking a too affectionate interest in their handsome young guest he was filled with jealousy and wrath, even though Bellerophon proved completely unresponsive. Some authorities say that, like Phædra in the story of Hippolytus, and like Potiphar's wife in the Bible, Anteia denounced to her husband as a traitor the man whose love she had failed to win. Be that as it may, the indignant Prœtus sent the youth to the court of his father-in-law, Iobates, King of Lycia, with a letter stating that the bearer was an unconquerable hero and at the same time requesting that he should be put to death. The same law of hospitality which deterred Prœtus from killing his guest now stayed the hand of Iobates, but fate intervened and gave him the opportunity he sought, by which he would be able to put the young man's valour to the test and—as he believed—get rid of him at the same time.

The land of Lycia was then being ravaged by an awful monster called the Chimæra, which had the head of a lion, the body of a goat, and the tail of a dragon. Breathing flame from its terrible nostrils, this beast spread desolation wherever it went, and Iobates suggested to Bellerophon that to destroy it would be a deed worthy of a hero.

Bellerophon agreed, but before setting out on this adventure he decided to consult a soothsayer called Polyidus, who advised him strongly to get possession of the winged horse Pegasus which had sprung from the Gorgon's blood. Athene had caught and tamed the beautiful creature, and its home was on Mount Helicon, the haunt of the Muses.

Bellerophon, directed by Polyidus, spent a night in a temple dedicated to the goddess of wisdom, who appeared to him in a vision, and, placing a golden bridle in his hand, bade him catch Pegasus as the winged horse descended to drink at the fountain called Pirene (or, according to other authorities, the fountain called Hippocrene).

Holding fast to the bridle, which was quite real, the young prince made his way to the indicated place and waited eagerly for Pegasus to appear. Presently he heard the beat of the great silver wings, and a moment later the marvellous steed was standing with its shapely head bent to drink from the pool below the fountain. Bellerophon stepped forward, and at the sight of the golden bridle Pegasus, who had been inclined at first to rise swiftly into the clouds, became tame and submissive, and allowed himself to be bridled like any ordinary horse. Bellerophon then jumped on his back, and they flew towards the land of Lycia, where far below dark patches of burned earth and scorched grass marked the track of the Chimæra.

Swooping down, Bellerophon fearlessly attacked the monster, which breathed forth huge spouts of glowing flame, and writhed hither and thither in its efforts to elude his sword-thrusts and at the same time to drag him and Pegasus to the ground. Thanks to the fleetness of the immortal steed, and to the strength and skill of Bellerophon's sword-arm, the struggle was not a long one, though violent while it lasted. The dreaded Chimæra lay dead, and its conqueror returned joyfully to Iobates with the cheerful tidings that his behest had been fulfilled, and his dominions were to be ravaged by the monster no more.

To Iobates these tidings were far from being cheerful, for though he was glad to be rid of the Chimæra he had hoped to be rid of Bellerophon also. Dissembling his disappointment, the King next suggested that the young prince should subdue a tribe of warriors called the Solymi, believed to be invincible, but Pegasus again played a decisive part, and it was soon demonstrated that the Solymi were not invincible at all. An expedition against the Amazons followed, and ended in the same way. Iobates, much impressed by these things, came to the conclusion that Bellerophon was no ordinary mortal, but a man singularly favoured by the gods, and gave him the hand of his daughter in marriage.

For a time the two lived very happily, and several children were born to them, one of whom, their daughter Laodamia, later bore to Zeus a son called Sarpedon, who figured with distinction in the Trojan war.   But the gods withdrew their favour, and many sorrows befell the man to whom they had once been so kind.

According to some authorities it was the presumptuous conduct of Bellerophon in attempting to fly up to the abode of the gods which made them angry.   Zeus sent a gadfly to sting Pegasus, usually so tractable when bestridden by his only mortal rider, and the irritated animal, rearing and plunging, flung Bellerophon to the earth far below.

> Bold Bellerophon (so Jove decreed
> In wrath) fell headlong from the fields of air.
>   WORDSWORTH

It is also said that to punish Anteia for her treachery Bellerophon took her for a ride on the winged horse and deliberately let her fall off, though nobody seems to have suggested that this rather cruel form of revenge displeased the gods.   They were themselves apt to be vindictive, and presumption would seem to them a much graver sin.

Whatever the reason may have been, the gods certainly ceased to show any goodwill towards Bellerophon.   Two of his children died, he became lame and blind, and ended his days wandering in solitude in a place called the Aleian Plain—the ' Plain of Wandering.'

Milton, in the seventh book of *Paradise Lost*, compares his own fate with that of Bellerophon:

> Descend from Heav'n, Urania—by that name
> If rightly thou art call'd—whose voice divine
> Following, above th' Olympian hill I soar,
> Above the flight of Pegasèan wing!
> The meaning, not the name, I call: for thou
> Nor of the Muses nine, nor on the top
> Of old Olympus dwell'st, but, Heav'nly-born,
> Before the hills appeared or fountain flowed
> Thou with Eternal Wisdom didst converse,
> Wisdom thy sister, and with her didst play
> In presence of th' Almighty Father, pleased
> With thy celestial song.   Up-led by thee,

Into the Heav'n of Heav'ns I have presumed,
An earthly guest, and drawn empyreal air,
Thy temp'ring; with like safety guided down,
Return me to my native element,
Lest, from this flying steed unreined (as once
Bellerophon, though from a lower clime)
Dismounted, on th' Aleian field I fall,
Erroneous there to wander and forlorn.

Shakespeare, in describing Henry, Prince of Wales (afterwards Henry V), says:

I saw young Harry, with his beaver on,
His cuisses on his thighs, gallantly arm'd,
Rise from the ground like feather'd Mercury,
And vaulted with such ease into his seat,
As if an angel dropp'd down from the clouds,
To turn and wind a fiery Pegasus
And witch the world with noble horsemanship.

In *Henry V* he makes the French Dauphin most mythologically minded when describing his horse:

Le cheval volant, the Pegasus, *chez les narines de feu!* . . . the basest horn of his hoof is more musical than the pipe of Hermes. . . . It is a beast for Perseus; he is pure air and fire.

CHAPTER XXV

THE TROJAN WAR

NEREUS, the sea-god, had a daughter called Thetis, upon whom Zeus looked with a favourable eye. But the All-Highest, having heard from the Fates that she would bear a son who would be greater than his father, decided not to add her to the long list of his loves, but to give her in marriage to Peleus, King of Phthia. To grace the wedding he promised that, with Hera and other Olympians, he would be present in person.

Here again we find an example of the resemblance between the classic myth and the folk-lore of the fairy-tale—the uninvited guest who uses magic powers to punish the people who neglected to send the invitation. Eris, the disagreeable and unpopular goddess of discord, was not among those whom Nereus summoned to his daughter's wedding-banquet, but this did not prevent her from appearing there. She flung into the middle of the joyous company an apple bearing the inscription, " For the fairest." Hera, Athene, and Aphrodite each considered that it should be given to herself, and the dispute between the three goddesses and their supporters threatened to turn the banquet into a wild scrimmage. Finally it was decided that the verdict should be pronounced by a certain handsome shepherd who tended his flocks on Mount Ida, and whose name was Paris.

Though he earned his bread in this humble way Paris was a king's son. His father and mother were Priam and Hecuba, King and Queen of Troy. An oracle having declared in his infancy that he would bring destruction on his native city, he was exposed on a hillside and left to die; but, as usually happened when such things were done, some shepherds came along in the nick of time and rescued the child.

THE JUDGMENT OF PARIS

Paris grew up so exceptionally good-looking that all the nymphs and shepherdesses on Mount Ida were in love with him. He himself fell in love with the nymph Œnone, and they led a very happy life upon " many-fountain'd Ida."

Then one day the three goddesses suddenly appeared to him,

> And at their feet the crocus brake like fire,
> Violet, amaracus, and asphodel.
>
> TENNYSON

Placing the fatal golden apple in his hands, they bade him choose to which of them it should most justly be given. They then proceeded most barefacedly to offer him bribes in order to influence the verdict. Hera promised him power and riches; Athene, fame and splendour in war; and Aphrodite, the loveliest of mortal women for his wife. This last suggestion pleased Paris better than the others, and he handed the golden apple to the goddess of love.

Not long after he abandoned both Œnone and Mount Ida, to say nothing of his sheep, and under the guidance of Aphrodite sailed to the shores of Greece.

HELEN

Tyndareus, King of Lacedæmon (otherwise Sparta), a city-state of Laconia, had a wife called Leda, who found favour in the eyes of Zeus. Of the four children born to Leda two, Castor and Clytemnestra, were mortal like their father, Tyndareus, and two, Polydeuces (Pollux) and Helen, were immortal, like their father, Zeus. Agamemnon, King of Mycenæ, married Clytemnestra, with results disastrous to himself, as will be seen later. His brother, Menelaus, wooed Helen, and won with her the kingdom of Sparta.

Now Tyndareus foresaw that the husband of the loveliest woman on earth would be exposed to many dangers and vexations; so he suggested that all Helen's suitors should pledge themselves by oath to help the successful suitor to regain possession of his wife should anyone attempt to kidnap her, and also to make no such attempt themselves.

> This was cause
> To Tyndarus [1] her father of much doubt,
> To give, or not to give her, and how best
> To make good fortune his: at length this thought

---

[1] Other authorities say that it was Odysseus who made this cautious suggestion.

Occurr'd, that each to each the wooers give
Their oath, and plight their hands, and on the flames
Pour the libations, and with solemn vows
Bind their firm faith that him, who should obtain
The virgin for his bride, they all would aid;
If any dar'd to seize and bear her off,
And drive by force her husband from her bed,
All would unite in arms, and lay his town,
Greek or Barbaric, level with the ground.

EURIPIDES (*Potter's tr.*)

This oath was the cause of the Trojan war.

PARIS AND HELEN

Aphrodite, who never did things by halves, took charge of the tactful and appreciative young shepherd who had given her the golden apple destined " For the fairest." She counselled him first to return to Troy and make himself known to his parents, and then obtain from his father, King Priam, permission—and the necessary ships—to make a voyage to Greece.

Troy, as may be seen from the maps at the end of this book, was a city on the Asiatic side of the Hellespont, not far from the river Scamander, in which goddesses were wont to wash their hair in order to give it a rich golden tinge.

When the Trojan war broke out most of the attacking forces came from what was roughly called ' Argos,' and were sometimes called the ' Argives.' The plain of Argolis comprised several important city-states, including Mycenæ, Argos itself, and Tiryns. (The Nemean lion and the Lernean Hydra were both natives of this plain.) In speaking of the two sides engaged in the struggle before the walls of Troy it is more usual, however, to describe the hosts of Menelaus and Agamemnon as the ' Greeks.'

Let us now return to Menelaus, King of Sparta, who had lived happily for several years with Helen, and to whose palace there came one fine day a young prince from Troy. It was a little unfortunate that when Aphrodite promised to give Paris the loveliest woman in the world for his wife that woman should already have been the wife of another person; but a trifle like that would not deter a goddess from keeping her word, and it was owing to the influence, if not to the explicit advice, of the Queen of Love that young Paris took advantage of the temporary absence of Menelaus to carry Helen off with him to Troy.

This was an act of hideous treachery, for Menelaus had received the young prince with much kindness, and had observed all the sacred duties of hospitality. When the King of Sparta returned from his journey and found that the Queen had fled with their Trojan guest he sent messengers in haste to all those other suitors who had bound themselves with a great oath to come to his aid in just such circumstances as these. All hastened to obey his call, with one exception. Odysseus, King of Ithaca, having been rejected by Helen, had married her cousin Penelope, and they had an infant son called Telemachus.

When Palamedes, an astute and observant man, arrived at Ithaca with the summons from Menelaus Odysseus proceeded to feign madness in order to escape from his oath. Harnessing an ox and a horse to a plough, he started ploughing a field, which he then sowed with salt. Palamedes took the infant Telemachus and laid him down in one of the furrows, and when he saw how carefully the supposed madman guided his team so that the ploughshare should not hurt the child he concluded quite rightly that Odysseus was shamming, and prevailed upon him to go to Aulis, on the shore of the Eubœan Sea, where the chieftains were keeping tryst.

With one voice these chieftains declared that their leader should be Agamemnon, who was Helen's brother-in-law twice over, as he had married her sister, and she his brother. Odysseus, however, was very useful to them because of his extreme cunning, and it was thanks to this cunning that they were able to enlist among their number the valiant Achilles, son of Thetis and Peleus.

ACHILLES

Various marvellous myths cling round the childhood of Achilles. According to the Roman poet Catullus, the three Fates came to the wedding of his parents and foretold that their son should go forth to battle against Troy, when the Trojans should fall before him like ears of corn beneath the sickle, but that in that war the young warrior should perish. Another version makes Chiron, the wise Centaur, foretell that Achilles, who was his pupil, should fall fighting against Troy, which city, unless he fought against it, might never be taken.

All the legends agree that Thetis tried to give her infant son immortality, but some say that she did it by plunging him in the Styx, and others that the method employed was to anoint him all over with ambrosia and then dip him into a fierce fire. Whatever means she chose, she held the infant by the heel, so that, though all the rest of his body was invulnerable, that one spot might be struck with a mortal blow. (Compare the Germanic legend of Siegfried, who bathed in dragon's blood, which made all his body invulnerable except a patch on his shoulder to which a leaf had adhered while he was bathing.)

Still anxious about her darling, Thetis sent him, disguised as a girl, to the court of Lycomedes, King of Skyros. It was there that Odysseus discovered him, and tricked him into betraying himself by the expert and interested way in which he handled some warlike weapons when they were placed before him among feminine ornaments. Odysseus had disguised himself as a wandering merchant, and had thus obtained the opportunity of spreading forth all these objects before the ' ladies ' of the palace.

THE GREEKS AT AULIS: THE SACRIFICE OF IPHIGENIA

The great chiefs of the host which sailed from Aulis against Troy were Agamemnon and his brother Menelaus; Diomed, son of Tydeus, and his friend Sthenelos; Nestor, ancient and wise, son of Neleus; Odysseus, son of Laertes of Ithaca; Thoas the Ætolian; Idomeneus, King of Crete, with whom was his friend Meriones; Tlepolemus, son of Herakles; Eumelus, son of Admetus and Alcestis; and Achilles, with his friend Patroclus, and their followers, the Myrmidons.

When all the ships had assembled off the coast of Bœotia, ready to take the assailing armies to the coast of Asia Minor, adverse winds delayed their departure so long that a soothsayer had to be consulted. Calchas was his name, and he was held in such high esteem that when he said that in order to obtain fair winds they must sacrifice to Artemis the elder daughter of King Agamemnon nobody felt that this cruel decree could be disobeyed. Iphigenia, the princess thus condemned to die, was at home in Argos with her mother, Clytemnestra, when a messenger arrived from the Greek camp bidding the Queen hasten at once to Aulis with her elder daughter, whose hand had been sought in marriage by Achilles. This message was a heartless ruse, invented by Calchas, Menelaus, Odysseus, and the reluctant Agamemnon, to lure Iphigenia to her death. It is at this point that the *Iphigenia in Aulis* of Euripides begins, and we cannot do better than tell the rest of the story as it is told in the play.

The opening scene is before Agamemnon's tent by the seashore, and the hour is somewhere between midnight and dawn.

Agamemnon, torn by remorse, seeks to dispatch a trusty old servant with a second letter to Clytemnestra, warning her to pay no heed to the first, but Menelaus meets and intercepts the messenger, and while the two kings are quarrelling a herald enters, announcing the arrival of Clytemnestra with her daughter Iphigenia and her small son Orestes. For a moment Menelaus almost relents, and it seems as if he will help his brother to avert the sacrifice; then they both remember that Odysseus is in the secret, and that there is no hope of any relenting on the part of the King of Ithaca.

Clytemnestra arrives at this juncture with her two children, and when Iphigenia flings her arms round her father's neck she sees that his eyes are full of sorrow, and asks him if it will be long before he comes home, and tells him that she wishes she could go with him to Troy.

Presently she withdraws into the tent, and Agamemnon, after vainly endeavouring to induce his wife to return to Argos and leave Iphigenia with him, has also departed. Then Achilles enters, and is surprised to find a lady of stately mien alone upon the shore. Still stronger is his surprise when the words of greeting spoken by Clytemnestra reveal to him who she is, and for what purpose she has brought her first-born child from Argos to Aulis. A moment later the old servant rushes in and blurts out the terrible truth.

Everything now depends on the reactions of Achilles. As his name had been used to " lure the victim to the net of death," he declares that it is his duty to defend Iphigenia from that fate; but

Iphigenia
M. Nonnenbruch

Captive Andromache

Lord Leighton

(Page 226)

By permission of the Berlin Photographic Co., London

he suggests that Clytemnestra should first try the effect of a little tactful pleading upon her husband. Tact was not the Queen's most prominent characteristic, for she adopts a hectoring and dictatorial tone which could hardly fail to harden the resistance of Agamemnon. In vain does Clytemnestra rail; in vain does the victim herself weep and plead. Agamemnon points to the ships lying at anchor in the straits between Bœotia and Eubœa, and to the camp noisy with armed men. If they do not win their way to Troy will not the Trojans attack them in their own homelands?

By now news of the coming of Iphigenia has spread through the host. There are tumults when it is known that Achilles is minded to cheat Artemis of her prey. Even his own faithful Myrmidons cast stones at him. Their leader, among whose faults cowardice was not numbered, was still ready to defend the unfortunate maiden, even if Calchas and Odysseus should try to drag her to the altar by her long, shining hair. But Iphigenia herself has in the meantime been reflecting:

> Mother, I have been thinking. Listen now!
> I will choose death, and freely will I choose.
> Fear I have banished wholly from my heart.
> Artemis asks my life. Can I say nay?
> Then let my life be given. Conquer Troy!
> EURIPIDES

With beautiful selflessness she refuses to let Achilles risk his life for her; she will not allow her mother to come with her to the sacrificial altar; she begs that Clytemnestra will forgive Agamemnon for his share in the tragedy—a fruitless prayer. Then, chanting a hymn to Artemis, goddess-Queen of the land of Aulis, she is led away.

At this point the play of Euripides is believed by scholars to have broken off, though there are some fragments attached to it which have been ascribed to his son, Euripides the younger. One such fragment is the speech of a messenger who comes to Clytemnestra with wonderful tidings. He tells how just as Calchas was about to deal the fatal blow the victim vanished from his sight, and upon the altar he found a hind. Artemis had relented at the eleventh hour, and though she would not restore Iphigenia to her sorrowing mother, neither would she exact her blood as the price of favouring winds for the Argive fleet.

N

In another play, *Iphigenia in Tauris*, Euripides describes what happened to the young princess after she had been wafted miraculously to the remote land of the Taurians, where she served as a priestess in a temple of the goddess Artemis Taurica.

PROTESILAUS AND LAODAMIA

The wind changed, as Artemis had promised through the soothsayer that it would, and the ships bearing the Greek warriors moved over the " wine-dark sea " towards the shores of the land known as the Troas, or the Troad, watered by the Scamander and dominated by the walled city of Troy. One of the legendary kings of the city, Ilus by name, had built on that spot a fortress called after him Ilion, or Ilium, and it must be remembered that most Roman and some English poets call Troy itself Ilium. Christopher Marlowe makes his Dr Faustus exclaim, when Mephistopheles calls up the vision of Helen,

> Was this the face that launch'd a thousand ships,
> And burnt the topless towers of Ilium?

When, however, the " thousand ships " came to anchor off the country where " topless towers " stood there was a general relucance on the part of the warriors to disembark.

> The Delphic oracle foretold
> That the first Greek who touched the Trojan strand
> Should die.
> WORDSWORTH

At last one braver than the rest, Protesilaus, leaped ashore, only to be slain by Trojans as soon as his foot had touched land.

When the news of his death reached Thessaly, his home, where his wife Laodamia was anxiously counting the days till his return, she implored the gods either to let her die also or to suffer her to see her lord once again, were it but for a little space.

> Such grace hath crowned thy prayer,
> Laodamia! that at Jove's command
> Thy husband walks the paths of upper air:
> He comes to tarry with thee three hours' space.
> Accept the gift, behold him face to face!
> WORDSWORTH

When, at the end of those three hours, Hermes appeared to lead Protesilaus down to the abode of the dead again Laodamia died of grief, and so was able to follow him thither.

Nymphs planted elm-trees upon the grave where this faithful man and his wife lay buried.

> Upon the side
> Of Hellespont (such faith was entertained)
> A knot of spiry trees for ages grew
> From out the tomb of him for whom she died;
> And ever, when such stature they had gained
> That Ilium's walls were subject to their view,
> The trees' tall summits withered at the sight:
> A constant interchange of growth and blight!
>
> WORDSWORTH

THE DAUGHTER OF CHRYSES

For nine long years the Greek hosts besieged the city of Troy. In the skirmishes before the walls they prevailed, but they could not fight their way into the city itself, and many of them began to grow weary for their homes.

It was their wont to divide their forces, one part remaining encamped before Troy, while the other part ravaged the towns of the surrounding plain for all those things of which the Argive army had most need. And hence came the great dispute which brought so many evils in its train.

One of the places which were thus sacked and despoiled was called Chryse, and there was in it a temple sacred to Apollo, served by a priest whose name was Chryses. The Greeks took much plunder from the city and from the temple, and they took also the fair maiden Chryseis, who was the daughter of the priest. Her they gave to Agamemnon as his share of the spoils.

Eager to ransom his child, Chryses came to the Greek camp, carrying his sacred staff, and bringing with him a great store of gold. But though many of the chieftains were willing to accept the ransom-money and let the maiden go, Agamemnon would not agree. " Begone, old man! " he cried wrathfully to the priest. " It shall go ill with you if you linger here. When I have taken the city of Troy I will bear your daughter away with me to my land of Argos."

Full of sorrow, the priest departed, and as he walked by the seashore he made his prayer to the god whom he served, and called upon Apollo to punish the Greeks for their cruelty.

Apollo heard him, and came down from Olympus, and loosed his golden arrows of death, first upon the dogs and the beasts of burden, and then upon the men. And the black smoke rolled along the edge of the sea as they burned the bodies of the dead.

Hera, who loved the Greeks, beheld these things, and she bade Achilles summon all the chieftains in council.

" Surely," said the son of Thetis, " some god is wroth with us. Let us ask some soothsayer what we may do."

Then Calchas the seer rose up, and, braving the wrath of Agamemnon, bade them send the daughter of Chryses back to her father without ransom, and, moreover, he demanded that with her they should send a hundred beasts to be sacrificed to Apollo.

Agamemnon was terrible in his fury at these words, but Achilles swore that if he would give up the maiden Chryseis the other chieftains would see him requited three- and four-fold after Troy should have fallen.

Then there broke out a fierce quarrel between the King of Argos and the chief of the Myrmidons, either defying and up-braiding the other most bitterly. Achilles was in the act of draw-ing his sword from its sheath when suddenly he felt a more than mortal hand holding him by the hair. It was Athene, who had been sent from Olympus by Hera to bid the young warrior be more patient. Obeying the goddess, he sheathed his sword; but he swore a mighty oath by the gold-studded sceptre of the Greeks that a day would come when Agamemnon would regret that he had wronged the most valiant warrior in his host.

Now it chanced that to Achilles also a maiden had been appor-tioned as his share of the spoils. Her name was Briseis, and she abode in that part of the camp where were the tents of the Myrmidons.

Agamemnon, having delivered up Chryseis according to the words of Calchas, insisted that Achilles should surrender Briseis, and sent two heralds to fetch her from the tent of the hero. Great was the wrath of Achilles, and when he had bidden his friend Patroclus that he should deliver the maiden to Agamemnon's messengers he prayed to his mother, Thetis, that she should implore Zeus to aid the sons of Troy against the Greeks.

THE WRATH OF ACHILLES AND ITS SEQUEL

Meanwhile Odysseus had conducted Chryseis safely to the house of her father, and sacrifices had been made to Apollo, and hymns sung, and libations poured forth, and the priest had prayed the archer god to turn aside his anger from the Greeks.

After twelve days, during which Thetis knew that Zeus had been absent from Olympus, feasting with the devout people of Ethiopia, the silver-footed goddess ascended to the mountain of the gods, and, kneeling before the king of the gods, with her left hand she clasped his knee and with her right his beard. And she prayed to him that the men of Troy might prevail against the Greeks, who had put dishonour upon her son.

Zeus, knowing that Hera loved the Greeks, and that already she had reproached him for showing too much favour to the Trojans, nevertheless promised that he would be mindful of the prayer of Thetis, and he confirmed the promise with a nod; " and the hair waved about his head, and all Olympus was shaken."

All-Highest though he was, Zeus did not choose to come openly to the aid of the men of Troy. While gods and men slept he sent a deceiving dream to the tent of Agamemnon, which spoke to him in the likeness of Nestor, whom the King held in high honour. And the false Nestor spoke, saying, " Awake, Agamemnon, and hearken unto the words of Zeus. The day of doom is come for the city of Troy. Set thy warriors in battle array, for the gods fight with thee."

So the King arose, and put on his tunic and his mantle, and girt himself with his sword, and took in his hand the sceptre which was the sign of his sovereignty over all the princes of Greece. And he called his chiefs together, and told them of his dream, and the heralds bade all the host assemble. Then the King made a trial of their valour by feigning discouragement and speaking irresolute words of a truce with Troy and an inglorious return to Argos. But even as the host wavered, and seemed about to surge towards the ships, Hera, seeing what was happening, sent Athene to urge Odysseus to speak words of courage and cheer to the faint-hearted Greeks.

There was a scene of much confusion, for Odysseus remonstrated with Agamemnon, and the bandy-legged, ill-favoured

Thersites mocked him, and the Greeks knew not whether to depart or to abide. But Athene stood beside Odysseus in the likeness of a herald, and the King of Ithaca lifted up his voice and spoke like a man inspired, bidding all men take heart again, and not set sail for home until Troy had fallen.

So Agamemnon gave orders that every man should sharpen his spear, and look to his chariot, and give his horses abundance of fodder, for on the morn they would make yet another attack upon the city of Priam.

And he prayed to Zeus for victory, but as yet the All-Highest heard him not.

THE DUEL BETWEEN PARIS AND MENELAUS

When the Trojans saw that their enemies were massing and marching upon them they came forth with cries like the cries of a flock of cranes; but the Greeks fought in grim silence. The sons of Priam were foremost among the Trojans—Hector of the glancing helm, and Paris of the yellow locks.

Paris rushed forth, crying to the Greeks that he was ready to do battle against the most valiant of their host, but when Menelaus, whom he had so bitterly wronged, leaped from his chariot to take up the challenge, the young prince started back as a man does who has come upon a snake in a lonely glen. His brother Hector rebuked him, and Paris, knowing that the rebuke was just, felt ashamed, and said that he was willing to meet Menelaus man to man, to decide the quarrel between them, the victor to take possession of Helen without further fighting between the Trojans and the Greeks.

Hector went boldly towards the Greeks and gave them this message, and Menelaus was glad; but first it was agreed that a sacrifice should be offered on either side to the gods, as a pledge of good faith.

Then to Helen, where she sat at her loom, came Iris, disguised as Laodice, Priam's fairest daughter, and told her how Menelaus and Paris were to fight for her, and she would be the wife of him that prevailed. And Helen wrapped herself in a white mantle, and went forth to the place where Priam sat on the wall with the elders of the city. And the old men said, when she drew near, "Small wonder that many a man has suffered much for this woman, for she is divinely beautiful. Yet it were better she should depart in the ships, lest she bring a curse on Troy." Priam spoke to Helen, and asked her who was the most majestic of the Greek chieftains, whom they could see encamped below the wall. And Helen told him that it was Agamemnon; and that the broad-shouldered man walking with long strides was Odysseus; and that the very tall one was Ajax, the bulwark of the Greeks. She marvelled at the absence of her brothers, Castor and Polydeuces, not knowing that they were dead.

After the sacrifice had been offered, and the libations poured forth, Hector and Odysseus marked out the ground for the duel, and drew lots, by shaking two pebbles in Hector's helmet, as to which combatant should be the first to throw his spear. The lot fell to Paris, and the spear-point struck the shield of Menelaus without piercing it. Then Menelaus, praying to Zeus, flung *his* spear, and it passed through the corslet of Paris without wounding him. The gods did not favour Menelaus, for when he smote his rival upon the helmet the sword broke into four pieces in his hand, and when he seized Paris by the helmet and began to drag him towards the Greek camp Aphrodite loosened the helmet-strap, so that it set Paris free, and afterwards, when Menelaus came rushing forward with a fresh spear, the goddess caused a mist to hide Paris while she snatched him out of the throng and bore him away to his own chamber within the walls of Troy. "No son of Troy would have hidden him for friendship's sake, for they all hated him like death."

And Agamemnon spoke, saying that since their champion had vanished from the field the Trojans should deliver up Helen, and also pay tribute to him to make good all the cost and trouble he had had during the nine years that he had besieged Troy.

OLYMPUS INTERVENES

Now, while yet the truce held between the Trojans and the Greeks, the high gods in council debated these matters, and while Zeus was inclined to favour the men of Troy, who had always been his devout and faithful votaries, Hera and Athene were violent champions of the Greeks. And Athene went down disguised as a Trojan, and urged Pandarus, the son of Lycaon, to shoot an arrow at the unsuspecting Menelaus. Pandarus was very proud of his bow, fashioned from the horns of a wild goat slain by himself, and while he strung his bow his comrades hid him with their shields. Then he fitted a sharp arrow into the bowstring and took careful aim, and Athene, who did not wish the wound to be mortal, guided the arrow to the spot where the golden clasps of the belt of Menelaus met, just beneath the breastplate.

Agamemnon, when he saw his brother's blood gushing forth, was full of dismay, and also of anger against the Trojans. He did not know that it was at the bidding of Athene that they had broken the truce. And forthwith he sent word through all the Greek host to make them ready for battle. And he himself walked among the warriors, reminding them of the valiant deeds of their fathers. And when the battle began the gods on either side urged the mortals on to victory. Ares, god of war, was with the Trojans, but with the Greeks was Athene, the goddess of wisdom.

DIOMED DOES VALIANTLY

In the two days' battle which ensued no man fought better than Diomed, " who raged in the battle so furiously that you could not tell with which host he was, whether with the Greeks or with the sons of Troy." Athene stood beside him, after he had been wounded slightly by an arrow from the goats'-horn bow of Pandarus, and she gave him new strength and new keenness of sight, saying, " Into thy heart have I breathed the spirit that was in Tydeus thy father. But fight not against any of the immortals if by hap thou meet them in the fray, save only Aphrodite."

Then Diomed raged like a lion against the men of Troy, and many fell before his onslaught. And Æneas, the son of Anchises and Aphrodite, came forth to do battle with him, driving his chariot, in which Pandarus stood, poising his spear and aiming at Diomed. But the spear glanced aside, and when Diomed flung his own spear the aim was true, and the sharp point clove Pandarus through the head. Æneas leapt forward to guard the body of his comrade, but Diomed seized a great stone and flung it at him, and it struck Æneas on the hip-bone. Seeing the peril of the son whom she had borne to Anchises, Aphrodite snatched Æneas up in her arms, and wrapped her shining veil about him. Then Diomed was very wroth, and he wounded the goddess on the wrist, so that the sacred *ichor* which flows in immortal veins gushed forth. She uttered a loud cry and let her son fall, and Apollo hastened to catch him and veil him in mist.

"Get thee gone, daughter of Zeus!" cried Diomed; and Aphrodite, faint with pain and leaning upon Iris, departed, and went up to Olympus in the chariot of Ares, which the god of war relinquished to her. And when she reached Olympus Zeus strove to comfort her, saying, "My daughter, deeds of war are not for thee. Leave them to Ares and to Athene."

Meanwhile Apollo had carried Æneas away, and had laid him, sorely hurt, in his own temple within the walls of Troy, where Artemis and Latona tended him, and healed him of his wound. And the god made an image of the hero, as if he were lying dead, and the Greeks and the Trojans fought to get possession of it. On the side of the Trojans was Sarpedon the Lycian, the son of Zeus and Laodamia—not of that Laodamia who was the wife of Protesilaus, but of a daughter of Bellerophon bearing the same name. And he urged Hector, the son of Priam, to fresh deeds of valour.

Presently Apollo restored Æneas to their midst, whole and strong, and the battle waxed fiercer than before, for Ares fought at Hector's side in the likeness of a mortal man. This thing was displeasing to Hera and Athene, and they sought the leave of Zeus to descend and check the rage of the god of war.

When their chariot touched the earth Hera assumed the form of the brazen-lunged Stentor, whose voice was as loud as the voices of fifty men, and taunted the Greeks with cowardice, while Athene rebuked Diomed for being no true son of his father Tydeus, who was small of stature but doughty in battle. Diomed made answer: "Nay, goddess, I heed thy commands. Ares is fighting against us, and I was bidden to wound none of the immortals but Aphrodite."

But Athene bade him drive his chariot straight at Ares, who only that morning had vowed to help the Greeks and had now changed his mind.   And she thrust Sthenelos out of the chariot, and herself seized the reins and lashed the horses, having donned meanwhile the Helmet of Hades to make herself invisible.

In the skirmish which followed Athene turned aside the spear which Ares flung at Diomed, and guided the spear which Diomed aimed at Ares.   And the god, being wounded in the loin, shouted with pain, and Diomed saw him go up to Olympus " as a thunder cloud goes up when the south wind blows hot."

There was amazement upon Olympus when Ares showed his wound, but Zeus would not listen to him when he begged the All-Highest to rebuke Athene for her intervention.   All that Zeus would do was to summon Pæan, the healer, to sprinkle sweet and healing herbs upon the body of the wounded god, whom Hebe bathed and clad in fair raiment before he sat down by Zeus, forgetful for the moment of his anger against the men of Greece.

HECTOR AND ANDROMACHE

Things were going ill with the Trojans.   When Hector entered the city by the gate called the Scæan gate the wives and mothers of the absent warriors crowded round him, clamouring for news. All he would answer was that they had best say their prayers. To his own mother, Queen Hecuba, he spoke at more length, bidding her go to the temple of Athene, with all the other mothers of Troy, and offer the most beautiful robe in her possession to the goddess, imploring her at the same time " to keep this dreadful Diomed from the walls of Troy."

While Hecuba was setting about this deed of worship Hector went to the house of Paris and bitterly upbraided his brother for the sorrow he had brought upon his native city.   And Helen said to Hector, " O my brother, would that I had died on the day of my birth!   And would that the gods had given me for my husband a man of understanding who feared the blame of other men, and not such a man as this.   Truly, Zeus has meted out unto us an evil portion, and our story shall be told in days that are as yet to come."

And Hector took leave of her, and went to his own house, seeking his wife, Andromache, but she was not to be found.   And the maidservants said that she had gone to the watch-tower by the Scæan gate, and that the nurse had gone with her, carrying her infant child, Astyanax.

So Hector hastened to the gate, and his wife came forth to meet him, saying, " O Hector, thy valour will slay thee! Thou hast pity neither for thy wife, nor for thy young babe. If thou diest better it were that I should die also. What comfort have I save in thee? My father is dead—Achilles slew him—and my seven brothers were all slain in one day by the great Achilles. My mother too is dead. Have pity then. Stay here with me."

" Nay," answered Hector, " I know that Priam, and his people, and Troy itself, are doomed. But it is not for this, nor for them, that I grieve. It is for thee, when thou shalt be led away captive, and shalt weave and draw water in the land of Greece. And some man, seeing thee, shall say, ' This captive woman was the wife of Hector of Troy.' "

Then he stretched forth his arms to Astyanax : but the child was afraid of the shining bronze helmet and the nodding plume of horsehair, and shrank back into the arms of his nurse. Hector laughed, and doffed the helmet and set it on the ground. And he took the child in his arms and kissed him, and prayed to Zeus that some day this son of his should be a great man among the Trojans and a joy to the heart of his mother.

But Andromache wept, striving to smile through her tears, and Hector stroked her with his hands, saying, " Grieve not. No man shall slay me unless it be ordained ; and from what is ordained no man, be he never so valiant, may escape. Begone to thy house. Ply the shuttle and the loom, and set tasks to thy handmaids, and leave to men the thought of battle."

He took his helmet and donned it again, and Andromache departed to their house, looking back often over her shoulder as she went.

And Hector went his way till he met Paris, who ran to him radiant in newly burnished armour, and together they issued forth from the Scæan gate and wrought valiantly against the hosts of the Greeks encamped before the city.

HECTOR AND AJAX

Athene, looking down from Olympus, saw that Hector was lay-ing many of the Greek chieftains low, and as she descended to earth she met Apollo, who said to her: " Thou comest, O Athene, to help the Greeks.   Well, let us stop the battle for this one day. But thereafter they must fight until the fate of the city is fulfilled."

" How," asked Athene, " shall we stop the battle? "

" By stirring up Hector to challenge the most valiant of the Greeks to single combat," the sun-god suggested.

So the god and the goddess put this thought into the heart of Helenus the seer, who was one of the sons of Priam and Hecuba. And Helenus spoke to his brother Hector according to the thought which Apollo and Athene had put into his heart.   Then Hector was glad, and he stretched forth his spear, holding it by the middle, to keep back the Trojans, and Agamemnon, perceiving his pur-pose, did the same along the foremost ranks of the Greeks.

Then Hector lifted up his voice and spoke to the men on either side, saying that he would fain meet in single combat the man who should stand forth as the champion of all the Greeks.   For a moment there was silence in the Grecian host, and Menelaus, ashamed that no younger man had taken up the challenge of Hector, cried out that he himself would fight with him.   But Agamemnon drew him back, reminding him that he was no longer young, and that even Achilles had been unwilling to meet Hector face to face.   And Nestor stood up and lamented that there was none both willing and worthy to be the champion of the Greeks. And it was decided that nine chieftains should draw lots, and the lot fell to Ajax, the son of Telamon, who came forth with long strides, brandishing his spear and holding up before him the huge sevenfold shield of bull's-hide and bronze which Tychius the smith had made for him.

(It is of this shield that Shakespeare is thinking when he makes Mark Antony say, " The sevenfold shield of Ajax cannot keep the battery from my heart.")

Hector flung his spear first, and it pierced six folds of the shield, only to be bent aside on the seventh.   Then it was the turn of Ajax, and the spear flung by him went through Hector's corslet and made a gash in his tunic without wounding him.   They took each a fresh spear, and again that of Hector was deflected by the sevenfold shield; but the spear of Ajax grazed Hector's neck, so that the blood welled up.

Then Hector caught from the ground a large stone and hurled it with all his might at the centre boss of the great shield, which rang aloud, but did not break. Ajax retorted with a yet larger stone, which clove Hector's shield asunder and laid him low; but Apollo helped him to his feet.

Next they drew their swords and would have renewed the fight, but the heralds stepped between them, and it was agreed that for that day there should be no more fighting. And to show that they parted in friendship Hector gave Ajax a silver-studded sword with its scabbard and belt, and Ajax gave Hector " a buckler glorious with purple."

Both the Greeks and the Trojans rejoiced, and there was joy that night in either host, because each had been loth to lose so valiant a man. And Nestor counselled the Greeks that for the time they should cease from war, burn their dead, and make a camp, with a wall and a trench, so that they might get safely to their ships if they were hard pressed by the men of Troy.

Next day a herald came from Troy, saying that Paris would yield up all the treasure which he had taken with Helen, and much more besides, but that Helen herself he would not yield up. And when the Greeks refused this offer the herald asked for a truce that they too might burn or bury their dead.

This was granted. And the next evening, at sunset, ships came from Lemnos bringing fresh supplies of weapons and of wine for the Greeks. And that night the Greeks feasted in their camp, and the Trojans in their city, but thunder rolled all through the night, for Zeus was planning evil against Troy.

And the next day the king of gods and men called all the gods into council upon the summit of Olympus. And he spoke sternly to them all, threatening to cast down into the dark depths of Tartarus any god or goddess who should go to the aid either of the Greeks or of the Trojans. For a moment the gods sat mute. Then Athene said, " We know, Father Zeus, that your word is law. But we are sorry for the Greeks. If we hold aloof from the battle may we not at least give counsel to them? "

And Zeus said that this they might do.

THE BATTLE OF THE PLAIN

Then was fought a long and fierce battle on the plain, wherein Greeks and Trojans strove with all their might to gain the victory. The men of Troy once fled, but Zeus dropped a thunderbolt in front of Diomed's chariot and stayed the pursuit. And when Hector saw that Diomed had turned back he cried to the Trojans that Zeus was with them, and to his chariot-team he spoke lovingly, reminding the horses how Andromache had cared for them, and bidding them bear him fast into the fray, that he might win from Diomed the breastplate wrought by Hephæstus.

And so fierce was the onslaught of Hector that it was the turn of the Greeks to fly, and they would have been utterly overcome had not Hera put it into the mind of Agamemnon to rally his shaken host.

Through all these days of tumult and stirring Zeus favoured the men of Troy, and Hera bestirred herself on the side of the Greeks. And the fortunes of battle swayed to and fro; and many valiant deeds were done, and many mighty men were laid low.

Athene, who also loved the Greeks, stood by Hera in her chariot when they were minded to descend to earth and mingle in the fray. But Zeus saw them from Mount Ida, and bade Iris of the shining wings hasten and tell them that if they intervened he would smite their chariot asunder with his terrible lightnings.

And when the sun went down the Greeks were glad, for it brought them a respite from fighting; but the men of Troy grieved, for they thought that if they could fight but a little longer they would surely prevail, and drive the Greeks into the sea.

Hector called the Trojans to council, and bade them tend their horses, and fetch bread and meat and wine from the city, and keep the watchfires alight upon the walls, lest the Greeks should take to their ships and escape under cover of darkness : for in the morning it was his purpose " to wake the war beside the ships."

So Hector spake; the Trojans roar'd applause;
Then loosed their sweating horses from the yoke,
And each beside his chariot bound his own.
TENNYSON

THE APPEAL TO ACHILLES

Meanwhile the disheartened Greeks had resolved to appeal to Achilles to come to their aid. And Agamemnon declared that not only would he restore the maiden Briseis, but send many gifts with her—tripods, and cauldrons, and horses, and " seven women skilled in handicrafts."

Three of the chieftains, accompanied by two heralds, made their way to that part of the beach where were the ships and the tents of the Myrmidons,[1] and there they found Achilles, playing the harp and singing lays of ancient heroes, while his friend Patroclus sat listening to him.

After they had all eaten together Odysseus spoke earnest words to Achilles, urging him to forget his anger and to come and save the Greek host from the fury of Hector. And Achilles answered at great length, reminding them of the hardships he had endured, and the exploits he had performed, while Agamemnon remained among the ships, taking more than his just share of the spoils; and he spoke very bitterly of the loss of the maiden Briseis, whom he had loved. And he said that he would not rise and fight until Hector should slay the Greeks "even unto the tents of the Myrmidons."

THE WAR GOES ON

All these episodes, and many of great interest though of less importance, are recorded by Homer in the *Iliad* in language of incomparable beauty and vigour, with marvellous skill in suggesting character and personality, and with great dexterity in the handling of the plot.

It is impossible in these pages to do more than touch upon the outstanding events in the tale of Troy, that tale of heroism and treachery, endurance and stratagem, love and sorrow and enmity, in which gods and goddesses act their parts as well as the mortals whose lives they so strangely make and mar, and the clash of bronze mingles with the murmur of the sea.

---

[1] The Myrmidons were so called because they were descended from the ants (*myrmekes*) changed by the gods into men and women to repopulate the plague-stricken island of Ægina.

Zeus intervened in what is usually called the Battle at the Wall, when he sent a blast of wind to drive the dust from the plain of Troy towards the Greek ships; and in the Battle by the Ships it was Poseidon who had pity on the Greeks, and who, assuming the form of Calchas, bade them stand firm against the onslaught of Hector.

THE DEATH OF PATROCLUS

When word came to the tents of the Myrmidons how hard pressed were the Greeks by Hector the heart of Patroclus was filled with sorrow, but in the heart of Achilles there was no pity.

And Patroclus, anxious to aid the Greeks, and knowing that the Trojans would be sore afraid if they thought that the great Achilles had forgotten his wrath against Agamemnon and was coming forth against them, begged of his friend that he would let him don his corslet and helmet, and take his silver-studded sword and his shining shield, and lead the Myrmidons into battle.

It happened that as the two friends were speaking of these things the Trojans drew near the Greek ships, setting fire to them as they came, and Achilles, seeing the flames leap up to the sky, said, " Gird on my armour quickly, Patroclus, and I will call my Myrmidons together."

And the Myrmidons went forth to battle, fifty times fifty in number, their shields as close together as a builder sets the stones when he builds a wall, while Achilles poured out a libation to Zeus, and begged the All-Highest to give good fortune to Patroclus and to all them that went with him.

When the Trojans beheld the helmet and the shield of Patroclus they thought that it was Achilles, and they fell back in haste upon the trench which they had dug, where many of their chariots were broken. But the chariot-team of Achilles over-leaped the trench, and Patroclus raged to and fro, seeking Hector that he might slay him. In that battle perished Sarpedon, the great chieftain of Lycia, and Hector and all the Trojans made lamentation for him. Zeus sent Apollo down from heaven to lap the dead Sarpedon in a mantle such as the gods wear, and Sleep and Death bore him to his own land of Lycia.

Now Achilles had warned Patroclus not to go too near to the

Homer
Harry Bates

208

Laocoön
Vatican
(*Page 226*)
From a photograph by D. Anderson

walls of Troy, but Patroclus forgot these words, and thrice he climbed up the corner of the city wall.   As many times did Apollo thrust him back again, saying, " It is not for thee, Patroclus, nor for Achilles, a mightier man than thou, to take the city of Troy."

And Apollo stirred up Hector to go and match himself against the friend of Achilles.   And Patroclus threw a great stone at Cebriones, who was driving Hector's chariot, and when the charioteer fell headlong Patroclus mocked him, and cried out that he was a marvellous driver, who would be able to gather up many oysters from the bed of the sea if he dived so well from a ship— even in stormy weather.

Apollo stood behind Patroclus in the fight which followed and darkened his eyes and broke the spear in his grasp, so that he knew not which way to turn.   And Hector saw him, and thrust at him with his spear so that he fell, and the Greeks, seeing him fall, cried aloud for terror.

And Hector stood over him and said, " Now can the great Achilles avail thee nothing."

Patroclus answered, " Thou braggest overmuch, Hector.   It was Apollo who slew me, and not thou.   But death is near thee— at the hand of the great Achilles."   And so saying he died.

Over the body of Patroclus a fierce battle raged, for there was not one of the chieftains who would not have been joyful to capture his battle-gear—the armour of Achilles.   It was Hector who stripped off the armour, and who would have dragged the body away by the feet had not Ajax, the son of Telamon, put his shield before it.

(In the host of the Greeks there were two chieftains called Ajax —the Greater, who was the son of Telamon, and the Lesser, who was the son of Oïleus, King of Locris.)

Zeus looked down upon his holy city of Troy, and he saw Hector, who had sent the armour of Patroclus towards Troy, run after the men who were carrying it, and himself put on the helmet and the corslet, and gird on the silver-studded sword of Achilles. And Zeus liked it not.

The chariot-team of Achilles stood apart from the fray with drooping heads, knowing well that Patroclus was dead, nor could Automedon, their driver, persuade them to move, until Zeus, pitying them, said, " Hector shall not possess these also."   And

o

then the horses obeyed their driver again, and Hector could not overtake them.

Menelaus now sent Antilochus, the son of the wise Nestor, with a message to Achilles, telling him that Patroclus was dead, that Hector had taken his arms, and that the Trojans were fighting over the body. But since Achilles had no arms—having given what he had to Patroclus—the Greeks recked not that the chief of the Myrmidons might overcome Hector and the men of Troy.

THE GRIEF OF ACHILLES FOR PATROCLUS

When Achilles heard that Patroclus had been slain he cast dust upon his head, and lay upon the bare earth, weeping and tearing his hair. Thetis his mother heard him, even in the depths of the sea, and rose up, and came to him, and asked what grieved him so sore. And when he had told her she entreated him not to desire the death of Hector, for she knew that when Hector should die Achilles should not live long after. But when she saw that his heart was set on avenging Patroclus she promised that she would go to Hephæstus and get from him fresh armour for her son.

THE REARMING OF ACHILLES

Now, though Zeus had hitherto favoured the Trojans rather than the Greeks, he was wroth with Hector, and he had pity on the body of Patroclus, stripped of the armour of Achilles and dragged to and fro in the tumult. So he sent Iris to Achilles, saying, " Arise, son of Peleus, or Patroclus will be a prey for the hounds of Troy."

And when Achilles asked how this might be, seeing that he had no shield or sword, Iris bade him go to the trench and stand there, and then the Trojans would cease from fighting.

He obeyed her behest, and Athene flung her Ægis about his broad shoulders, and set a shining flame upon his forehead, and when he shouted to the Trojans his voice clanged like a trumpet. The men of Troy fell back, trembling for fear, and the Greeks lifted up the body of Patroclus and bore him to the tents of the Myrmidons with great lamentation.

While Achilles and his men washed and anointed the body of Patroclus Thetis went her way to the house of Hephæstus. Now when the blacksmith of the gods had been cast down from high heaven Thetis and her sister had harboured him in their home in the depths of the sea, and he remembered these things, and was glad to be of some good service to the mother of Achilles. And when Thetis had told him what she desired he said, " Fear not. I will make your son such arms that men will marvel when they look upon them."

Forthwith he went to his smithy, and blew the fire with the bellows, and took his hammer in one hand and his tongs in the other. And in the fire he melted bronze, and gold, and silver, and tin.

First he made the shield. He set on it the embossed images of the earth and the sea, the sun and the moon, and all the stars. And therewith he wrought two cities, one at peace, with a bridal procession passing through the streets, and one at war, beleaguered by an army, with sentinels standing on the walls. Other images there were also. Fields being ploughed and reaped, and vineyards in the time of the grape-harvest, and sheepfolds, and men and maidens dancing. Then he made a shining corslet, which was brighter than flame, and a great helmet crested with gold, and greaves of bronze. As a hawk swoops from its eyrie, Thetis swooped down from Olympus, and sought that part of the seashore where were the ships and the tents of the Myrmidons. And she found her son still lamenting over the dead Patroclus.

" Come, my son," she said ; " it was the decree of the gods that this man should die. Look what Hephæstus has made for thee— armour such as never yet was borne by mortal man ! " And the armour clashed aloud as she cast it down before him.

Then Achilles looked upon the glorious shield, and corslet, and helmet, and greaves, and was glad. And he made himself ready for battle.

When Achilles was armed he went to Agamemnon, and all the Greeks gathered round. And the twain made their peace, and they were of one mind that the Greeks should go forth and assail the men of Troy. But the crafty Odysseus said, " It is ill fighting and fasting. Let a feast of reconciliation be spread, and let every man eat."

These words did not please Achilles, who was in no mood for feasting, but Odysseus had his will.   And presently all the gifts that Agamemnon had offered to Achilles were brought by Odysseus to the tents of the Myrmidons—the tripods, the cauldrons, the horses, the seven women, and the fair Briseis.

But from the feast Achilles sat apart, for his heart was heavy within him, thinking of how in times past he had feasted with Patroclus before going into battle.   And when Zeus saw this he spoke to Athene, and she descended from Olympus, and filled Achilles with nectar and ambrosia, so that he should not faint for hunger in the hour of battle.

Then Achilles rose up, and took his shield, and with it the great spear which Chiron had given to his father Peleus, and he spoke to his horses, the piebald and the bay, bidding them not to leave him dead on the field, as they had left Patroclus.

And Hera gave a voice to the bay horse, which said, " Surely we will save thee, mighty Achilles; yet thy doom draws near, decreed not by us, but by the gods.   It was not because of us that Patroclus fell.   Hector had the glory, but the slayer was Apollo.   So shalt thou die also, by the hand of a man, but at the behest of a god."

And Achilles answered, " Why do ye speak to me of my doom? It is known to me.   But I will not cease from fighting till I have made those Trojans weary of war."

ACHILLES AND ÆNEAS

Seeking eagerly for Hector, Achilles went into the thick of the battle.   And Apollo came and stood by Æneas, the son of Anchises, and reminded him that he had bragged of his desire to meet Achilles face to face, and that, though he had fled before him at the capture of Lyrnessus, he too was the son of a goddess, even of Aphrodite, who among the immortals was of more account than Thetis.

Taking courage from these words, Æneas hurled his spear at Achilles, and with such good aim that it pierced the two outer folds of bronze upon his shield.   When Achilles in turn took aim the shield of Æneas was cloven, but the son of Anchises was not hurt.   They would have grappled then in deadly combat, Achilles wielding his sword, and Æneas poising a great stone in both his hands, but there befell a marvellous thing. It was not decreed that Æneas should die, for he and his sons were destined to rule over Troy in the years to be. So Poseidon lifted him up and swept him through the air, and set him down far to the rear of the battle. And the sea-god plucked from the shield of Æneas the spear which transfixed it and laid it down at the feet of Achilles, who wondered much, and said, " Surely Æneas spoke truly when he boasted that he was dear to the gods." That he did speak truly was to be proved later.

And he rushed again into the fray, and among those whom he laid low was the young Polydorus, the last-born of the sons of Priam, who had been forbidden by his father to go to the battle. Apollo had warned Hector not to meet Achilles face to face, but when Hector saw his brother lying wounded unto death he could not stand aside any longer, and as he ran forward Achilles rejoiced, saying within himself, " Here comes the man who slew Patroclus." But in the duel which followed Athene turned aside the spear of Hector, and Apollo would not suffer the spear of Achilles to find its mark. So Achilles strove with Hector no more for that day, but by the river Xanthus (Scamander) he slew innumerable Trojans, who leaped into the water as locusts leap when they are driven from the fields by fire.

THE RIVER SCAMANDER

Now when the river-god of the Scamander found his waters all choked with dead men and dead horses, so that they could not flow into the sea, he rose up above his banks, and prayed Achilles to depart and to do no more slaughter in that place. And Achilles answered that though he was willing to depart from the river he would not cease from slaying the Trojans until he had met Hector again in battle. Then the river-god rose up yet higher, and called aloud to Apollo to obey the behest of Zeus, who had bidden him succour the sons of Troy. And when Achilles saw Scamander overflowing the banks and following him fast across the plain he was afraid; and the waters rose until they broke upon his shield, and when he took hold of a tall lime-tree for support the tree came crashing down, and its roots tore a great hole in the bank of the river. And Scamander smote him across the shoulders with a mighty wave. Then Achilles called aloud to Zeus and to all the gods to save him from the river. " Surely," he cried, " it would be better that Hector should slay me than that I should die like some poor shepherd boy swept away by a swollen stream! "

Poseidon and Athene heard his prayer, and they came and took him each one by the hand, saying that it was not his doom to be drowned in Scamander.

All the plain was flooded by this time, and armour and dead men and battle-gear were tossing on the waves. And Scamander cried to his brother, the river-god Simois, urging him to brim over his banks and drown Achilles, lest holy Troy should perish utterly.

Hera looked down from heaven, and when she saw the dark waves surging towards Achilles she called to Hephæstus to help the son of Thetis, whom he had armed with his own hands, but whom Scamander threatened to destroy. And she summoned the west wind and the south wind to blow across the plain of Troy and dry up the floods, while Hephæstus breathed upon the river, and kindled a great fire along the banks, so that the eels and the little fishes writhed to and fro in the water, and the willows and the tamarisks shrivelled up. Then Scamander yielded, and swore that he would cease helping the men of Troy if Hephæstus would stay his fiery breath and suffer the river to flow quietly to the sea. And Hephæstus departed, and the floods subsided, and the plain was as it had been before, the willows and tamarisks put forth fresh shoots, and the little fishes swam at their ease in the cool water.

THE STRIFE OF THE GODS

But there was strife among the immortal gods, for some of them loved Troy, and others loved the Greeks, and Zeus looked on while the battle raged. Ares thrust his spear at Athene, but it could not pierce her terrible Ægis; and Athene caught up a large and ancient boundary-stone, and with it smote Ares upon the neck, so that he fell to the earth. Aphrodite would have helped the god of war to rise, but Hera sent Athene to hinder her. Then

Poseidon said to Apollo that it ill became them to stand aside, and
that since Apollo was helping the men of Troy, whom the sea-god
desired to see conquered, they might well fight it out themselves.
But Apollo answered, " O Earthshaker, I will not fight with thee
for the sake of these wretched men.   They perish like the leaves
of the wood.   To-day they eat the fruits of the earth : to-morrow
they have ceased to be."

Now Apollo feared to do battle against Poseidon, who was the
brother of his father Zeus, but his sister Artemis was angry, and
taunted him with cowardice, and asked him of what use was his
famous bow.   But when Hera saw this she was angry likewise,
and she rebuked Artemis, and smote her upon the head with her
own arrows, and Artemis fled, leaving her bow behind and all her
arrows lying in the dust.

THE DEATH OF HECTOR

Meanwhile Priam, standing upon the wall of Troy, saw the
Trojans fleeing towards the city.   And he told the keepers of the
gates to hold the wickets open, so that the fugitives might swiftly
enter in.   And Achilles pursued the Trojans up to the very gates
of Troy.

Apollo then put courageous thoughts into the mind of Agenor,
the son of Antenor, who stood and faced the pursuing Achilles,
and flung his spear at him.   The spear glanced off the brazen
greave, but Achilles was very wroth, and would have slain Agenor
had not Apollo caught him up and set him within the city.   Thereupon Apollo assumed the outward shape of Agenor, and made as
if he were flying from Achilles, who sped after him; and while
those two ran swiftly upon the plain all the Trojans were able to
get safely within the gates.

Then the god revealed himself to Achilles, and said, " Lo, all
the sons of Troy are within their gates, while thou art here, far
from them, striving to slay me, who am an immortal god."
Achilles was very angry, but he dared not touch Apollo, though
he spoke bitter words to him before he turned back towards Troy.

Priam, watching from the walls, saw the glorious armour that
Hephæstus had made shining like the brightest of the stars—men
call it Orion's Dog—which is at its full splendour in the time of

vintage; and he groaned aloud, for he knew that his son Hector was eager to meet Achilles in the field.

And the aged King of Troy stretched forth his hands to Hector, saying, " Of many valiant sons hath Achilles bereft me. Two are missing this day, though perchance they live yet, and are held captive by the Greeks. Yet what matters it, so long as thou art still in the land of the living? Have pity on me, and on Troy, and on all of us. Losing thee, we lose our best defender. Come within the city wall, my son, and go not forth to meet that proud, revengeful man."

And Hecuba, his mother, wept, praying him not to go.

But Hector heeded not. Once indeed, for a little space, he mused how it would be if he were to lay down his shield, and doff his helmet, and lean his spear against the wall, and seek parley with Achilles, offering to yield up Helen and all the wealth of Troy if the Greeks would depart and leave the city in peace. But he told himself that Achilles would slay him where he stood, and that there was nothing for it but to do battle against him.

Meanwhile Achilles came forth, with his gigantic spear across his right shoulder, his armour glowing like fire. And Hector turned from him and fled past the watch-tower, past the ancient, wind-blown fig-tree, along the wagon-track beneath the walls, as far as the source of the Scamander. That river rises from two springs, one hot and the other cold, and there in stone troughs the women of Troy used to wash their garments in the peaceful days or ever the Greeks came to that land.

Achilles put forth his utmost speed, pursuing Hector, who fled as if his feet were winged, and three times they ran round the city, while the gods looked down.

Zeus had pity upon Hector, remembering how the tamer of horses had been wont to offer sacrifices to him, both upon Mount Ida and within the citadel of Troy, and he asked the other gods if it were not better that they should save him from the hand of Achilles. But Athene said, " Lord, what is this thing that thou sayest? Hector is doomed. Save him if thou wilt. Reverse his doom if it so please thee. But we, the other gods, will not say that it is well done." Zeus made answer, " I am loth to see Hector die. But it must needs be."

And now the two runners approached for the fourth time the

twin fountains at the source of the Scamander; and Zeus held up
the great scales of Fate—Fate who is stronger than even the
greatest of the gods; and on one scale he put the doom of Hector
and on the other the doom of Achilles. And the scale of Hector
dropped, even unto the realms of the dead. Then Apollo, who
had been at Hector's side helping him on, said that there was no
more hope, and left him. But Athene stood near Achilles, and
spoke words of cheer to him, bidding him pause to take breath,
while she gave Hector courage to turn and meet him. The goddess assumed the shape of Deiphobus, whom Hector loved best
of all his brothers, and came to him, saying, " Let us stand together and do battle against this man, and peradventure we shall
prevail."

Achilles drew near, and Hector of the waving plume said to
him, " Three times I have fled before thee about the walls of
Troy, but now I will meet thee face to face. Let us make a pact
between us that the victor shall treat reverently the body of the
vanquished." Achilles frowned and answered, " With thee,
Hector, will I make no pact. One of us two must die, and surely
it will be thou. Athene shall avenge all my companions whom
thou hast slain."

He threw his great spear, but Hector by crouching down escaped
death, and Athene plucked it from the earth and gave it back to
Achilles.

Then Hector, with defiant words, flung his long-shafted spear,
and so good was his aim that he struck his opponent's shield fair
and square upon the midmost boss. But against the craftsman-
ship of Hephæstus the spear-point made by a mortal smith could
avail nothing. The spear glanced aside and rebounded, and
Hector turned—as he thought—to Deiphobus to give him a fresh
one, and behold, Deiphobus was not there.

Then Hector said, " This is the hour that the gods have decreed
for my death. Deiphobus is far away, within the walls of Troy,
and Athene has deceived me; nor will Zeus or Apollo stand near
me any more."

He drew his sword and rushed towards Achilles, but before he
could strike a blow his opponent had run forth to meet him, with
head bent low, his plume streaming in the wind, his spear-point
shining like the evening star. For one moment he pondered as

to the spot where he should drive the weapon home, for Hector was wearing the armour of Patroclus; but just where the neck joined the shoulder there was an unguarded chink, and there did Achilles thrust his spear with such fury that it stood out behind Hector's neck.

Then Achilles cried aloud, " Now, Hector, thou hast fallen before me, and the dogs and the vultures shall devour thee; but to Patroclus, whom thou didst slay, the Greeks shall give rites of burial." Hector, nigh to death, made answer, " Great Achilles, I pray thee let not the dogs of the Greeks devour me! My father and mother will pay thee a rich ransom, bronze and gold, if but the men and women of Troy may give me the rites of burial."

" No ransom will I take," said Achilles, " nor could Priam buy back thy body for its weight in gold."

Then Hector uttered his last words. " I know," he said, " that thy heart is of iron. Yet beware of the vengeance of the gods, in that day when Paris and Apollo shall lay thee low beside the Scæan gate."

And as soon as Achilles saw that Hector was indeed dead he stripped off his armour, and the Greeks gathered round, marvelling at the comeliness of Hector; and each man, forgetful of the reverence which all men owe to the dead, as he came thrust his spear into the body of the most valiant of all the sons of Troy.

Then Achilles had a cruel thought. He tied thongs of oxhide about the ankles of Hector, and with that once noble head trailing in the dust he dragged the dead hero behind his chariot down to the Greek camp by the ships.

Priam saw this thing from the city wall, and had his remaining sons not restrained him he would have rushed forth to kneel before Achilles and beg for the body of Hector. Hecuba too lamented for her son, but as yet Andromache knew not what had befallen.

The wife of Hector was sitting in her house, wearing an embroidered purple mantle, and on her head was the diadem that Aphrodite had given her on her wedding day. And even as she bade her maidens make the bath ready for Hector when he should return from battle she heard a cry of lamentation from the city, and rose up, and hastened like one distracted to the wall.

And she looked down from the wall, and saw the horses of Achilles dragging Hector down to the sea, and fell fainting to the ground.   And then from her head dropped the diadem, the gift of Aphrodite, which she had worn first on the day that Hector of the waving plume led her from the house of her father to be his wife.

THE FUNERAL RITES OF PATROCLUS

The Trojans lamented for Hector.   And Achilles made ready to pay the rites of burial and of burning to Patroclus.   He bade his Myrmidons drive their chariots thrice round the place where the body of his friend lay upon a fair bier, with the mangled body of Hector lying in the dust hard by.   And then, refusing to let the blood and mire be washed from his limbs, he lay down in an open place near the sea.

And as he slept the ghost of Patroclus came and stood by his head, saying, " Make haste to bury me, Achilles, for until that be done the shades of the dead will not let me draw near them. Give me thy hand, for when my bones have been consumed to ashes I shall return from Hades no more.   But let thy ashes be laid by mine, so that we may be together, as we were in our youth in the house of thy father."   And even as Achilles stretched forth his hands the ghost flew away as smoke flies on the wind.

On the morrow they made a great pyre of wood, and on it they laid the body of Patroclus, and with it they burned the bodies of four horses and two hounds and twelve Trojan youths whom Achilles had taken captive on the banks of Scamander.

And after a time Achilles bade his Myrmidons quench the flames with wine, so that the bones of Patroclus might be gathered up and placed in a golden urn against the day when the two friends should be reunited in death.

When all was done Achilles set about instituting funeral games in memory of his friend, and for the chariot-races he offered five prizes: the first, a woman-slave skilled in needlework, and with her a three-footed kettle of bronze; the second, a mare six years old; the third, a fair new kettle of bronze; the fourth, two talents of gold; and the fifth, a two-handled cup.   But in the races he himself would not take part, for he knew that the first prize would fall to him, since his horses were not of mortal breed, having been given to Peleus, his father, by the god Poseidon.

Five chieftains took part in the race—Menelaus, Eumelus, Meriones, Diomed, and Antilochus. Eumelus was the first to get ahead, but Diomed soon overtook him, and might indeed have proved victorious had not Apollo knocked the whip out of his hand. Athene gave him back his whip, and she also broke the yoke of Eumelus, so that it seemed as if victory must lie between Menelaus and Diomed. But at that moment Antilochus remembered the counsels which his father, Nestor, had given him before the race began, and urged his horses to make their utmost effort even as the chariots drew level with the turning-point, which was by an old tree-stump and two white stones, and by craft he was able to get ahead of Menelaus and win the second place, for the first place was won by Diomed.

A great dispute broke out among the Greeks, both those who had watched the race and those who had taken part in it. Achilles pitied Eumelus, who was a skilful charioteer, but who was constrained to return on foot, dragging his broken chariot and driving his horses before him. And Menelaus was wroth with Antilochus, whom he suspected of fraud. But the son of Nestor courteously offered to yield up the second prize to the elder man, and the heart of Menelaus softened towards him, and he said that he in his turn would yield up the mare to Antilochus, himself taking the kettle of bronze. The fourth prize was given to Meriones, but to Nestor Achilles gave the two-handled cup, because it was only old age which hindered him from taking part in the funeral games.

The best contests were wrestling and boxing, and both were hotly contested. The prize for boxing was divided between Ajax the Greater and Odysseus. These two contended also in the foot-race, and Ajax would have won had not Athene aided Odysseus, as was her wont.

In the single combat with spears Diomed overcame Ajax: and in the weight-throwing contest Polypœtes was the victor. Then there was the archery contest, in which a wood-dove was tethered to the top of a tall mast set upright in the sand. Teucer might have been victorious, but he omitted to pray to Apollo when drawing his bow, and the first prize went to Meriones, who vowed a hundred lambs to the god of the silver bow.

THE FUNERAL RITES OF HECTOR

Now Zeus had compassion upon Priam, who was lamenting over his son Hector, and the All-Highest sent Thetis to Achilles to tell him that it was the will of the gods that he should give up the body of Hector to his father in exchange for ransom. And Achilles bowed to the will of the gods.

Then Iris went, at the behest of Zeus, to the place within the walls of Troy where Priam sat weeping with his mantle over his face. And she spoke to him, saying, " Be comforted, Priam, son of Dardanus, for Zeus has sent me to thee. Go now to Achilles, bearing gifts to ransom the body of Hector, thy dear son. Fear nothing, and take no man with thee save an ancient herald, who will help thee to bring Hector home."

Priam rose up eagerly to obey, but Hecuba, his wife, would fain have held him back. Not heeding her fears, he loaded a wagon with fair raiment, cloaks and tunics and rugs, three-footed cauldrons, talents of gold, and a cup of great beauty which the Thracians had given him. He took leave of his nine remaining sons with bitter words, saying that he wished they had all died instead of Hector, and bidding them yoke the mules to the wagon, while he himself, with the herald, harnessed the horses to the chariot.

Before he set forth Hecuba brought a great cup of water that he might wash his hands, and he took it from her, and poured forth a libation to Zeus, praying the god to send him a good omen. And Zeus sent a mighty eagle, which flew high above the city, and they all were glad.

Then Priam and the herald, whose name was Idæus, set off towards the seashore where the ships of the Myrmidons were, and Zeus sent Hermes, in the likeness of a fair youth, to go with them and to make them invisible until they reached the tent of Achilles.

Feigning to be one of the Myrmidons, the messenger of the gods spoke comforting words to Priam, telling him that the body of Hector was still fair and seemly, and that the gods still loved the dead man who had been valiant and upright in his life. And Hermes leaped into the old King's chariot, and seized the reins, and the horses and the mules and the wagon received new strength and speed, and they came swiftly to the tent of Achilles, while the sentinels lay sleeping with the slumber that the god had made to fall upon them. Only at the last moment, when Priam stood before the tent of Achilles, did Hermes reveal himself, and declare for what purpose he had been sent by Zeus.

Priam entered the tent, and found Achilles sitting by a table, with two of his comrades attending on him, for he had but newly finished his repast. No man saw the aged King of Troy until he knelt down before Achilles, and then they all gazed at him with wonder. " Think of thy father," prayed the old man, clasping the hands of Achilles : " he is old, even as I am, but he has this comfort—that he awaits the return of his son. Alas for me, the greater number of my many sons are now dead, and to ransom the body of the best and most valiant of them all have I come as a suppliant to thy feet. Have pity on him and on me! "

At these words Achilles wept, thinking of his home and of Patroclus. Then he raised up Priam, and said, " Surely thou art an iron-hearted man thus to come to the man who slew thy son! Nevertheless, lamentation avails nothing. The gods will that men should suffer. Great gifts did they give to Peleus, my father ; but this evil also, that I am the sole son of his house, and must abide far from him, here beneath the walls of Troy. And as for thee, old sir, the gods gave thee lordship over all the land between Lesbos and Phrygia and the Hellespont ; but this evil also, that there is ever strife and slaying about thy city walls. As for thy son, weep no more. Weeping will not bring him back from the dead."

Achilles went from the tent, taking two of his comrades with him, and they unyoked the mules and the horses, and Idæus the herald handed over to them the gifts which Priam had brought for ransom. Two cloaks and a tunic Achilles left, wherewith they might enfold the body of Hector. And he gave orders that the body should be washed and anointed, and when this had been done he himself lifted it on to a litter. And his comrades lifted the litter on to the wagon. After that Achilles invited King Priam to eat with him in his tent, and he agreed that for eleven days there should be a truce, while the Trojans performed the rites of burial for Hector. When the old man grew weary the comrades of Achilles made a couch for him outside the tent, in a place where no chieftain of the Greeks would be likely to see him.

For if Agamemnon had known that Priam was in the tents of the Myrmidons it would have gone ill for the King of Troy.

Hermes came and stood by Priam while he slept, and bade him rise up for fear that word of his presence might come to Agamemnon. The old man trembled, and roused the herald, and the two, with the chariot and the wagon and the body of Hector, passed through the hosts of the Myrmidons, no man seeing or hearing their passing.

As they drew near the walls of Troy Priam's daughter Cassandra—she who had the gift of prophecy—called out to the people of Troy that they should go forth and meet Hector. And in the twinkling of an eye the streets were empty, and all the men and women, with pitiful lamentations, gathered round the wagon. They carried Hector to his own house and laid him on his bed, while the minstrels made sorrowful music, and the women wailed.

Andromache mourned for her husband, and Hecuba for her son, and it comforted them to see Hector lying fair and stainless, despite the cruel deeds of Achilles. Fair and tranquil he lay, as men lie whom Apollo has slain swiftly, and who have felt no pang. Last of all Helen made lamentation. "Would that I had died," she said, "ere ever I had come to Troy! Never hast thou, O Hector, spoken one bitter word to me. I have no friend left in all this city. Therefore well may I weep for thee."

Then Priam bade his people gather wood for the funeral pyre, not fearing the Greeks, since Achilles had promised a truce until the twelfth day.

For nine days they made ready the pyre, and on the tenth they laid the body of Hector upon it, and when the flesh was all consumed they poured wine upon the flames, and gathered up the bones and laid them in a golden coffer. Over this they spread robes of purple, and when they had piled great stones over all they heaped up a mighty mound of earth. And while these things were being done sentinels kept watch, lest the Greeks should arise and fall upon them.

So they buried Hector, the tamer of horses.

THE DOOM OF TROY: THE DEATH OF ACHILLES

It is at this point—the funeral rites of Hector, the tamer of horses—that Homer's *Iliad* ends. Perhaps some day by some amazing stroke of good fortune some one may discover an ancient papyrus or parchment with a continuation of the greatest of all epics, showing what befell after Hector's death; but in the present state of our knowledge we can only patch the story together from the works of poets living at a later date than Homer.

According to these poets Memnon, King of Ethiopia, a son of Tithonus, Priam's brother, and Aurora, the goddess of the dawn, came with ten thousand armed men to the aid of Troy. In the battle which followed he slew Antilochus, the son of Nestor, but was himself slain by Achilles.

Homer does not describe the event which he so often predicts and foreshadows—the death of Achilles; but in the *Odyssey* he mentions the burial of the ashes of Achilles and Patroclus in a golden urn beneath a high mound on the shores of the Hellespont. Other poets give varying accounts of the manner in which death came to the proud son of Thetis and Peleus, but the earliest and most generally accepted version says that he was slain by Apollo, disguised as Paris, during a desperate assault upon the Scæan gate.

Another version of the story tells how Achilles fell in love with Polyxena, one of the daughters of Priam, and, coming unarmed to the temple of Apollo to be married to the princess, was fatally wounded by the treacherous Paris, who smote him upon his vulnerable heel. (Homer does not refer to the legend of the heel of Achilles.) Odysseus and Ajax the Greater rescued the body of Achilles from the Trojans, and then themselves fought a fierce duel over his famous armour. Ajax, having been declared the loser, killed himself for rage, and incidentally provided Sophocles many years later with the subject for a fine tragedy. The fate of Ajax the Lesser was equally unhappy. Having incurred the wrath of Athene, he was drowned on the voyage homeward from Troy.

THE DEATH OF PARIS

Priam and Hecuba had a son called Helenus who was a sooth-sayer. Odysseus had the good fortune to capture this prince, and the Greeks forced him to reveal that the most fatal thing for Troy would be the bow and arrows of Herakles.

This famous bow, together with its deadly arrows, had been, as we know, bequeathed to Philoctetes by the dying hero, and were still in his possession. He had been left at Lemnos, suffering from a poisoned serpent-bite in one of his feet, but Odysseus now went in quest of him, and after Machaon, the son of Æsculapius, had cured his wound he took an active part in the siege and helped to conquer the city.

Among the victims of the famous bow was Paris himself, the foolish youth who had brought disaster on his city and all his people. In his agony—for he was not slain outright—he remembered that his first love, Œnone, was skilful in the healing art, and implored her to help him. Remembering his faithlessness, the nymph refused. But after his death she was sorry for her refusal, and, leaping upon his funeral pyre, allowed herself to be devoured by the flames, so that her ashes and his were mingled.

THE WOODEN HORSE

Another revelation made by Helenus was that Troy would never fall while the Palladium, the ancient image of Athene, was still within its walls. But when Diomed—some say helped by Odysseus—entered the city in disguise in order to steal it he carried away only a clever imitation, and still the Trojans would not yield to the Greeks. At last Athene put a stratagem into the mind of Epeius, one of Agamemnon's chieftains. At his suggestion the Greeks made as if to depart, burned their tents, hoisted their sails, and put to sea. But upon the deserted shore they left a great wooden horse, which excited the curiosity of the Trojans. Cassandra warned her countrymen not to touch the horse, even though Sinon, one of the Greeks, pretending to be a deserter from the attacking host, declared that it was an offering to Athene, and that if it were dragged within the walls of Troy the city would never be taken. Another warning was uttered by

P

Laocoön, the priest of Apollo, who with his two sons was thereupon strangled by two serpents sent from the sea by the resentful
Poseidon.

Believing the treacherous Sinon rather than the far-seeing Cassandra and the cautious Laocoön, the Trojans dragged the horse
into the city. And while they were feasting triumphantly the
Greek chieftains who had lain all that time concealed in the hollow
body of the beast crept out and unbarred the city gates. And so
the Greeks entered Troy, and put the inhabitants to the sword,
and " burned the topless towers of Ilium."

Among the most ruthless of the conquerors was Neoptolemus,
son of Achilles. The name of this youth had been Pyrrhus,
which means ' yellow-haired,' but when he came from his native
isle of Skyros to join the Greek host they called him Neoptolemus,
or ' new soldier.' When the Greeks stormed Troy Neoptolemus
broke down the gates of Priam's palace and, having slain the boy
Astyanax, Hector's son, brutally murdered Priam himself.
Another story relates that it was Odysseus who, fearing lest
Hector's son should be as valiant a man as his father, flung him
down from the walls of Troy. This is the version immortalized
by Euripides in his tragedy *The Trojan Women*, though there it is
a herald and not Odysseus himself who kills Astyanax.

Troy was reduced to ashes, and the womenkind of its dead
defenders were portioned out as slaves among the victors.

Andromache was handed over to Neoptolemus, though some
years later she became the wife of Helenus the seer; Hecuba fell
to the lot of Odysseus, but according to one legend she was
changed into a phantom hound and haunted the ruins of Troy;
Cassandra was given to Agamemnon, whom in vain she warned of
the fate awaiting him at the hands of Clytemnestra and her lover
Ægisthus; and Polyxena was sacrificed on the grave of Achilles.

Menelaus was driven ashore on the coast of Egypt. The subsequent adventures of Odysseus and Æneas, and the tragic end of
Agamemnon, will be related in further chapters of the present
book.

As for Helen, the unconscious but fatal cause of so much death
and disaster, she went back to her husband, Menelaus. We shall
meet her in the *Odyssey*, sitting in the palace of that much-
forgiving King.

THE TALE OF TROY IN LITERATURE

The great Homeric epic has been like a vast quarry from which later and lesser poets have carted away many loads of stone. Greeks and Romans, Italians, and Frenchmen, and Englishmen have all turned to the tale of Troy, borrowing, imitating, continuing, distorting, but always keeping their mind's eye fixed upon the windy plain watered by the Scamander, where once stood the " topless towers of Ilium."

Long before the Renaissance opened up the wonders of the original Greek epics and tragedies Latin versions, quaintly translated into French and Italian, had familiarized the medieval world with the men and women whose names, personalities, and misfortunes form the rich fabric of classical literature.

In the Elizabethan period Greeks and Trojans strutted and mouthed upon the London stage, and were as well known to the occupants of the cheapest places, the ' groundlings,' as they were to the gallants sitting in the privileged seats upon the stage itself. Shakespeare, who, like Chaucer, took the pseudo-classical story of Troilus and Cressida as a subject, also alluded both seriously and humorously to various people and incidents in the tale of Troy.   In *Hamlet* the Prince of Denmark quotes from an imaginary play about Æneas, in which the hero gives to Dido, Queen of Carthage, a most lurid account of the murder of Priam by Pyrrhus (Neoptolemus).

> The rugged Pyrrhus, he whose sable arms,
> Black as his purpose, did the night resemble
> When he lay couched in the ominous horse.
>
> .   .   .   .   .
>
> With eyes like carbuncles, the hellish Pyrrhus
> Old grandsire Priam seeks.
>
> .   .   .   .   .
>
>   Anon he finds him
> Striking too short at Greeks; his antique sword,
> Rebellious to his arm, lies where it falls,
> Repugnant to command: unequal match'd,
> Pyrrhus at Priam drives; in rage strikes wide;
> But with the whiff and wind of his fell sword
> The unnerved father falls.

And so on—up to the " instant burst of clamour " raised by Hecuba when " she saw Pyrrhus make malicious sport " hacking poor Priam to pieces.

It is a moot point whether Shakespeare meant us to take this—as Hamlet certainly appears to take it—quite seriously. The style is so ridiculously high-falutin' and over-coloured that it is rather difficult to believe that the clever young Prince of Denmark honestly admired it. Was he pulling the leg of Polonius? One only hopes that he was.

Shakespeare seems to have been unable to catch any of the authentic flame from the Homeric altar. His handling of the Trojan theme in *Troilus and Cressida* is strangely inadequate. Perhaps if he had been able to read the original Greek, instead of depending on Latin translations or adaptations, he would have done better things.

CHAPTER XXVI

THE ADVENTURES OF ODYSSEUS

NONE of the Greek chiefs who took part in the siege of Troy seems to have had a very safe and swift journey home, but the most perilous and long-drawn-out voyage of all was that of Odysseus (whom the Romans called Ulysses), King of Ithaca. Homer's tale of his adventures, the *Odyssey*, begins ten years after the city of the Trojans crashed in smoke and flame. Poseidon, the sea-god, hated the wily King, but while he was absent being feasted by the pious Ethiopians the gods upon Olympus met in council to consider what should be done to deliver Odysseus from the snares of the nymph Calypso, who had held him captive for seven years on her island of Ogygia.

After some discussion it was agreed that Hermes should go to Calypso's island and tell her that it was the will of the gods that Odysseus should return to his home, while Athene went to Ithaca, where Penelope was keeping at bay—not without some difficulty —the numerous suitors who wished to persuade her that her long-absent husband must be dead, and each of whom was eager to take his place. Penelope's plan was to promise them that when she had finished weaving a burial-robe for her father-in-law, Laertes, she would choose a second husband; but every night she un-ravelled all the web she had woven on her loom during the day. This had continued for four years, but now one of the suitors had discovered the ruse, and all were very angry.

Athene, disguised as Mentes, King of the Taphians, reached Ithaca and was courteously received by young Telemachus, who confided to the inquisitive but sympathetic stranger his sorrow for the mysterious disappearance of his father, Odysseus, and his resentment at the continual presence of the hungry and stubborn suitors of Penelope in the halls of the palace. The false Mentes counselled the youth to call all the suitors together and bid them return for a time each to his own house, while Penelope sojourned with her father, Icarius of Sparta.

" When these things are done," said the stranger, " fit out a ship with twenty oars, and go in quest of your father. First to Pylos, and then to Sparta, to the dwelling-place of Menelaus. If news of thy father's death reach thee come home, raise a mound in his memory, and let thy mother take unto her another husband. And then contrive some means to slay these suitors, who have battened upon thy father's house too long."

Telemachus would fain have offered a rich token of friendship to the stranger, but the goddess departed, flying " like a sea-eagle," and the prince realized that he had been honoured by a visit from an immortal. (Men were always on the alert for such visits in those days.)

THE QUEST OF TELEMACHUS

After a night spent in musing upon the counsels of Mentes (as we must call Athene while she is bearing the name and the out-ward form of the aged King of the Taphians) Telemachus called an assembly of all the people, including the suitors, and Alitherses the soothsayer stood up in their midst and declared that great evil was coming to the suitors, and that Odysseus should yet return.

Mentor, a wise old man whom Odysseus had placed in charge of his household, rebuked the suitors for their obstinacy and the people for their disloyalty to the memory of their King, and finally it was decided that Telemachus should be given all things needful for his voyage, though few thought that the undertaking would have any fortunate outcome.

The aged nurse, Eurycleia, who had held Odysseus as a baby in her arms, helped the young man to store his ship with twelve jars of wine, " not of the best," and twenty measures of barley-meal, and promised, weeping, that for twelve days she would keep the secret of his departure from the Queen.

Then Telemachus went down to the ship, led by Athene, whom we must now call Mentor, for she had assumed the name and form of the faithful steward. And when the wine and the meal had been carried aboard by stealth, and libations had been poured forth to the gods, more especially to Zeus, they raised the pine-tree mast, and hauled up the sails with ropes of oxhide, and the wind filled the sails, and the water foamed about the keel. And Athene, in the likeness of Mentor, went with them.

TELEMACHUS AT PYLOS

As the sun rose the ship reached the shores of Pylos, the dwelling-place of Nestor, the wisest of the Greeks.   There the travellers were hospitably received, and Peisistratus, Nestor's son, gave them wine in a cup of gold.   And after they had poured forth a libation to Poseidon Telemachus revealed himself, and declared what was his purpose in coming thither.

Nestor, in whose mind the name of Odysseus had waked many echoes of the long struggle for Troy, then related the various misfortunes which had befallen the Greek chieftains after the city of Priam was sacked and burned.   Most grievous of all was the fate of Agamemnon, slain by Ægisthus, his wife's lover, with the aid of the cruel Queen, who had never forgiven her husband for sacrificing their first-born child, Iphigenia, upon the seashore at Aulis.   Menelaus, driven with five ships as far as Egypt, dwelt for seven years in that land, while Ægisthus ruled at Mycenæ. But in the eighth year Orestes, the son of Agamemnon, came from Athens to avenge his father's death.   Diomed and his people, and the Myrmidons, reached their homelands at last, as did also Philoctetes and Idomeneus.

In conclusion Nestor counselled Telemachus to go to Sparta and ask Menelaus if he had had any tidings of the fate of Odysseus. And the next day, after a heifer with gilded horns had been sacrificed to the gods, and Telemachus had been bathed, and anointed with oil, and robed in a rich mantle, the young prince set off for Lacedæmon in a chariot driven by Peisistratus.   But Mentor did not go with them, for the goddess, in the likeness of a sea-eagle, had taken wing for Cauconia, purposing to rejoin the seafarers on a later date.

> Departed the grey-eyed goddess Athene,
> Likened in form to an osprey; and all were filled with amazement.
>
> HOMER (*Cotterill's tr.*)

TELEMACHUS IN SPARTA

When Telemachus and Peisistratus reached the palace of Menelaus they found a scene of feasting and mirth, for Neoptolemus was being married to Hermione, the daughter of Menelaus and

Helen. The two strangers were welcomed with much honour, but until they had been bathed and banqueted they were not asked either their names or the reason of their coming.

After the banquet Menelaus overheard one of his guests saying to the other that the hall of the palace was as goodly with gold and amber and ivory as the hall of the Olympian Zeus himself.

Then Menelaus said, " No hall of mortal man can be compared with the halls of the gods. Yet I have wandered far in my time, and gathered much gear. Alas, while I was absent my brother was cruelly slain. Would that I had only a third part of all that is mine, if but the men who fell before the walls of Troy were alive at this hour! And most of all do I lament Odysseus, though no man knows if he be dead or living."

When he heard these words Telemachus held up his purple cloak to hide the tears which sprang to his eyes at the sound of his father's name, and in that moment Menelaus recognized him, though as yet saying nothing. When the fair Helen came in after the banquet, holding a distaff of gold and followed by three maidens, one of whom carried a pannier of purple wool, she saw the strangers, and said to her husband, " Who are these? One of them is marvellously like Odysseus. It must be Telemachus, his son, whom he left in Ithaca as an infant when for my sake he went to fight against Troy."

And Menelaus answered, " Madam, it must truly be he. For he has the hands and feet of his father, and the colour of his eyes and hair. And just now he wept behind his mantle when I spoke his father's name."

Then Peisistratus said, " True, O King Menelaus. This is the son of Odysseus, who comes to see if thou canst perchance help him to find his father."

And after they had exchanged courteous greetings, and tears had been shed over the calamities that the gods had inflicted upon so many of those who fought beneath the walls of Troy, Helen put a drowsy herb called nepenthe in their wine, which made men forget their sorrows. And they slept.

MENELAUS AND THE OLD MAN OF THE SEA

On the morrow Telemachus revealed to the King of Sparta the purpose of his coming, and Menelaus then related the following story:

"There is an island called Pharos, one day's journey distant from the land of Egypt, and there I was held becalmed for twenty days when I was on my way homeward from that land.

"All our corn was eaten, and my crew, smitten with hunger, tried to hook little fishes out of the sea, while I wandered sadly alone. In my hour of need Eidothea, daughter of Proteus, the Old Man of the Sea, took pity on me, and told me that if I could catch and hold her father when he came from the sea-depths to count his flock of seals he would tell me what god I had offended, and how I might make atonement and get me a fair wind for home.

"Furthermore she counselled me to take three of my most faithful comrades, and wrap myself and them in four seals' hides which she gave us, and lie down among the seals; and she warned us that when we had laid our hands upon Proteus he would change his shape many times, and only if we held him fast would he answer my questions. She also gave us ambrosia to put under our nostrils, that we should not be sickened by the reek of the raw hide.

"At noon all the seals ranged themselves upon the shore, and we with them, and when the Old Man of the Sea had counted them, and we with them, he lay down to sleep. Then we rushed upon him and held him fast, nor would we loosen our hold, even though he took the shape first of a lion, then of a snake, then of a leopard, then of a wild boar, then of running water. Lastly he turned himself into a flowering tree. And finding that we still held him fast, he spoke, asking what I would have of him.

"To my questions he answered that it was Zeus whom I had affronted, and that I must go back to the land of Egypt, offer sacrifice to him, and set sail again for Sparta, if I would fain have favouring winds. Then he told me the hard fate of Agamemnon, my brother, slain in his own palace most falsely by his wife's lover, Ægisthus; and lastly he told me that Odysseus was with the nymph Calypso on her island.

Him I beheld on an island, and plentiful tears he was shedding,
Held in Calypso's halls; for the sea-nymph still with compulsion
Keepeth him there all hopeless of reaching the land of his fathers,
Since no ship well-fitted with oars he possesseth or shipmates,
Such as to help him to traverse the wide expanses of ocean.

HOMER (*Cotterill's tr.*)

" Next day," said Menelaus, " I returned to the river of Egypt,
the stream that flows from heaven, and made due sacrifice to the
gods.   Then I raised a great mound to the memory of Agamemnon, my brother.   And, the gods giving me fair winds, I returned
to my own country."

Menelaus would fain have kept Telemachus with him for many
days, but the young man was eager to be gone, and, declining a
proffered gift of chariot-horses on the plea that in Ithaca there
was pasture only for goats, he made ready to depart.

Meanwhile Athene had taken on the shape of Penelope's sister,
Iphthime, the wife of Eumelus, and had visited in a dream the
Queen of Ithaca, who was lamenting the departure of Telemachus.

" Fear not for thy son, Penelope," said the dream sister, " for
he has a mighty guardian, none other than Athene, by whom I am
sent to comfort thee."

But when Penelope prayed for tidings of her husband,
Odysseus, she was vouchsafed no answer.

HERMES IN OGYGIA

The high gods sat in council upon Olympus, only Poseidon
being absent, and Zeus decreed that Hermes should go to the isle
of Ogygia and tell the nymph Calypso that Odysseus must return
to his own country and his own people.

It was a fair island, and when Hermes, wearing his golden
sandals and carrying his magic wand, alighted there he found the
nymph sitting in a cave spinning, and singing with a sweet voice.
Round the cave was a grove of poplars and cypresses; grape-vines
clustered about the entrance, and through meadows sweet with
violets flowed the waters of four silver fountains.

When Hermes had told Calypso the will of Zeus concerning
Odysseus she was grieved, for she had saved the wanderer's life
when the Most-High had smitten his ship with a thunderbolt on

the voyage homeward from Troy, and she asked nothing better than to keep him always with her, but she knew that she must obey.

So she went to where Odysseus sat weeping and gazing over the sea, and told him to take his axe and cut down trees, and from them to hew beams to make a raft, that he might win back to Ithaca; and when he feared some evil stratagem she swore by the Styx that she meant him no ill.

Then they supped together, and the next day Calypso gave him an axe and an adze, and showed him where the trees were growing that best suited his purpose. He felled twenty, and lopped them, and the nymph brought him also a gimlet, that he might make holes in the wood. And when he had clamped the beams together with wooden pegs he fashioned a mast and a yard-arm and a rudder, and round about he put a fence of wicker to keep out the waves.

Next day he pushed the raft out over the water, laden with wine and water and goodly garments, and with words of good counsel from Calypso in his ears he hoisted sail, and departed from Ogygia. And all night he slept not, but watched the stars.

For seventeen days he sailed, and sighted no land; and then on the horizon he saw the island where dwelt the folk called Phæacians, whose King was called Alcinous.

THE WRATH OF POSEIDON

And it befell that Poseidon, returning from the land of the pious Ethiopians, saw the raft with Odysseus at the helm moving across the waters. And in his wrath he stirred the sea with his trident, and summoned all the winds that blow, and caused a great storm to break upon the face of the deep.

The raft was tossed hither and thither, and once Odysseus was swept into the sea, but he succeeded in climbing aboard again, though the rudder was broken, and he was at the mercy of the waves. Then the sea-goddess Ino had pity on him, and rose from the depths of the ocean, and gave him a scarf to wrap under his breast, so that, discarding the rich raiment which had almost dragged him to death, he might swim to the land of the Phæacians.

And she warned him that when he reached land he must throw the scarf into the sea, at the same time keeping his eyes turned the other way.

And Odysseus swam for two days and nights, while Athene chained up all the winds except the north wind, which was bearing him towards the island. But even when he drew near the wrath of Poseidon was upon him, for there were only jagged rocks and steep cliffs rising sheer out of the sea.

Then he prayed to the river-god whose current he could feel thrusting outward from a gap in the cliffs, and the river made the current more gentle, so that Odysseus was able to struggle to land. Before he lay down to sleep he flung the scarf of Ino into the sea, and she rose and caught it in her hands. Then beneath a thicket of wild olive the King of Ithaca, sorely wearied and stained with sun and salt water, laid him down to sleep.

> Up to a coppice he went, and found trees nigh to the water
> Standing apart in the open, and 'neath two bushes he hid him.
> HOMER (*Cotterill's tr.*)

ODYSSEUS AND NAUSICAA

Meanwhile Athene had visited Nausicaa, the daughter of the Phæacian King, in a dream, bidding her rise early next morning and go a-washing in the river.

Alcinous and his wife, Queen Arete, were already astir when their young daughter came to them to ask if she might fill a wagon with raiment, and robes, and coverlets, and go with her maidens to the mouth of the river, taking food and wine with them, and a jar of oil to anoint their limbs after bathing.

Consent was readily given, and when the gay band had washed all the clothes, spread them out to dry, bathed themselves, and been refreshed with what we should call a ' picnic lunch,' they began to play a ball game, singing as they did so. Perhaps by pure mischance, or maybe at the will of Athene, the ball went wide and fell into the water. The cry of dismay uttered by Nausicaa aroused Odysseus, whose olive-tree thicket was close to the mouth of the river, but still louder were the cries of all the maidens when, haggard and travel-stained, the seafaring King of Ithaca emerged and came towards them. But he spoke fair and courteous words, which reassured the princess, and she told her companions to give the stranger food, raiment, and oil.

Athene now gave to the newly fed, washed, and anointed Odysseus such an air of splendour and majesty that Nausicaa remarked to her companions that he was like unto one of the immortal gods, adding, " Would that such a man might be my husband, and dwell here always! "

To Odysseus she said that she could not take him back to the palace with her, lest he should be seen on the way, and some one of the baser sort might say, " Who is this man with Nausicaa? Perhaps he is her chosen husband. For she looks with scorn upon the men of Phæacia."

So when the wagon came near to the gates of the city Nausicaa whipped up her mules and went on ahead, and Odysseus tarried in a small grove of poplars sacred to Athene, where he made his prayer to the grey-eyed goddess that she would protect him from the wrath of Poseidon, and grant him a safe return to Ithaca.

The goddess heard, but dared not as yet appear to him, for fear of the wrath of the sea-god. The reason for that wrath will soon be made plain.

ODYSSEUS IN THE HOUSE OF ALCINOUS

When Odysseus reached the palace of Alcinous he marvelled at its beauty, for the walls were of bronze, and the golden doors swung upon hinges of silver. Fifty women were in that house, grinding corn and weaving purple cloth; and round about was a garden, with an orchard full of delicious fruit.

Odysseus entered the great hall, where the chiefs of the Phæacians were feasting together, and knelt down, as Nausicaa had bidden him, before the Queen, Arete, whom he begged to show him grace and favour, and to send him home safely to his native land. But where that land was he said not as yet.

When he had made this supplication, which the Queen received in silence, he went and sat down by the hearth. But the oldest among the chieftains said that it was not fitting that he should remain there, and Alcinous bade him come and sit in a place of honour, and they gave him meat and drink, and an attendant poured water on his hands.

Then Alcinous spake fair words, promising to speed the stranger upon his homeward way.   Presently, when all the chieftains had withdrawn, and Odysseus found himself alone with the King and Queen, he told them how he had escaped in a raft from the island of Calypso, and of his sufferings before he was cast ashore in their country.   He told them also how Nausicaa had found him on the shore, and they blamed her that she had not brought the stranger to the palace herself.   But Odysseus, who did not wish the maiden to be rebuked, said that it was his own desire that he should come later, and alone.

Then Alcinous said, " Gladly would I have such a man as thou for my daughter's husband, but no man would I detain here against the wish of his own heart.   My ships are the best that sail the sea, and my rowers the most skilful of all that ply the oar. To-morrow thou shalt set forth for thy home, wherever it may be."   All this time no man had known the name of their stranger-guest, not even Nausicaa, of whom he took leave with fair and gentle words, promising to remember her always and honour her as a goddess.   But after the banquet Demodocus the minstrel, inspired by Apollo, sang of the Wooden Horse and of the doom of Troy, and the heart of Odysseus was softened, and his eyes filled with tears; and Alcinous, marking these things, said, " Tell us why thou dost weep?   Hadst thou a kinsman or a friend who died among the warriors who perished before Troy? "

ODYSSEUS TELLS HIS OWN STORY: THE LOTUS-EATERS

Then the stranger revealed himself, saying, " I am Odysseus, the son of Laertes.   My dwelling is in the rocky island of Ithaca, far to the west, towards sunset.   Great troubles did the gods inflict upon me on my way homeward from Troy."

And he told them his story, and what he and his comrades had done after Troy had fallen.

First he told how they had sacked a city called Ismarus, and how many of their number had perished through lingering to make merry, so that reinforcements came up to help the citizens. When they put to sea again, as many as had escaped death,

Zeus sent a great storm to delay them, but at last, after nine days, they reached the land of the Lotus-eaters. The lotus is a wondrous fruit, for whoso eats thereof forgets at once home and country and all loved things, and asks only to remain dreaming among the waterfalls and the blossoming trees for ever.

Some of the seafarers who went ashore returned bearing branches laden with the deadly fruit, and some of them actually tasted of it, and were very reluctant to sail forth again. Tennyson, in his poem *The Lotus Eaters*, thus describes their home:

> A land of streams! some, like a downward smoke,
> Slow-dropping veils of thinnest lawn, did go;
> And some thro' wavering lights and shadows broke,
> Rolling a slumbrous sheet of foam below.
> They saw the gleaming river seaward flow
> From the inner land: far off, three mountain-tops,
> Three silent pinnacles of agèd snow,
> Stood sunset-flush'd: and, dew'd with showery drops,
> Up-clomb the shadowy pine above the woven copse.

THE CYCLOPS

The wind sank down, and Odysseus and his men took to their oars, and presently they came to the country of the Cyclopes, the one-eyed giants. But they thought it more prudent to cast anchor off a pleasant island near by, where the nymphs of the place were friendly towards them.

Next day Odysseus took with him twelve of his bravest men, and, carrying a goatskin full of a specially choice wine and a wallet full of corn, they made their way to the mainland and entered a vast cave, where they found pens full of sheep and goats, and baskets full of cheeses, and many pails of milk. But the Cyclops Polyphemus, the owner of all this, was absent.

In the evening he returned, and the light of the fire which he kindled in the cave revealed the presence of strangers.

" Who are ye? " he roared, in a voice of thunder. " Are ye merchants? Or are ye pirates? "

Trembling, Odysseus replied that they were Greeks on their way home from Troy, and reminded the giant that Zeus favoured those who dealt mercifully with strangers. This reminder merely angered Polyphemus, who seized two of the intruders, dashed their heads on the earth, tore them limb from limb, and proceeded to make his supper off them, washed down with deep draughts of milk. After which he went to sleep.

Next day he breakfasted on two more of Odysseus's men, and then went out, having first rolled a large rock against the mouth of the cave. During his absence the crafty wits of the King of Ithaca got to work. Leaning against the wall was the trunk of a large olive-tree which the giant was drying in order to make a staff for himself. Odysseus cut off a long piece of this tree, and he and his men hacked one end until it had a sharp point, and they dried it in the fire before putting it in a dark corner of the cave.

At dusk Polyphemus returned, killed and ate two more men, and squatted down by the fire. Then Odysseus came forward with the wineskin in his hand and invited the giant to drink. The wine was sweet and darkly red, a gift from the priest of Apollo at Ismarus as a thanksgiving because Odysseus had spared the temple when he destroyed the city, and when the Cyclops had quaffed a bowl full of it he called for more.

" Such wine," he cried, " must the gods drink in heaven! Our grapes yield none such."

After a second draught he became very sleepy, but before he went to sleep Odysseus told him that his name was No Man, and asked what gift he would give him in exchange for the wine.

" I will eat all the others before I eat thee," growled the giant, and straightway lapsed into slumber.

This was the moment for which Odysseus had been waiting. He and his comrades took the stake of olive-wood and thrust it into the fire, and presently it burst into flame. Then they took it up and drove it straight through the single eye in the centre of the giant's forehead.

The monster leaped up, roaring with anguish, blind and helpless. And his brethren, who lived in the caves round about the mountain, heard him shouting, and called out to know if anyone was hurting him.

" No Man," he answered, in a terrible voice. " No Man is hurting me! "

" If," they said, " no man is hurting thee we can do nothing. Pray to our father Zeus." And they composed themselves again to slumber.

Circe

Sir E. Burne-Jones

By permission of Mr Frederick Hollyer

Odysseus and the Sirens
Herbert J. Draper
By permission of the Corporation of Hull

Groping with his great hands, Polyphemus rolled away the stone by the door of the cave, thinking to catch his enemies one by one as they came forth. But Odysseus thought of a cunning device to trick him. Among the flocks in the cave were some rams, very large, with fleeces thick and long. Under the bellies of these rams he bound his six surviving comrades with osier-twigs from the giant's faggot heap. As he could not do the same for himself, he chose the longest beast, and, clinging fast to its wool with both hands, was able to get out of the cave unperceived when the sheep went forth to pasture in the morning.

Glad were they who had stayed near the ships when they saw Odysseus and his six companions, driving seven rams before them; but they would fain have lamented those who had not returned, only they feared lest by their weeping the giant should discover where they were.

When they put to sea Odysseus stood up in the ship and shouted to the Cyclops that he was justly punished for his cruelty; and in his fury the giant broke the top off one of the hills and flung it towards the place where he had heard the voice. It fell so near the ship that the backwash of the wave it made carried it again towards the shore. The rowers pushed off in haste, and Odysseus made signs to them to row with all their might, but before they were very far on their way he called aloud to the giant, telling him that he was Odysseus, the son of Laertes, of Ithaca.

Then Polyphemus cried that the oracle was fulfilled which foretold that he should be blinded by that man; and he prayed to his father Poseidon that Odysseus should never reach his home, or, if he should, that he might come thither alone, and find sore trouble waiting for him.

Presently they came to the island of wild goats where they had left the rest of their company, and they shared among them the sheep they had taken from the Cyclops, the great ram being adjudged to Odysseus as his portion.

ÆOLUS: THE LÆSTRYGONES

Next morning they sailed until they came to the floating, bronze-walled island of Æolus, where the king of the winds feasted them kindly. And when Odysseus asked his help he gave

Q

him, bound in an oxskin, all the winds that would blow him off his homeward course, and this leathern bag he fastened to the deck of the ship with a thong of silver.   Moreover, he caused a mild west wind to blow, and it bore the ship towards Ithaca, so near that those on board could see the men who tended the beacons on the hill-tops.

But, being very weary, Odysseus fell asleep; and his comrades, thinking that the leathern bag contained rich spoils from Troy, loosed it from the silver thong.   And the winds rushed out with a great tumult, and drove them back to the island of Æolus, their master.   But this time, perceiving that Odysseus was hated of the high gods, the king of the winds would not help him.

Next, after rowing till their backs and their arms were weary, they reached Lamus, the stronghold of the giants called Læstry-gones, in whose land the night is as the day.   These creatures fed on human flesh, and before the seafarers could get away they had speared several of them as if they had been fishes and devoured them.   This was the fate of all the men upon all the ships save that of Odysseus, who cut the hawser with his sword just in time and cried to his men to row hard—which they were not loth to do.

CIRCE'S ISLAND

Next Odysseus and his small surviving band came to the fair island of Æææ, where dwelt the enchantress called Circe.   The wise chieftain went ashore and climbed to a hill-top, whence he could see the smoke rising from her palace.   Just as he was con-sidering whether he should go alone to that dwelling or return to the ship and plan a search-party a huge stag, going to the river to drink, crossed his path.   Odysseus flung his spear and pierced the beast through the heart.   Then he bound the feet with green withes, slung the carcass across his shoulders, and hastened down to the ship, where his anxious comrades welcomed him with joy. All that day they feasted upon venison and sweet wine, and at night they slept on the shore.

On the morrow they drew lots as to who should lead half the company—twenty-two men—upon an expedition into the heart of the island, and the lot fell to Eurylochus.   When he and his companions reached the open space in the wood where stood Circe's palace wolves and lions ran forward and fawned upon them as a dog fawns upon the master who is about to give it a bone. And as they paused in terror they heard the voice of Circe, singing at her loom.

One of the strangers, called Polites, charmed by the beauty of the voice, said that it were well they should make their presence known. And they cried out, and Circe came forth and beckoned them within. Only Eurylochus did not enter, for he feared some snare. For a long time he waited, but of all his comrades not one came forth again. They had all been changed into swine by a touch of Circe's magic wand and a draught from her magic cup.

> Who knows not Circe,
> The daughter of the Sun, whose charmèd cup
> Whoever tasted lost his upright shape,
> And downward fell into a grov'ling swine?
>
> MILTON

Eurylochus fled back to the seashore, and when he had told his story Odysseus girt on his silver-studded sword, and took his bow, and, disregarding the prayers of his companions, set forth himself to find the lady of the island.

As he passed through the thick wood that girdled her palace Hermes came to him in the guise of a fair youth and said, " Is it to rescue thy comrades that thou art come? Circe has changed them into swine. But take this herb—it is called moly, and the root is black, but the flowers are milk-white—and she will not be able to harm thee. When she has set food and wine before thee, and has smitten thee with her wand, rush at her with thy sword drawn and make her swear by the oath that binds even the gods that she will not hurt thee."

Thereupon the messenger of the gods winged back to Olympus, and Odysseus, with a heavy heart, drew near the palace of Circe.

The enchantress came forth to meet him.

> How shall I name him?
> This spare, dark-featur'd,
> Quick-eyed stranger?
> Ah! and I see too
> His sailor's bonnet,
> His short coat, travel-tarnish'd,
>   With one arm bare.
>
> MATTHEW ARNOLD

Graciously she welcomed him, set him in a carven chair, and offered him wine in a cup of gold.   When he had drunk she smote him with her wand, saying, " Go to thy sty, and wallow with thy fellows there! "   But the herb of Hermes broke the spell, and Odysseus flung himself upon her with his sword upraised as if to slay her.

Falling upon her knees, Circe cried aloud, " Who art thou who canst drink of that cup and take no hurt?   Surely thou art Odysseus, homeward bound from Troy, of whose coming to this island Hermes warned me.   Let us be friends."

But Odysseus was wary, and he made her swear the oath by which even the gods were bound that she would do him no harm, before he would sit and eat with her.

When she had sworn that oath her maidens prepared a bath, and mixed wine for him, and set wheaten bread upon the table. But Odysseus sat silent, thinking of his companions.

" Why dost thou sit silent, Odysseus? " asked Circe.   " Dost thou fear me, despite mine oath? "

And when he had told her what was in his mind she rose and led him to the sties where she kept her swine.   She unbarred the doors, and the swine ran out, grunting as is their wont, and she touched each one with her wand, and rubbed him with a magic herb.   Then the snouts and tusks fell from their faces, and the bristles from their bodies, and they were men again, only fairer than before.   When they saw Odysseus they wept for joy, and Circe herself was stirred by pity.

For a whole year the King of Ithaca and his companions dwelt upon the island of Æ--a, but when the year was spent their heart turned towards home.   Then Circe told Odysseus that he would never win back to his own country till he had descended to the realms of the dead and had spoken with Tiresias the seer.   And she told him how to reach that place, and what offerings to make, and how to dig a trench and sacrifice a black ram and a black ewe near the confluence of the rivers Phlegethon and Cocytus. " Then," she said, " many ghosts will come to taste the blood of the sacrifice, but do not let them taste of it till thou hast had speech with Tiresias, who will tell thee how to return to thy home."

THE DWELLINGS OF THE DEAD

Next day the ship sailed with the two black-fleeced sheep on board, and a favouring wind, sent by Circe, to speed the travellers on their way.   And at nightfall they came to the gloomy land of the Cimmerians, upon the frontiers of the domain of the dead. And everything befell as the enchantress had foretold.

When the blood of the ram and the ewe ran down into the trench which Odysseus had made the ghosts of the dead gathered round.   Among them was Elpenor, the last of the companions of Odysseus to die, and he begged that upon his grave might be set up the oar which he had been wont to ply among his comrades on the ship.   And the mother of Odysseus came, who had died while he was fighting before Troy, but though he wept to see her he would not let her come near until he had spoken with Tiresias.

At last came the ancient seer, and Odysseus sheathed the sword with which he had been guarding the trench, and when the ghost had drunk of the blood the doom was spoken.

" Great peril and toil shall be thine, Odysseus, ere thou comest to thy home.   But if, when ye come to the island of the three promontories, where graze the oxen and the sheep of the Sun, thou and thy men harm them not, ye shall not perish.   If thou alone shouldst escape, the ship of a strange people shall bear thee home, and thou shalt find trouble there.   But, having avenged thyself upon thine enemies, thou shalt travel to a far land where men know not the sea, eat no salt with their meat, and have never seen a ship.   There shalt thou make a threefold sacrifice to Poseidon.   Afterwards shalt thou return to thy home, and offer a sacrifice of a hundred beasts to all the gods.   And thou shalt die an old man, in peace, with thy own people about thee."

Odysseus answered, " So be it, Tiresias."

And then others of the spirits came and drank of the blood, and were able therefore to speak to the wayfarer who had come from the land of the living to the realm of the dead.

The mother of Odysseus told him how things were in Ithaca when she had died of grief for his absence; and after that there passed before him a great many of the souls of famous women of old years, Alcmene and Leda, and Eriphyle among them.   Then came the soul of Agamemnon, and spoke bitter words of his death at the hands of Ægisthus when he returned to his own palace at Mycenæ. And after him came the pale shadows of Patroclus and Achilles, and Ajax and Antilochus.

Achilles prayed for news of his aged father, Peleus, and of his son, Neoptolemus. And Odysseus said to him, " Evil is my doom, wandering far from my native land. But well is it with thee, O Achilles, who in life wast honoured like a god, and in death art king among the dead."

" Nay," Achilles made answer. " Speak no such words of comfort to me. Rather would I be a hireling in the house of some poor man, and dwell among the living upon the earth, than reign over the whole realm of the dead."

And when Odysseus had told him of the valiant deeds of Neoptolemus, his son, " the soul of Achilles departed with great strides through the meadow of asphodel."

Other famous shades did Odysseus behold—Orion, the great hunter; Tantalus, chin-deep in his pool; Sisyphus, heaving at his heavy stone; and lastly the shade of Herakles, but the shade only, for the hero himself sat among the Olympians with his wife, Hebe, the daughter of Zeus.

As thousands of the dead thronged round him, uttering mournful cries, Odysseus was smitten with terror lest Persephone should keep him in her dark domain. So he made what haste he could to the upper world, and climbed aboard his ship, and the great stream of ocean carried them back to the island of Circe.

At sunset they beached upon the isle of Ææa, and slept near the ship that night. The next day Circe feasted them royally, and spoke words of good counsel concerning what should befall them upon their journey homeward to Ithaca.

THE SIRENS : SCYLLA : THE OXEN OF THE SUN

Three warnings did Circe utter: concerning the Sirens, the six-necked sea-monster Scylla, and, as Tiresias had also said, the oxen of the Sun. Then she took her leave of the stranger-king who had been her guest for a year, and the ship, borne by a friendly wind, moved over the dark waters.

Presently the wind dropped, and they saw an island on the horizon. Then Odysseus, following the behest of Circe, took a large piece of wax and melted it in the sun, and with it sealed up the ears of his men, so that they should not hear the fatal song of the Sirens and perish upon the rocks. And he ordered his men to bind him to the mast by his wrists and ankles, so that he should not leap madly into the water at the sound of that magic melody:

> Steer, hither steer your wingèd pines,
>   All beaten mariners!
> Here lie Love's undiscovered mines,
>   A prey to passengers—
> Perfumes far sweeter than the best
> Which make the Phœnix' urn and nest.
>   Fear not your ships,
> Nor any to oppose you save our lips;
>   But come on shore
> Where no joy dies till it hath gotten more.
>   WILLIAM BROWNE OF TAVISTOCK

The Sirens, seeing a ship near their island, lifted up their voices in a song so incredibly sweet that even the stern Odysseus was bewitched and cried aloud to his companions to unbind him, so that he might follow the singers. But with their ears filled with wax they could hear neither the Sirens nor him, and, bending steadily to their oars, they drove the ship through the waves, and before long they were safe upon the open sea.

Then they continued their way until they saw a great fume and seething of spray and heard a sound like thunder, and Odysseus knew that they were drawing near the terrible rock of Scylla, with the whirlpool called Charybdis on the opposite side of the narrow strait that foamed between them.

Odysseus remembered that Circe had warned him that of the two perils the whirlpool was the greater, and that it would be better that Scylla should catch and devour some of his crew than that the whole ship should perish. So he steered as close to the great rock as he dared, under the cliff. And Scylla crawled out of her cave upon her twelve small feet, whimpering like a whelp and stretching out her six hideous heads. And before the ship could get clear through the strait she had seized six of the crew and carried them up to her cave to devour them as if they had been so many fishes.

Then the ship sailed on again, and came to the island of the three promontories. Then Odysseus, hearing the bleating of sheep and the lowing of kine, knew that near by were the pastures where grazed the immortal flocks of the Sun, and, remembering the warnings he had received, he would fain have rowed past the island. But his men were weary, and Eurylochus prevailed upon him to beach the ship, so that they might sleep that night upon the shore. Only he made them swear to touch neither ox nor sheep, and to be content with the food with which Circe had stored their ship.

But for a month the south wind blew without ceasing, and they might by no means leave the island. And their stores were all eaten, and they roamed about snaring birds and catching fishes, and sore pressed by hunger.

It chanced one day that while their leader was asleep Eurylochus spoke to the others and said, " Let us sacrifice to the most high gods the best of the oxen of the Sun. And we will vow to build a goodly temple to the Sun-god when we reach Ithaca. But if he slay us now in his wrath so had I liefer perish than die slowly for lack of food."

When Odysseus awoke from his slumber and returned to the seashore his nostrils were filled with the savour of burning flesh, for his followers had sacrificed the fattest of the oxen of the Sun, pouring out libations of water, since they had no wine, and, for lack of barley, sprinkling green leaves, while they made their prayer.

One of the two nymphs who had charge of the flocks and herds flew to the Sun to tell him what had befallen, and in his wrath he swore that if Zeus would not punish the wrongdoers he would descend from the sky and, leaving the world of men in darkness, go down and give his light to the realms of the dead.

But Zeus said, " Shine still upon the earth. I will break the ship of these sinners asunder with one of my thunderbolts in the middle of the sea."

So Odysseus and his followers sailed away, and a dark cloud hung over them, and the west wind swooped upon their ship and snapped the mast asunder. And then did Zeus fling his terrible thunderbolt, full of sulphurous fumes, and, as he had promised, the ship was broken asunder. Of all those on board none escaped death but Odysseus himself, and he, clinging to the mast and keel, which were still afloat, and to which he bound himself with a leathern thong, was driven past Scylla and Charybdis, and floated for nine days, using his hands as oars, till he reached the island of the nymph Calypso.

When Odysseus had ended his story there was silence for a time throughout the palace hall of Alcinous. Then the King of the Phæacians spoke, saying, " Odysseus, now that thou hast come to my house thou shalt be thwarted no longer. And each of us will give you a tripod and a cauldron."

And this seemed good to the chieftains, and the next day these gifts were brought to the seashore, and they were stowed under the benches of the ship, so that they should not get in the way of the rowers.

THE GATHERING OF THE PHÆACIANS

Next day Athene in the likeness of a herald called all the people together that they might hear the story of the stranger who had thus mysteriously arrived in their midst. And when they were assembled in the palace the King's blind minstrel Demodocus sang a song concerning the dispute between Odysseus and Achilles, and Odysseus wept, covering his face with his mantle. Afterwards they had sports, wrestling and running and tossing quoits, and Odysseus, being challenged, flung a quoit farther than all the rest.

And great and beauteous gifts were given to Odysseus, and a coffer, bound with strong cords, in which he might carry them. When this had been done an ox was sacrificed to Zeus, and the minstrel sang:

> But Odysseus
> Ever and ever was turning his eyes to the sun in its splendour,
> Longing to hasten its setting, so eager he felt for departure.
> HOMER (*Cotterill's tr.*)

So, at last, the moment came to depart. They made libations to Zeus, and Odysseus, with fair and courteous words, took his leave of Arete, from whom he received a fresh robe and tunic, a sheet and a rug, and a gift of bread and wine. Then he climbed aboard the ship that had been made ready, and laid him down and slept. The Phæacians bent to their oars, and the ship sped over the waves so swiftly that not even a hawk could have kept pace with it.

THE RETURN TO ITHACA

When the morning star rose they were within sight of the harbour of Phorcys in Ithaca, which lies between two high cliffs. Near by grew an olive-tree, and there was a cave sacred to the nymphs. In this harbour the seamen beached their swift ship. Then they lifted Odysseus out, still asleep upon the sheet and the rug that Arete had given him. Beside him, under the olive-tree, they set all the other gifts that he had received in their country. Then they put forth again to sea.

But Poseidon was very wroth when he saw these things, and complained to Zeus. And in his anger he sank the Phæacian ship upon her homeward way.

When Odysseus awoke Athene had spread a mist about him, so that he did not know where he was, and imagined that he had been abandoned in some desert. Then he counted his spoils, tripods, and cauldrons, and raiment, and found nothing missing. Yet none the less did he lament his evil fortune.

Athene now came to him in the guise of a young shepherd, of whom he asked the name of the land in which he was. When the supposed shepherd had told him that it was Ithaca he was very glad; but he dissembled, for he was ever cunning, and said that he was on his way from Crete to Elis, or to Pylos, whither he had made a covenant with certain Phœnicians that they should carry him.

Then Athene laid aside the guise of the shepherd lad and said, " It were a clever fellow who could outwit thee! Even here, in thine own land, thou art wary still. But let this be. For I am Athene, the daughter of Zeus. Let us hide this gear of thine, for thou hast yet much to endure ere thou comest into thine own."

Odysseus spoke to her reverently, as a man speaks to the high gods when they vouchsafe to speak with mortal men, and he prayed her to tell him if this were in good sooth Ithaca. And when she had assured him that it was he knelt down and kissed the earth, and prayed to the nymphs, greeting them lovingly. And in their cave he stored the rich gear he had brought from the land of the Phæacians.

Then Athene said, " Lo, I will wither thy flesh, and rive thy head of its bright hair, and thine eyes also of their brightness. Neither thy wife nor thy son shall know thee. Get thee to the hut of the faithful swineherd Eumæus, and I will go to fetch Telemachus, who is seeking news of thee in the house of Menelaus."

Then the goddess departed, and Odysseus, changed to a withered and ragged old man, went down to the place where the swine were kept, guarded by four fierce dogs. And because the suitors of Penelope were great eaters the hogs were not as many as they had been wont to be aforetime.

The dogs would have pulled the stranger down, but the swineherd called them off, saying, " Surely, old man, it had been a grief to me if these hounds had devoured thee. I have other griefs enough, sorrowing for my lord, and tending fat swine for strangers to eat. But come now into my hut."

And the faithful swineherd led the supposed beggar into his dwelling, and spread a goatskin upon a heap of brushwood that he might rest, and gave him pork cooked upon spits, and wine in a bowl of ivy-wood, to refresh him.

While Odysseus ate and drank Eumæus told him about the wickedness of the suitors, and how they revelled and wasted the substance of the royal house.

Then the beggar said, " Friend, who was this lord of thine? I have travelled far, and peradventure I have seen him."

Eumæus answered, " All wayfarers talk after that fashion, and not a tattered fellow comes here but the Queen must see him and question him. But I am sure that Odysseus is dead."

Then said his guest, " Hearken unto me. Odysseus will yet return; yea, at the waning of the moon he will come, and take vengeance on his enemies. And when this shall be I will claim of thee the reward of a bringer of good tidings."

But the swineherd would not believe him, and began to speak of other matters, the absence of Telemachus among them. And he questioned the stranger, who invented a long and false story of his life and adventures to satisfy the curiosity of the old man.

At eventide the other swineherds came, driving the swine home; and Eumæus, who was chief over them all, took a fine hog and killed and roasted it.   Then he divided it into portions, one for the nymphs, one for Hermes, others for the rest of the company, but the best portion, which is the chine, he gave to the stranger.   And when Odysseus lay down to sleep he covered him with his own mantle.

TELEMACHUS RETURNS

Now all this while Telemachus was tarrying in Sparta at the house of Menelaus, and to him came Athene, telling him that Penelope's father and her brethren were desirous that she should take another husband, and that it behoved him to return home. And she counselled him to avoid the strait between Samos and Ithaca, where some of the most valiant of his mother's suitors were lying in wait to destroy him; and also that when he reached Ithaca he should place his own gear in the hands of some trusty woman until such time as he should take to him a wife.   Likewise she bade him, when he returned to Ithaca, that he should send his companions to the city, but himself remain for the night in the hut of Eumæus the swineherd.

Next morning he told Menelaus that he must away, and the King and Queen gave him many rich gifts at parting; a cup of silver and gold wrought by Hephæstus, and a robe embroidered by the hands of Helen herself.

So Telemachus went forth in the chariot with his friend Peisistratus, the son of Nestor, of whom he took leave at Pylos, where the ship was waiting, for he feared that if he should return to the house of Nestor the old man would constrain him to tarry there, which he was loth to do.

While the ship was being made ready for sea there came a man running, a fugitive from Argos, who had slain one of his kinsmen, and who was even then pursued by the avengers of the dead. Theoclymenus was his name, and he was a soothsayer.   Telemachus agreed to take him on board, and Athene sent a favouring wind, and they sailed towards Ithaca.

In due course they reached the island, and beached their ship, making it fast with anchors at the bows and hawsers at the stern.

And before he went, as Athene had bidden, to the hut of Eumæus Telemachus counselled Theoclymenus the soothsayer to seek shelter in the house of Eurymachus, " for," he said, " he is of all the suitors the most honoured among men."

Even as he spoke a hawk was seen flying on his right hand, with a dove in her talons; and the soothsayer declared that the omen was good.

Odysseus and Eumæus meanwhile were making breakfast ready in the hut, and presently Odysseus said, " I hear footsteps, but the dogs do not bark. This must be a comrade or a friend."

Even as he spoke Telemachus stood in the doorway, and Eumæus ran to meet him, and kissed him as if he had been his long-lost son.

The supposed beggar would have made way for the young man, but Telemachus would not suffer him to do it. And they spoke together, Telemachus promising food and clothes and a weapon, but warning the old man not to go to the palace, because the suitors gathered there were haughty and high-handed men.

Then Odysseus said, " Why dost thou bear with these things ? Do thy people hate thee ? "

" Nay," answered Telemachus; " but I have no kinsmen to come to my aid. Perhaps these men will slay me, but that shall be as the gods ordain."

And, turning to Eumæus, he bade him go and advise Penelope of his return, but secretly.

When the swineherd was gone Athene stood before Odysseus, but Telemachus could not see her, and knew not why the dogs whimpered as if for fear. The goddess beckoned Odysseus to come forth from the hut, and when he was come she said, " Reveal thyself to thy son, and concert with him how ye twain may slay the suitors. And lo! I am with you."

Then she touched him with her wand, and he appeared suddenly comely and fair again, clothed no longer in rags, but in a robe of linen and a goodly tunic. Having done this, she vanished, and when the King of Ithaca went back into the hut his son gazed at him in wonder, deeming he must be one of the immortal gods.

" Nay," answered Odysseus, when he asked him if this were indeed so, " I am no god, but thy father, for whom thou hast sought sorrowing."

Then they embraced each other, and the young man wept, and little by little the tale of the wanderings of Odysseus was told, and he drew from his son the names and the number of the suitors, and the places whence they came. Then Odysseus said, " In the morning go back to the palace and mingle with the suitors. Presently I will come in the guise of an old beggar, and if they use me ill do thou endure it, even if they should thrust me out of doors. And mark well. At a certain sign from me take all the weapons in the palace and stow them in thine own chamber. And if they ask why thou hast done this thing say that it is because the smoke has stained them. Say also that if there should be strife over the wine-cups it were better that no such weapons were at hand. Keep two swords, none the less, two bucklers and two spears, for thyself and me. And say no word to anyone—not to Laertes my father, nor to Penelope, nor to Eumæus either."

Meanwhile the ship of Telemachus had cast anchor, and a herald had gone to Penelope to tell her of her son's return; and at the palace he encountered the swineherd, who had also been sent thither on a message. And it was Eumæus to whom the Queen hearkened.

The suitors were very wroth when they heard these tidings, and took counsel together how they might slay the young man, disregarding the words of Amphinomus, who alone among them had misgivings.

Before Eumæus returned to his tent Athene changed Odysseus back to the likeness of a beggar man, for she did not wish the swineherd to recognize his master. And meanwhile another ship had entered the harbour, bearing those of the suitors who had sought to waylay Telemachus in the strait between Ithaca and Samos. These joined their brethren in the palace, bringing their spears and shields with them.

ODYSSEUS IN HIS OWN HOUSE

Next day Telemachus, after some speech with Eumæus and with the supposed beggar, went to the palace, and his old nurse, Eurycleia, saw him coming, and was the first to kiss him. Then came Penelope and kissed him upon the cheek and upon both his eyes, praying him to tell her what news he had heard of his father. But Telemachus made answer, " Of these things I cannot speak now.   Get thee in, and vow a sacrifice to the gods.   As for me, I must go and fetch a stranger who came with me from Argos, and whom I would fain bid to thine house."

Theoclymenus the seer was the stranger of whom he spoke, and when he had brought him, and they had set meat and drink before him, Penelope asked again for news of her lord.   Telemachus told all that he had heard from Nestor and from Menelaus, and when he had finished the seer said, " Hearken unto me, O wife of Odysseus : at this very hour thy lord is in this land.   The omens are clear."

" The gods grant it, stranger," answered Penelope.

Meanwhile Eumæus and the supposed beggar were making their way to the palace, and in the courtyard they found the dog Argus lying neglected on a dunghill.   Odysseus had reared this dog himself in the old days, but he departed for Troy before Argus had come to his full growth.   While he was strong and swift men had used the dog to hunt wild goats, and roe-deers, and hares : but now he was old and helpless, and no man regarded him.   But he knew his master, and moved his ears and wagged his tail, though he was too weak to come to him.

Then said Odysseus, with tears in his eyes, " Surely, Eumæus, it is strange that a dog of so good a breed should be left to die on a dunghill."

" His master died in a far land," answered the swineherd, " and the women-slaves neglect him.   Slaves are ever careless when their lord is far away."

Even as he was speaking the dog Argus died.   Twenty years he had waited, and he saw his master again at last.

After that they went into the hall where the suitors sat at meat. Telemachus sent servants with food to the beggar man, and a message that he might pass among the company asking alms from them.

So Odysseus went round his own palace hall, telling a tale of hardships and loss in far lands, and how he had been sold as a slave in Cyprus.

Some of the suitors had compassion upon him, and others marvelled, but Antinous, who had the falsest heart of them all, mocked him with bitter words of scorn, and when he rebuked him he caught up a footstool and smote him with it.   But Odysseus, for all that he seemed old and feeble, never flinched, and the other suitors upbraided Antinous, and reminded him that sometimes the immortal gods walk in the guise of beggars among mortal men.

When Penelope heard how a poor man and a stranger had been smitten in her house she said, " So may Antinous himself be smitten by Apollo the Archer! "

Then she told Eumæus to bring the stranger to her, that she might question him.   And at that moment Telemachus sneezed, and the heart of his mother rejoiced at the happy omen.

But Odysseus, feigning to fear the suitors, prayed that the Queen would wait until the setting of the sun before she should have speech with him.

THE CONTEST BETWEEN ODYSSEUS AND IRUS

Now there was a beggar that dwelt in the city, Arnæus by name, large in bulk, but not as strong as he was large.   The suitors had nicknamed him Irus, after Iris, the messenger of the gods, for oftentimes he would do errands for them.   This fellow, seeing a rival in the palace hall, said, " Give place, old man, lest I drive thee forth."

" There is room enough for us both," answered Odysseus, but Irus would not listen, and challenged him to a fight.

Antinous laughed aloud, and cried that this was the best sport he had ever seen, and that they must watch the contest.   And he proposed that whichever proved the victor should sit with them at meat, and should have his choice between three goats' paunches which had been prepared for supper.   Telemachus promised that no man should strike a foul blow while the older man was fighting with the younger, and to this the suitors agreed.

Odysseus girded himself for the fray, and when they saw his broad shoulders, and his mighty arms, and the strength of his thighs, they said among themselves that it would go ill with Irus that day.   Irus himself would fain have slipped away, but Antinous would not suffer it, and the fight began.

Odysseus debated in his mind whether he should slay the fellow

Mourning Penelope
Vatican
Photo Brogi

Clytemnestra

Hon. John Collier

By permission, from the original picture in the Guildhall Art Gallery   257

outright or fell him to the earth. And it seemed to him that the second was the better way. So he smote Irus upon the jawbone with such force that the bone broke in two, and the man lay groaning, with the blood streaming from his mouth. All the suitors laughed, and Antinous gave the best of the goats' paunches to Odysseus, and Amphinomus gave him two loaves, and pledged him in a cup of wine.

Then Odysseus said to Amphinomus, " Let no man do wrong, for Zeus will punish evil deeds at last. He who is absent will one day return. Get thee gone ere he comes."

But the other, not heeding the warning, went away with a heavy heart, feeling his doom upon him.

Then Athene put it into the heart of Penelope to show herself to the suitors, and she caused a deep sleep to fall upon the Queen, to whom while she slept she gave grace and beauty such as Aphrodite has. When Penelope came forth and stood at the hall door with a handmaiden at either side of her the suitors gazed at her in wonder, and each prayed to the gods that she might yet be his wife.

She questioned her son concerning what had befallen the stranger, and he told her that things had not happened as the suitors would have wished, since it was the stranger who had prevailed in the fight.

" Would," said the young man, " that all the suitors were even as their messenger Irus is now—for he sits at the gate wagging his head, and cannot stand upon his feet, so sore hath this stranger smitten him."

Eurymachus spoke fair words to Penelope then, praising her wisdom and her beauty, but she answered that her beauty had departed when Odysseus went to Troy: but that, since he had bidden her take another husband when their son had grown to man's estate, she feared that day had now come. And she lamented moreover that her suitors were of such a strange sort that instead of bringing gifts they devoured her substance.

Thereupon the suitors sent hastily for rich gifts, broidered robes, amber necklaces, and earrings of rare workmanship, and they swore that until she had chosen a husband from among them they would not depart from her halls.

Then the Queen retired to her own chamber, and the suitors amused themselves with music and dancing. And there arose a

R

dispute between Eurymachus and the supposed beggar, but it was passed over for the time; and at the behest of Telemachus the suitors betook themselves to slumber.

ODYSSEUS AND EURYCLEIA

Odysseus now bade Telemachus that he should help him to hide the armour that was in the hall. And the young man told Eurycleia to shut the women-slaves up until this had been done, but she demurred, asking who should then bear the lamp for him. Telemachus answered, " This stranger shall bear the lamp." But when all the women were shut up Athene came, and took a lamp of gold, and walked before them. And so all the weapons were stored away as Odysseus had willed, and while Telemachus went to his chamber to sleep Odysseus remained alone by the dying fire in the deserted hall.

Presently Penelope came forth with her maidens, and bade Eurycleia bring a bench with a fleece upon it so that the stranger should sit while he told her his story. But at first the supposed beggar prayed her not to ask his name, or his country, or what things had befallen him, lest, thinking on his sorrows, he should weep, and her maidens might deem that he was drunk with wine.

Penelope reassured him none the less, and told him of her own sorrow—how she was beset by unwelcome wooers, and how she had beguiled them by promising to choose from among them whenever she had finished weaving grave-clothes for her father-in-law, Laertes. For three years she had deceived them, un-ravelling every night the yarn she had woven during the day, but the fourth year her women-slaves betrayed her.

When she had told Odysseus these things he related his adventures, but not those he had had in truth. He invented a tale of hardships and peril, feigning to be a grandson of Minos, King of Crete, and describing how he had entertained Odysseus for twelve days on his way to Troy. Penelope wept when he described the sea-purple mantle and the golden clasp of Odysseus, for these had been gifts from her to her husband in the old days, but the supposed beggar assured her most earnestly that Odysseus lived yet and would soon return.

Then she would have had her handmaidens spread a bed for him and prepare a bath, but he would have none of them. Only he prayed that if there were in the household some old woman true of heart she might wash his feet. So Penelope called Eurycleia, who had carried Odysseus in her arms as a baby, and while she made ready the bath he sat with his face turned aside, fearing lest she should recognize him. More especially did he fear that she might know him by the scar upon his leg, which he had received from the tusk of a wild boar when he was hunting upon Parnassus.

When the old woman had brought the shining cauldron full of water, and had knelt down before the stranger, she took hold of his scarred leg and passed her hand down it, and let the foot drop so suddenly that the cauldron fell on its side with a clang, and the water was spilled on the ground. Then her eyes filled with tears, and she faltered forth, " Surely thou art Odysseus, my dear child! "

And she looked towards Penelope, but Odysseus in haste bade her keep silence, for no man must know of his coming till he had avenged himself on the wooers.

Penelope, still not recognizing him, then told the stranger of a dream she had had, of an eagle that had slain a flock of geese in the palace, and a voice had said, " These geese are thy suitors, and the eagle is thy husband." And Odysseus said it was a good dream.

THE BOW OF ODYSSEUS

While Odysseus lay wakeful that night Athene came to him and bade him have faith in her and let his heart be troubled no more.

There followed conversations between Odysseus and various members of the royal household, a woman grinding at a handmill, a swineherd, a goatherd, and Philœtius the neatherd. This last, lamenting how the suitors devoured the herds which he had tended for his absent master, declared that he would have fled long since had he not nursed the hope that Odysseus might yet return. And Odysseus swore a solemn oath to him that this thing should come to pass.

And after a while the suitors came to feast, and Ctesippus of

Samos spoke taunting words to the supposed beggar, and hurled a bullock's foot at him, whereat Telemachus could scarcely contain his wrath. And suddenly Theoclymenus the soothsayer lifted up his voice, saying that he beheld terrible omens:

> " Yea and the walls are spattered with blood, and the beautiful alcoves,
> See too, crowded with ghosts is the porch and crowded the courtyard,
> Hurrying down to the darkness of Erebus! Out of the heaven
> Withered and gone is the sun, and a poisonous mist is arising."
>
> <div align="right">HOMER (<i>Cotterill's tr.</i>)</div>

But the suitors scoffed and jeered, holding the seer for a madman.

Then it was that Penelope went and unhooked from its peg the great bow of Odysseus and a quiver full of arrows; and, standing by a pillar in the hall, she spoke to the suitors.

" Ye suitors who devour this house, here is the bow of the great Odysseus. Let my son Telemachus set up twelve axes in a row. And he that can most easily bend this bow and aim an arrow most truly through the helveholes of the axes, him will I take for my husband and follow from this house."

She bade Eumæus bear the bow and arrow to the suitors, which he did weeping, while Telemachus set the axes in line. His father made him a sign that he was not to make any trial of strength for his own part, so he stood aside, and the first to bear the bow was Leiodes the priest, who alone of all the suitors was righteous at heart. But his hands were feeble, and he could not even shoot one arrow.

Then the string was greased to make it more supple, yet even so there was none of them that could bend the bow, till there remained only the two strongest, Antinous and Eurymachus. Odysseus had meanwhile followed the swineherd and the neatherd into the yard, and had revealed himself to them, and they wept for joy and came to stand by him.

When he returned to the hall Eurymachus had, with shame and sorrow, acknowledged that he could not draw the bow, and Antinous was declaring that it was his purpose to make essay on the morrow, having first made sacrifice to Apollo.

Then said the disguised Odysseus, " Let me try to bend this bow."

The suitors were angry at this, but Penelope would have it so, and promised the beggar great gifts if he should succeed.

Then Telemachus said, " My mother, the bow is mine, and no man shall say nay if I will that this stranger try his luck. But get thee to thy chamber with thy maidens, that men may take thought for the things which concern men." He did not wish her to see the deeds that he knew were shortly to be done in the hall, and Penelope, marvelling at his tone of authority, departed silently. And when Eumæus had handed the bow to his master he went and bade Eurycleia keep the women-slaves in their own quarters, whatever they might hear.

Gently Odysseus handled the great bow, to see if it had come to any harm, while the suitors watched him with disdain. Then when he had satisfied himself that all was well he strung it as a minstrel strings his harp, and twanged it, when it gave forth a note like the song of a swallow. He took an arrow, and fitted the string into the notch, and drew it as he sat. And the arrow passed clean through every ring of the axes, and stuck fast in the wall behind. He turned to his son, saying:

> " Now is the moment at hand! Let us serve the Achæans their supper
> While it is day!—and when supper is done find other amusement,
> Singing and dancing—for these are ever the crown of a banquet."
> Speaking, he nodded. At once, with his sharp sword girded about him,
> Telemachus, dear son of the godlike hero Odysseus,
> Laying his hand on a spear, sprang forth at the side of his father.
>
> H O M E R (*Cotterill's tr.*)

THE DOOM OF THE SUITORS

To the suitors Odysseus said, " This being done, I will aim at another mark."

The mark was Antinous, who was raising a cup to his lips, recking nothing of death. But the arrow-head passed straight through his neck, and he dropped the cup, and fell to the earth. When the others saw him thus laid low they sprang up, looking round for weapons, but on the walls was neither spear nor shield, and they were perplexed, not knowing whether Antinous had been smitten by chance or purposely.

Odysseus then revealed himself.

" Dogs," he cried, " ye thought never to see me here, and ye have devoured my substance and persecuted my wife, neither

fearing the gods nor being mindful of men.   But therefore is
doom come upon you all most suddenly."

They stood cowering, and only Eurymachus dared speak.   He
said, " If thou art indeed Odysseus thou speakest truly.   But
Antinous was more guilty than all the rest, and he has been laid
low.   We who remain will restore twentyfold all that we have
taken of thine, and pay back all that we have devoured."

But Odysseus answered, " Of paying back it is useless to speak
now.   My hands shall not rest from slaying till I am avenged
upon ye all."

Then Eurymachus turned to the other suitors, and urged that
they should flee to the city to get help, but even as he rushed towards the door an arrow struck him on the breast, and as Amphinomus followed Telemachus thrust his spear through him, nor
dared he pause to draw it forth lest he should be smitten first.

Running to his father, he said, " Is it time now to fetch arms
for us and for our helpers? "

" Yea," answered Odysseus, " and that hastily, lest my arrows
give out."

Telemachus ran to the armoury and armed himself, and likewise Eumæus and Philœtius, and brought arms, helmet, shield,
and two spears, so that Odysseus could arm himself likewise when
all his arrows were spent.

But Melanthius, the goatherd, stole up to the armoury, and
brought down arms for the suitors, for he was a traitor.   But the
two faithful servants, Eumæus and Philœtius, followed him when
they espied him creeping thither again, and, binding his feet and
his hands, fastened him by a rope to the roof-beam.

For a moment Athene, disguised as Mentor, stood in the hall
beside Odysseus and his son, but, thinking to try their valour yet
a little more, she changed herself into a swallow and sat up among
the rafters.

Then Agelaus exhorted his comrades to have courage, and to
hurl their spears all together.   Yet this availed them nothing, for
Athene caused all their spears to glance aside, and Odysseus and
Telemachus and the two herdsmen slew each his man again and
yet again.   Ctesippus grazed Eumæus in the shoulder, and
Amphimedon wounded Telemachus slightly, but Philœtius
struck down Ctesippus, and Telemachus slew Amphimedon, and

all the time Athene's bright Ægis flamed above their heads.   As birds are dispersed and torn by eagles the suitors scattered and fell on every side.

Leiodes the priest prayed for mercy, but because he had offered sacrifice on behalf of the other suitors Odysseus would grant him none.   But Phemius the minstrel, who had sung for them unwillingly, and Medon the herald, who had been their reluctant messenger, he spared.

At last there remained not one suitor alive.   Then Odysseus gave orders that the place should be cleared and cleansed and washed with water and purified with sulphur, before Eurycleia the nurse went to Penelope to tell her that her lord had returned from his wanderings at last.

But Penelope could not believe the glad tidings.   And she gazed upon the stranger, when he had come from the bath and Athene had made him fairer than of yore, not knowing for certain whether this were indeed her lord and not another.

Then he said to her, " Hearken, Penelope, and I will tell thee the fashion of my bed, which I myself made, with a bed-post of olive-wood and thongs of bright purple leather, and adornments of carving, of silver and ivory and gold.   But whether it be still in its place I know not."

Then by this token, known only to Odysseus and herself and one of her maidservants, the Queen perceived that it was indeed he, and with tears of delight she folded her arms about him.

Here the story of Odysseus may be said to end, though the *Odyssey* carries it a little further, describing how Hermes conducted the suitors down to the dwellings of the dead, and how they encountered the shades of Patroclus and Achilles, Ajax and Agamemnon; how Odysseus was reunited to his aged father, Laertes; and how the kinsfolk of the suitors made an abortive effort to avenge them.

Dante represents Odysseus as setting forth in his old age to sail " beyond the sunset," and Tennyson has made use of this idea in one of his finest poems, *Ulysses.*

> I am a part of all that I have met;
> Yet all experience is an arch wherethro'
> Gleams that untravell'd world, whose margin fades
> For ever and for ever when I move.

There lies the port; the vessel puffs her sail:
There gloom the dark broad seas. My mariners,
Souls that have toil'd and wrought, and thought with me—
That ever with a frolic welcome took
The thunder and the sunshine, and opposed
Free hearts, free foreheads—you and I are old;
Old age hath yet his honour and his toil;
Death closes all: but something ere the end,
Some work of noble note, may yet be done,
Not unbecoming men that strove with gods.
The light begins to twinkle from the rocks:
The long day wanes: the slow moon climbs: the deep
Moans with many voices.   Come, my friends,
'Tis not too late to seek a newer world.

CHAPTER XXVII

AGAMEMNON AND HIS FAMILY

OF all the Greek chieftains who lay encamped for ten weary years before the walls of Troy Agamemnon had the hardest fate.

His wife, Clytemnestra, had never forgiven him for sacrificing their first-born child, and during his long absence she took to herself a lover, a certain Ægisthus, a descendant of Pelops, and a kinsman of Agamemnon.

What befell when the King returned to Mycenæ Æschylus tells in the first of a trilogy, or series of three plays, devoted to the doom of that unhappy family. This play is called *Agamemnon*, and it opens upon the roof of the King's palace, where a sentinel is watching for the signal fire which shall proclaim that proud Troy has fallen. He sees it, and his announcement is confirmed by the words of a herald or messenger who enters shortly after; but the chorus of ancient Argive men, though celebrating the Trojan defeat, is full of foreboding and gloomy with thoughts of Clytemnestra's unforgetting mind.

Agamemnon arrives with his captive the prophetess Cassandra, who foresees both her fate and the King's, but to whose frantic words neither he nor any other man will pay any heed.

Clytemnestra now comes forward to greet her husband with hypocritical courtesy, and leads him into the palace, followed by Cassandra, who is preparing herself for death.

A terrible cry is heard from within—the death-cry of the King—and the play ends with Clytemnestra and Ægisthus glorying in their murderous deed.

Various tales are told as to the manner in which that deed was done. The most picturesque relates that as Agamemnon came from the bath his treacherous Queen handed him a tunic of which the sleeves had been sewn together; then as he struggled to put it on she smote him with an axe, and Ægisthus completed the crime she had thus cunningly and ruthlessly planned.

ORESTES AVENGES HIS FATHER

The second play of the three is called the *Choephoræ*, or libation-bearers, and deals with the adventures of Orestes, in whom many perceive a prototype of Hamlet.

This only son of Agamemnon and Clytemnestra had been living at the court of Strophius, King of Phocis, whose son Pylades became his greatest friend. The two young men visit the grave of Agamemnon, where, according to a funeral custom common among the ancients, Orestes dedicates a lock of his own hair.

Clytemnestra meanwhile has been haunted by terrible dreams, and has sent her daughter Electra, with a band of Argive women, to pour libations upon the tomb of the murdered King. Electra recognizes her brother's hair, and a pathetic reunion follows, when the princess urges the newly rediscovered Orestes to avenge their father Agamemnon. (In a play by Euripides on the same theme an old servant sees the footsteps of Orestes and a lock of his hair near the grave, but Electra hesitates to believe that they are really those of her long-lost brother.)

Apollo had already laid his commands upon the young prince to punish his guilty mother and her lover, and it is now arranged that Orestes and Pylades shall arrive at the palace feigning to be travellers who bring the news to Clytemnestra that her son is dead. Ægisthus, perhaps suspecting that things are not what they seem, questions the strangers, and is slain by Orestes, whose identity is thus revealed to his mother.

Terror-struck, she begs for mercy, but Electra urges her brother to show none, and, dragging her within the palace, Orestes kills her. (Note that in Greek tragedy deeds of violence such as this are always performed ' off-stage.')

THE TRIBULATIONS OF ORESTES

Now Clytemnestra was justly punished, and at the behest of Apollo himself, but in the eyes of the immortal gods the man who, even as an act of retribution, had murdered his mother was stained with a peculiarly horrible sin. Even as Orestes is pleading that his deed was not unpardonable the Furies appear, and by these terrible instruments of vengeance the unfortunate prince is pursued until he loses his reason.

The third play is called the *Eumenides*. The word means literally the ' gracious ones,' but it was a polite name for the Furies themselves, than whom no beings were ever less gracious. This play opens at the shrine of Apollo at Delphi, where the distraught Orestes, still pursued by the avenging Furies, implores the pity of the god. Touched with compassion, Apollo bids the young man go to Athens and appeal to Athene, but the ghost of Clytemnestra rises from the grave and stirs the Furies up to further violence.

The next scene is in the temple of Athene at Athens. She hears the pleading of Orestes and the fierce denunciations of the Eumenides, and decrees that the question shall be laid before a tribunal of Athenian judges, meeting upon the Areopagus, or Hill of Ares, where at a later date such tribunals were wont to assemble and promulgate their decisions. These judges were equally divided upon the question as to whether Orestes should continue to suffer or might now be purified from his sin, but Athene gave the casting vote in his favour. (According to another version of the story the judges were unanimous in acquitting Orestes.) Orestes was duly purified, either at Delphi or at Trœzen, and the Furies were consoled by being offered an honourable dwelling-place in Athens, on the flanks of the Areopagus, where later ages raised a shrine to them. It was upon this hill— Mars' Hill—that the Apostle Paul spoke to the Athenian people.

THE REUNION OF IPHIGENIA AND ORESTES

Euripides tells a picturesque story in the play called *Iphigenia in Tauris*. The elder daughter of Agamemnon and Clytemnestra, as has already been related, was snatched by Artemis from the sacrificial pyre and borne away to the land of Tauris, where for many years she served as a priestess in the temple of the goddess. The Taurians were a savage people whose wont it was to sacrifice any unfortunate seafarers wrecked on their coasts and to offer up their lives to Artemis, of whom they possessed an ancient image believed to have fallen down from heaven.

Now Apollo, according to this version of the tale, had told

Orestes that he could be purified of his sin and delivered from the unwelcome society of the Furies only if he should bring this sacred image from the peninsula of the Chersonese to the mainland of Greece. It was a perilous enterprise, for the Taurians regarded this image as the most holy and auspicious thing in their land, but Orestes, accompanied by the ever-faithful Pylades, determined to make the attempt.

They were captured, however, and delivered into the hands of the priestess Iphigenia, who had been haunted by the fear that a day would come when she would be called upon to make ready some hapless Greek for death. She offered to connive at the escape of one of the two if he would carry a letter from her to some one in the land of Greece. Each of the young men was eager that his friend should go, and finally Orestes prevailed upon Pylades to be the messenger of the priestess. The letter was handed to him—and the name upon the outer fold was the name of Orestes himself. The brother and sister were thus made aware of their relationship, and their reunion, as described by Euripides, is one of the most beautiful of the many ' recognition scenes ' in dramatic literature.

Iphigenia determined to aid and abet her brother and his friend in carrying off the sacred image, and to fly with them from the country of the Taurians. Their flight was discovered, and the Taurians, led by their King, Thoas, set off fiercely in pursuit; but Athene intervened to save them, declaring that all that they had done was according to the will of the immortal gods.

CHAPTER XXVIII

VIRGIL'S "ÆNEID"

IT will be remembered that among the Trojans who helped to defend their city against the Greeks was Æneas, the son of Anchises and Aphrodite. An early legend stated that he escaped from the flaming ruins and found refuge somewhere in Italy, but a Sicilian historian of the third century B.C., Timæus by name, seems to have been the first to identify him with the founder of the Roman state.

The idea took a firm hold upon the imagination of the Roman people, whose pride of race was flattered by the divine origin thus attributed to their city, and in the time of the Emperor Augustus Cæsar, just before the opening of the Christian era, Virgil began an immense epic, the *Æneid*, describing the wanderings and exploits of the fabulous Trojan. Æneas was a particularly interesting person in the eyes of the Emperor, for the Julian *gens*, to which his uncle Julius Cæsar, and therefore he himself, traced back their descent, claimed to be of the blood of Iulus (Julus), sometimes called Ascanius, the son of Æneas. Flatterers saw in the good looks of many members of the family evidence of their kinship with the goddess of love and beauty, and were not backward in saying so.

In giving a brief summary of the unfinished epic we will use, as Virgil naturally did, the Latin names of the immortal actors in the story.

THE ADVENTURES OF ÆNEAS

Æneas, having rescued his blind father, Anchises, carrying him upon his shoulders from the flaming city of Troy, set sail, with a small company of Trojan fugitives, for the land of Italy, the future cradle of the Roman State. With him went his friend Achates, the *fidus Achates* whose loyalty has become a proverb.

The journey to Italy occupied many years, and at the outset the travellers were opposed by Juno (Hera), who had not forgotten her hatred of Troy even though the city had vanished in smoke and flame.   The goddess persuaded Æolus to unleash his fiercest winds upon the little fleet, but Neptune (Poseidon) had pity on them, and seven came safely to anchor off the coast of Libya.

Walking in the forest, Æneas met his mother Venus (Aphrodite), disguised as a huntress.   She spoke gracious words to him, foretelling a great and glorious future for his descendants.   It is in Virgil's description of this remarkable interview that occurs the famous line:

Vera incessu patuit dea.
(The true goddess was revealed by her gait.)

DIDO AND ÆNEAS

The city of Carthage had been founded not long before, and over it ruled a young widowed queen called Dido, who received Æneas and his companions hospitably, and who—for so Venus willed that it should be—fell deeply in love with the young stranger.

At her request he related the story of the fall of Troy, and how he had fled, carrying his father, and leading by the hand his young son, Iulus.   His wife, Creüsa, tried to follow, but was lost, and when he ran back to seek her among the flames her ghost appeared to him, saying that her death was decreed by the gods, but that on the shores of the Tiber a happy fate, a kingdom, and a royal bride awaited him.

Æneas went on to tell how the oracle at Delos had commanded him to seek the land which was the cradle of their race.   He thought that Apollo meant Crete, but when he and his companions sailed to that island misfortune overtook them, and the household gods, which had been brought from Troy, appeared to him in a dream and revealed that Italy, not Crete, was the place indicated by the god.   Anchises at this juncture remembered that Cassandra also had spoken of the land of Hesperia, and the travellers determined to make their way thither with what speed they might.

Many vicissitudes chequered their journey; they landed on the island of the Harpies; they encountered Priam's son, Helenus, who bade Æneas visit the Cumæan Sibyl, and found a new city in the place where he should find a white sow with a litter of thirty young.   Having visited the land of the Cyclopes in Sicily, where the aged Anchises died, the young hero set sail with his small son and his faithful band of followers, and finally reached Dido's realm of Carthage.

The Queen's love for Æneas grew greater every day, and was noised abroad by the nimble-footed and many-eyed goddess of Rumour.   When the news reached Iarbas, a son of Jupiter (Zeus) and one of the Libyan nymphs, he was furious, for he had been rejected by Dido when he sought her hand in marriage.   He appealed to his divine father, who sent Mercury (Hermes) to Æneas with strict injunctions to leave Carthage for ever, instead of lingering there in the arms of the infatuated Queen.   These stories were all familiar to Shakespeare, who alludes to most of them.   When Cassius is boasting how he rescued Cæsar from drowning he says,

> I, as Æneas, our great ancestor,
> Did from the flames of Troy upon his shoulder
> The old Anchises bear, so from the waves of Tiber
> Did I the tired Cæsar.

And Lorenzo in the moonlit garden at Belmont exclaims,

> In such a night
> Stood Dido with a willow in her hand
> Upon the wild sea banks and waft her love
> To come again to Carthage.

Very reluctantly Æneas began to make ready to depart, but his intentions could not be hidden from Dido, who appealed to him most pitifully, with many tears, not to abandon her.   He steeled his heart, however, and, pleading that the decrees of the gods must not be set aside, resolved to follow where destiny beckoned. In vain Dido reproached him, in vain she wept; the Trojans continued to make ready their ships, careening the keels, and bringing fresh timber from the forest wherewith to make oars.

The Queen of Carthage then persuaded her sister Anna to help her to prepare a great funeral pyre in the inner court of the palace, giving as her reason that she wished to destroy every relic of the false Æneas, his arms, his garments, and the marriage-bed which he had thus deserted. (They were never, strictly speaking, married, but Dido claimed that their love was tantamount to wedlock.)

That night, as Æneas lay asleep on the deck of his ship by the poop, Mercury appeared to him, an auburn-haired and handsome youth, and warned him to set sail without further delay, for a favourable wind was blowing, and Dido was plotting evil things. Here occurs the familiar sentence,

> Varium et mutabile semper
> Femina.
>
> (Woman is ever a fickle and changeable thing.)

Æneas sprang up, cut the hawsers with his sword, and gave the order to depart.

THE DEATH OF DIDO

At daybreak Dido perceived that the harbour was deserted, and the first pale streaks of the rising sun touched the receding sails of the Trojan fleet. With terrible cries she called down curses upon the fugitives, and prayed that their descendants and the Carthaginians might be enemies to all generations. (This came to pass.) Then, full of despair, she rushed into the courtyard, and, climbing on to the pyre, gazed for the last time upon the Trojan raiment and the well-remembered couch that had been heaped up there at her behest. She took up the sword which Æneas had brought with him from Troy and plunged it into her heart.

Juno, looking down from heaven, beheld the unhappy Queen writhing in agony, gazing with dim eyes up at the sky which she could not now discern. The goddess, touched by pity, sent Iris, flying earthward on her dewy saffron wings, to release the spirit of Dido from its body, and so the Queen of Carthage descended to the land of the shades.

Far off the Trojans could see the flames mounting from the funeral pyre, but knew not what they were, and marvelled what omen of doom that dark, rolling smoke might be.

NISUS AND EURYALUS

Threatening clouds caused the Trojans to take refuge in a harbour of Sicily, where, as it was the anniversary of the death of Anchises, funeral games were duly held in his honour. In the foot-race contended two friends, Nisus and Euryalus, who were so dear to each other that each would rather that his friend had proved victor than himself.

Nisus was well ahead, followed by Salius, behind whom were Euryalus and the rest of the competitiors. Near the end of the course Nisus slipped and fell. But even in his dismay he remembered his friend, and as he struggled to his feet he so contrived it that Salius should stumble over him, thus giving Euryalus the chance—which he promptly seized—of gaining the lead and winning the race.

Nothing could more clearly mark the difference in outlook between the ancient and the modern world than the admiration demanded by Virgil for this " excellent youth," whom we should regard as totally deficient in the first elements of sportsmanship.

FURTHER VICISSITUDES OF ÆNEAS

Meanwhile Juno, still implacable against the sons of Troy, sent Iris to stir up discontent among the Trojan matrons who had followed their husbands on all their wanderings, and were very loth to put again to sea. While the menfolk were amusing themselves with boxing, wrestling, and racing the women went down to the shore and set fire to the ships. No sooner was this done than the doers of the deed were sorry, and scattered in all directions, hiding themselves in woods and caves. Æneas appealed to Jupiter, reminding him of his ancient love for Troy, and imploring him to save this poor remnant of the Trojan fleet; and hardly was the prayer uttered when a heavy storm of rain quenched the flames. All the ships save four were saved.

Nautes, one of the oldest and wisest of the company, now counselled Æneas to leave behind, under the leadership of his friend Acestes, all those who were too old or too fainthearted for further hardships. In this way room would be found in the

s

depleted fleet for the younger and more hardy. The ghost of Anchises endorsed this excellent counsel, and the next day Æneas and his companions set sail, under the favour of Venus, who begged Neptune to grant a calm passage to her son. The sea-god promised that every man should come safely into harbour except one. That unlucky one was the pilot, Palinurus, who fell asleep at his post at the helm, tumbled into the sea, and was drowned.

Sorrowing for his friend, Æneas himself took the helm and led his fleet to the shores of the land called Cumæ, where it was his purpose to consult the far-famed Cumæan Sibyl, as Helenus had said that he should. (The Sibyls were priestesses—or, some said, daughters—of Apollo, and they uttered divinely inspired prophecies. Their number is given variously as four or ten, but the higher is the more generally accepted estimate. There was one at Babylon, and another at Delphi; but the Cumæan, largely thanks to Virgil, is the best known. Tarquin, after some haggling, was said to have obtained from her a collection of oracles called the Sibylline Books, which were kept in a vault under the temple of Jupiter Capitolinus at Rome until destroyed by fire in the year 83 B.C. A second collection, garnered at great expense by the Emperor Augustus, was reduced to ashes by Stilicho in the fifth century A.D.) Reverently Æneas approached the sculptured temple of the prophetess, who received him kindly, and bade him sacrifice seven bullocks and as many ewes to Apollo. The Trojan obeyed, at the same time praying earnestly to the god who had ever pitied the struggles of Troy.

Now, inspired by the god, the Sibyl, foretelling great glory and great disasters, decreed that Æneas should descend to the realm of the dead, first obtaining the Golden Bough which should safeguard him on his journey. Here occurs the oft-quoted phrase,

Facilis descensus Averno.
(The descent of Avernus is easy.)

When Æneas, accompanied by the faithful Achates, returned to the seashore they saw stretched out upon it the dead body of their comrade Misenus, son of Æolus. Thus swiftly were the words of the Sibyl brought to pass, for she had told him that one of his comrades had perished, and had bidden him perform funeral rites before descending to the Stygian groves of the shades.

THE GOLDEN BOUGH

In order to procure faggots for the funeral pyre Æneas and some of his companions went into the dense forest, and with their axes felled great branches of ilex, ash, and oak. Two doves flew down and alighted on a patch of turf, and, recognizing them as birds sacred to Venus, his mother, the hero prayed for their help.

They rose into the air, and, following their flight with anxious eyes, he saw them, at the dark gates of Avernus, glide up together to the top of an ilex-tree, where through the branches he could clearly catch a gleam of gold.

> As in the wintry woods the mistletoe
> Blooms with strange foliage, borne by no tree,
> Circling with golden twigs the rounded trunks,
> So seemed the gleam of leafy gold amid
> The dusky ilex.

Æneas promptly grasped the precious Golden Bough and bore it back to the dwelling of the Sibyl.

THE DESCENT OF AVERNUS

Having performed the funeral rites of Misenus, he solemnly offered the appointed sacrifice at the entrance to the dark cave where the descent of Avernus began, and the Sibyl, warning him that he would need all his courage, plunged into the shadows.

Through the hollow palaces and intangible realms of Dis they descended, and past the threshold haunted by many horrors—Death, Disease, Old Age, Fear and Penury, Centaurs, Gorgons, Harpies, and evil Dreams.

A path led them to the river Acheron, where the gaunt and ragged ferryman, Charon, plied to and fro. On the bank, waiting to be ferried across, was a throng of shades as numerous as forest leaves falling when the chill of autumn begins. Here occurs the famous line,

> Tendebantque manus ripæ ulterioris amore
> (Stretching forth longing hands to the farther shore),

which has been variously interpreted as meaning that the ghosts were anxious to pass across, or regretted the shore they were about to leave. The Sibyl explained that those whom Charon took on his boat were souls whose bodies had received funeral rites. The others had to wait for a hundred years.

Æneas recognized Palinurus, whose body was still tossing in the sea, and the Sibyl consoled the unfortunate pilot by telling him that though his spirit might not yet cross the Styx, a time would come when his bones would be interred under a lofty mound, where offerings would be made in his memory, and the place would bear his name.

CHARON: CERBERUS: THE ABODE OF THE DEAD

When Charon would have refused to take Æneas and the Sibyl in his boat the prophetess produced the Golden Bough, and the ferryman had no choice but to make room for two more passengers in his crazy craft, which creaked with the weight, while marshy ooze rose between its rotten planks.

On the farther side Cerberus was making a hideous din with his three heads all barking at once, but the Sibyl tossed into his jaws a cake of wheat and honey drugged with a deadening herb, and the watch-dog of Hell sank helpless on the ground.

In a dreary myrtle grove the two travellers next saw the ghosts of those who had pined to death for love, Dido among them; and thence they passed to the remoter fields, where the shades of the great heroes dwelt. When the chieftains of the Greek host saw the armour of the Trojan warriors shining in the gloom they were sore afraid.

Then Tartarus, the terrible prison-house of evildoers, guarded by the watchful Tisiphone, loomed up on the left of their path. (Virgil's description of this castle, washed by the burning waves of Phlegethon, has been quoted earlier in this book.[1]) Finally they reached the entrance to Pluto's palace, where Æneas hung up the Golden Bough. The hero now beheld the Elysian Fields, the abode of the virtuous and happy shades, and here he was reunited for a brief moment with his father, Anchises.

The old man proceeded to utter prophecies (one hopes that the Cumæan Sibyl did not regard this as an invasion of her particular

[1] See page 97.

sphere), tracing the descendants of his son as far as Romulus, and then continuing the line to Cæsar, " and all the posterity of Iulus," with special reference to Augustus (Virgil's patron and friend), who was to establish a second Age of Gold in those fields of Latium where once Saturn reigned. This was the part of the *Æneid* which Virgil read aloud to the Emperor, and which drew tears from the eyes of Augustus by its touching reference to the death of his promising young nephew and adopted son, Marcellus.

Finally Anchises dismissed Æneas and the Sibyl through the ivory gate of Sleep.

THE TROJANS IN ITALY

After various other losses and adventures the Trojans reached the mouth of the Tiber, and disembarked upon the soil that was to be their children's heritage. There was already a king reigning there, a certain Latinus, who had a daughter called Lavinia. Nobody acquainted with the reliable character of pagan predictions will need to be told that this was the royal bride whom the ghost of Creüsa had promised to her widowed husband. Oracles and omens had also been active in Italy, and Latinus was not slow to realize that this was the stranger whom destiny had chosen to be the husband of his child. To show his appreciation of the fact he sent messengers to the Trojan camp with rich gifts, horses with purple housings and golden collars.

THE WRATH OF JUNO

The wife of Jupiter, looking down from the clouds, beheld Æneas and the Trojans rejoicing, and straightway called to her aid the snaky-locked Fury called Alecto. Unfortunately the hand of Lavinia had already been promised to her kinsman Turnus, chief of the Rutulians, and the Fury proceeded first to inflame the mind of Amata, the wife of Latinus, against the proposed alliance with a complete stranger and the bold repudiation of former promises. Having stirred up the Queen, Alecto flew to the palace of Turnus, and poured into his sleeping mind the story of the coming of the Trojans and all that might result from it.

The Fury then flew to the forest where Iulus, now a handsome youth, was hunting the stag. By misadventure he wounded a tame deer which was much beloved by Sylvia, the daughter of Tyrrheus, who was the ranger of the royal herds, and this deed so incensed the foresters that they attacked Iulus and his companions, and a desperate fight took place, the brothers and friends of Sylvia being urged on by Alecto. But Juno now felt that enough had been done, and sternly ordered the Fury to return to her dwelling on the gloomy bank of Cocytus.

WAR BETWEEN THE ITALIANS AND THE TROJANS

War now broke out on all sides in Italy, and Latinus, unwilling to listen to the clamour raised by his subjects, shut himself in a remote part of his palace in his city of Laurentum, and let events take their course. As he would not unbar the doors of the temple of Janus,[1] Juno herself descended from heaven, and with her own hand pushed them open.

Five great cities prepared for war; against the omens, against the oracles, the tribes of Latium were resolved to drive the Trojans forth, and to see that the hand of Lavinia was bestowed upon Turnus.

Virgil gives a long and most picturesque list of the various chieftains who hastened to fling themselves into the fray, and describes Turnus as being " taller than the rest by the whole of his head." Among his allies was Camilla, the warrior maiden, who led a troop of Volscian cavalry.

The air was full of the brazen notes of war-trumpets and the clang of arms.

TIBER AND ÆNEAS

Greatly perturbed at all these menacing preparations, Æneas lay down to sleep on the bank of the river Tiber, and beneath the shade of the poplars the god of the river appeared to him, robed in a garment of fine linen, with a crown of rushes on his head. " Go

[1] See page 289.

not hence, son of the gods," said Father Tiber. " Here is your home, here shall be your Penates. And where you shall find, under an ilex-tree, a white sow with thirty young, there shall Iulus found a city and call it Alba. Now hearken. On these shores dwells a race of Arcadians, who have built a city called Pallantium. They were followers of Evander, and his son Pallas is their leader. Seek alliance with these people, and when you have conquered you shall pay homage to me, dark blue Tiber, a river well loved by the immortal gods."

ÆNEAS AND EVANDER

Obedient to the words of the river-god, Æneas and his chosen companions set out next morning, and reached the city of Pallantium, where, in a grove outside the city wall, they found Evander and his son offering sacrifices to Hercules.

The old man was the son of the god Mercury and an Arcadian nymph, and sixty years before the Trojan war he had led a colony from Pallantium in Arcadia to the banks of the Tiber, where they founded a settlement at the foot of what was in after years known as the Palatine Hill. To him Æneas spoke courteous and friendly words, and the old man, who remembered Anchises, readily promised his aid against the followers of Turnus. He also undertook to obtain the aid of the Etruscans, who were in revolt against their King, Mezentius, an ally of the Rutulians. A sudden flash of lightning from the blue sky and a long roll of thunder startled them all, but Æneas interpreted it as a signal from his mother, Venus, and the whole company sacrificed before the altars of Hercules and of the little household gods.

This thunderclap was not the only token given by the goddess of her interest in the enterprise of her son. She brought him arms fashioned by her husband, Vulcan. Upon the shield the blacksmith-god had wrought prophetic images of all the descendants of Iulus, of Romulus and Remus, and of many future events in the history of Rome, culminating in the triumphs of Augustus Cæsar.

THE DEEDS OF TURNUS

Juno meanwhile sent Iris to Turnus, urging him to attack the Trojans during the absence of their chief. Nothing loth, the chief of the Rutulians mounted his piebald charger and led his hosts towards the Trojan camp. But the Trojans, remembering the counsels of Æneas, remained within their ramparts and would not come forth, and Turnus, in a fierce rage, gave the order that the Trojan ships, which were drawn up on the river-bank, should be set on fire. But Jupiter, faithful to a vow which he had made long since to the goddess Cybele, from whose sacred pine-trees the Trojan ships were fashioned, turned the whole fleet into as many water-nymphs.

Turnus, quite erroneously, imagined that this sudden and astonishing transformation was a token of Jupiter's displeasure with the Trojans, and was proportionately encouraged.

THE VALIANT DEED OF NISUS AND EURYALUS

Iulus and his companions, though the immediate danger had passed, longed for the return of Æneas; and the two young friends, Nisus and Euryalus, decided to go forth by stealth to Pallantium and urge the hero to return. Nisus would fain have gone alone upon this hazardous adventure, but Euryalus would not hear of it, and together they went to the leaders of the Trojans, who were at that moment holding a council as to what it were best to do.

Nisus declared that the Rutulians were drowsy with wine, and that he and his friend could easily make their way through the camp and thence to Pallantium, of which they had often seen the distant towers when they were hunting on the river-bank.

Delighted, Iulus promised rich reward if the exploit were safely carried through; and when Euryalus paused a moment to beg him to comfort his widowed mother if he should perish the son of Æneas answered, " Your mother shall be as mine; for great thanks are due to her who has borne so valiant a son."

In order to get through the Rutulian camp the two friends had no choice but to slay several of the sleeping warriors who lay across their path, among them the favourite soothsayer of Turnus.

Having armed themselves with the gear of their victims, they crept onward until they reached a wood, where they felt that they were no longer in any peril.

Little did they know that three hundred Latin horsemen, led by a captain called Volscens, were at that moment on their way to reinforce Turnus and his Rutulians. The captain caught a gleam of moonlight upon the helmet of Euryalus, and, looking more closely, perceived that two armed men were lurking among the trees. When he challenged them they fled, but his horsemen formed a ring round the fugitives, and after a desperate struggle, during which each of the faithful friends thought more of saving the other's life than of guarding his own, both were killed,

> Even as a fair flower mangled by the plough,
> Or weary poppies drooping under rain.

But Nisus, in his supreme effort to avenge Euryalus, had first laid Volscens low.

Great was the dismay of the Rutulians when they found so many dead men lying, stripped of their arms, in the camp, and greatly did they grieve for Volscens when his body was borne thither by his men. But they consoled themselves by wreaking vengeance on the lifeless bodies of Nisus and Euryalus, whose heads they fixed upon spears where the saddened Trojans could see them.

THE SIEGE OF THE TROJAN CAMP

There followed a fierce assault upon the Trojan camp which developed into a regular siege. Many deeds of great daring were performed on either side, but when a certain Numanus, a brother-in-law of Turnus, taunted the Trojans for remaining cooped up in their stronghold, and contrasted the austere habits of the Italians with the more luxurious ways of the invaders, Iulus grew so angry that, praying to Jupiter to direct his aim, he shot an arrow at the braggart which clove him through the head.

The god Apollo, pleased with this deed, descended to earth in the guise of an ancient armour-bearer and spoke to the young archer, telling him that it was he who had granted him this glory, but at the same time counselling him, by reason of his youth, to abstain yet awhile from war. Then he vanished suddenly with a rattle of the arrows in his quiver, and the Trojans realized that the god had been in their midst.

The fortunes of battle swayed to and fro, and sallies and counter-attacks succeeded one another with varying results. Once Turnus, hard pressed during an attack which took him right inside the camp, was forced to spring into the river and swim to the farther shore.   Just as in the tale of Troy as told by Homer, so in the story of Æneas as related by Virgil the gods concern themselves actively in the struggles of mortal men, take sides, argue among themselves, and on occasion intervene.   We see Juno still implacable against the Trojans, Venus pleading for them, and Jupiter saying yet again that even he cannot avert the decrees of fate.

Meanwhile Æneas, with a large body of reinforcements from Pallantium and Etruria, was hastening back to his friends.   The water-nymphs into which his ships had been transformed rose from the waves and told him what had happened during his absence.   They also urged him at dawn the next day to make an attack upon the Rutulian besiegers, promising him a great victory.

Æneas, a wise if not a dashing hero, knew better than to disregard advice offered in this supernatural manner.   The next day a fierce battle began, in the course of which Pallas was slain by Turnus.   Æneas, full of sorrow, attacked with even greater energy than before, and now the Trojans within the camp, led by Iulus, made a powerful sortie.   At one moment Turnus was nigh unto death, but Juno, with the permission of Jupiter, rescued him.

After that it seemed for some time uncertain whether the Trojans or the Italians would win the day, but when Æneas wounded Mezentius the tide began to turn in favour of the men of Troy.   The Etruscan King's young son Lausus perished in trying to save his father, who, with his faithful horse Rhæbus, was then slain by Æneas.

The next step was a request from the Italians for a truce, in order that they might bury their dead.   This was granted.

Meanwhile the Italians had sent messengers to crave the aid of Diomed, King of Ætolia, who had settled with a Greek colony in a part of Italy where they built a city called Agyrippa.   These messengers now returned, saying that the Ætolian prince could not help them, and that his advice was that they should make peace with the Trojans.

King Latinus then called his people together, saying that they were waging an ill-omened war against opponents of divine race, and suggesting that they should offer land to the Trojans, or, if the strangers did not choose to settle there, give them the means to build a fresh fleet. And a certain aged Italian called Drances, who was known to be a wise man, added his voice to that of Latinus in urging that peace should be made. He also blamed Turnus for all the misfortunes which had befallen the Italians.

But Turnus rose up and clamoured for the war to go on, and declared his willingness to meet Æneas, man to man, in single combat. While they were disputing Æneas and his forces were advancing against the city.

Foremost in the preparations to resist them was the warlike Camilla. She was the daughter of Metabus, King of the Privernates, who, having been driven forth by his rebellious subjects, took the infant Camilla in his arms and fled. Reaching the banks of the swollen river Amasenus, and being hotly pursued by his enemies, he tied the child to his spear, which, with a prayer to Diana, he hurled at the farther bank. He then swam across, and, finding Camilla uninjured, dedicated her to the goddess of the chase. Together father and child led a wild and lonely life in the forest, and Camilla grew up a fearless huntress, skilful with bow and arrow, an expert horsewoman, and warlike as any man.

In the battle for the city of Latinus she bore a leading part, and laid many Trojans low, but she was mortally wounded by one of the followers of Æneas, called Aruns. With her last breath the indomitable maiden sent a message to Turnus, bidding him take her place in the ranks of the defenders, and keep the Trojans from the city.

Diana, unable to save her votary, whose death had been decreed by fate, avenged her by sending Ops (Opis) to slay Aruns with a well-aimed shaft.

ÆNEAS AND TURNUS

The idea of a single combat between Æneas and Turnus was now revived, a truce was sworn, and the lists were prepared for the duel. Juno, anxious lest the Trojan should prevail, spoke to the nymph Juturna, the sister of the Rutulian leader, urging her to aid her brother, and hinting that she might contrive to break the truce, and thus start the war anew.

Assuming the shape of a warrior called Camers, she incited the Rutulians to start fighting again, and one of them hurled a spear which killed an unfortunate Trojan called Gylippus. Not unnaturally fighting broke out on all sides, and in the battle which followed Æneas, in the very act of urging his men to keep the truce, was wounded by an arrow,

> By what hand aimed, or by what wind propelled,
> Who was it, fickle chance or meddling god,
> To whom the Rutulians owed that grace,
> Remains unknown.

Turnus, when he saw Æneas retiring hurt, roused himself and incited his followers to fresh deeds of valour; but Venus, ever mindful of her beloved son, and seeing that the good old physician Iapis could not extract the arrow-head, descended in a cloud, bearing a spray of the purple-hued dittany which grows on Mount Ida. Unperceived by Iapis, she steeped this flower, with ambrosia and other immortal substances, in the water with which the wound was being laved, and immediately the blood ceased to flow, the pain died away, and the cruel barb came easily forth.

Æneas, full of fresh energy, rushed forward seeking Turnus, but the nymph Juturna, assuming the form of her brother's charioteer, seized the reins and so guided the horses of his chariot that the Trojan was not able to come to grips with his foe.

Finally Æneas ceased to pursue the elusive chieftain, and concentrated his attention upon the Rutulians, and the battle raged more fiercely and in wilder confusion than ever.

Venus now intervened again, inspiring her son with a determination to march against the city of Latinus and make a strong attack upon its walls. When this plan was put into effect there was chaos in the city, for some of the people were ready to defend their homes, and others were anxious to fling open the gates.

Amata, the Queen, looking forth from the palace, saw the enemy drawing near the walls, flaming brands soaring over the roofs, and no Rutulians to come to the rescue. Crying aloud that she was the source of all the evils that had befallen, she tore her purple robe into strips and hanged herself from a lofty beam.

Great was the sorrow of her husband Latinus, who cast dust upon his grey head, and of her daughter Lavinia, who tore her golden hair. And Turnus, far off, heard sounds of lamentation wafted from the city of Laurentum, and, disregarding the warlike promptings of Juturna and the desperate appeals of his friend Saces, he resolved to meet Æneas in single combat, feeling that his memory would then be honoured in spite of the ill-starred intervention of his sister, who had broken the truce and frustrated his desire for the duel.

So at last the two warriors met face to face, and there was a hush in both armies. The men who were handling the battering-ram ceased their labour, the people on the ramparts of Laurentum stood motionless.

Each combatant flung a spear before, with a loud clash of sword-blades upon shields, they met at close quarters, while Jove himself held the scales of fate. Turnus swung his sword and struck with all his might, but the faithless weapon snapped. Then he snatched up the sword of his charioteer, but against the armour wrought by Vulcan it splintered like an icicle. The unfortunate Rutulian had no choice but to flee. Hither and thither he ran, hemmed in by walls and people on two sides, and on the third by a broad marsh. Five times he completed the circle, hotly pursued by Æneas, and as many times they covered as much ground swerving this way and that.

Meanwhile Juno had been pleading with Jupiter for the life of Turnus, but the king of gods rebuked her for having incited Juturna to stir up the Rutulian chief against the Trojans, and for protecting him in the fight, since she well knew that destiny had decreed great honour and achievement to the son of Anchises. The goddess agreed, but she pleaded that if a royal marriage were to be celebrated and a new state established,

> Let it be Latium still, still let there be
> An Alban king, a Roman line made strong
> With old Italian valour. Troy has passed;
> Let her name pass as well

Jupiter promised that these things should be, and sent two Furies, called the Diræ, to give a sign to Juturna that the fate of

Turnus was sealed.   Knowing that against that decree she could do nothing, the nymph drew her blue mantle over her head and plunged weeping into the river.

The great epic ends with the death of Turnus at the hands of Æneas, and we have no description from Virgil's hand of the wedding of the victor and Lavinia, or of the foundation of the state which afterwards became Imperial Rome.

CHAPTER XXIX

THE LESSER GODS OF THE ROMANS

THE Romans, as we have already observed, adopted many of the traditional Greek gods and goddesses, sometimes identifying them with their own ancient divinities, but almost always altering their names. Thus Olympian Zeus became the Roman Jupiter or Jove, Hermes became Mercury, Athene became Minerva, Ares became Mars. Just how far the Roman idea of these immortal beings was characteristic of the people of Latium is a moot point among learned men. One school of thought holds that the Romans merely borrowed certain images and fables from the Greeks, and grafted them on to the natural Roman stem, while others teach that, apart from certain primitive divinities of agriculture, war, and fortune, the Romans were somewhat deficient in myths of the great gods, and had to go to the Greeks to learn how to practise a religion worthy of a mighty race.

We are not here concerned with the later stages of the religious history of Rome, when all sorts of Egyptian, Asiatic, and even Celtic cults got mingled with the traditional paganism, thus preparing the way for Christianity, but it is necessary to mention in passing the important part played by the Roman idea of a sacred city-state, and of the relationships between the priesthood, the governing power, whether king, republic, or emperor, and the general well-being of the Roman people. There was little idealism and not very much poetry about the myths and rituals of pagan Rome. Either as farmers or as citizens the Romans were practical men, who wished to propitiate the forces that might help or hinder them.

The land of Latium was, however, haunted and pervaded by local legends, woven round the gods of hearth and home, of vineyard and garden, flock and herd, and the husbandman's year was one long succession of pious observances, processions, dances, sacrifices, bonfires, and festivals.

The Roman gods had no human forms; they had neither the virtues nor the faults of mortal men; they did not inhabit temples, or reveal themselves to their votaries.   Such ideas, when we find them in the literature of Rome, are definitely derived from the mythology of the much-admired Greeks.

This kind of god, a national force rather than a being, was called a *numen*.   One such god, Jupiter Feretrius, was once believed to dwell in an oak-tree on the Capitoline Hill, at the spot where Romulus dedicated the first spoils won in a victory over an enemy in the field.   At a much later date a building called the *ædes* might be erected to enclose a patch of ground sacred to some *numen*. But we are still very far from the elaborate worship offered by the Greeks to the Olympians.

THE LARES AND PENATES

Speaking very roughly, we may say that the names given by the Romans to the Greek gods amounted to a sort of Romanization, or adoption into the Roman system of ideas.   We need not dwell upon the resemblances—or the differences—between the divinities of war, love, wisdom, and so forth as honoured among the isles of Greece or upon the seven hills of Rome.   What we are thinking about now is the sort of homely little god peculiar to the Roman people.

Foremost among these were the Lares and Penates, who in every house had a little shrine, or even a chapel, all to themselves. They were represented, after the art of sculpture developed, as youths wearing short tunics and carrying libation-bowls or drinking-horns, and their images were kept polished with wax.   It was important to keep them in a friendly humour, for the Penates took heed that there should be no dearth of food in the house, while the Lar was the guardian of the pastures and the cornfields outside.   The Lar was originally an Etruscan divinity, whose function it was to mark the boundary between one farm and another, and even after the Lares became associated with the Penates as the gods of home they still did open-air duty as the guardians of landmarks, boundaries, and highroads.   The Romans also paid almost religious veneration to the shades (Manes) of their ancestors, and in the family ceremonies held to honour the memory of the founders of the line the *paterfamilias* acted as priest, and his son as *camillus,* or acolyte.

OTHER DEITIES

An essentially Roman divinity was Janus, the god of gateways and of beginnings—hence our word for the month that begins the year—January. He has been described as "the opener and fastener of all things that are." To him was sacred the first hour of the day, and because he "looked before and after" he was represented with two faces, each seen in profile.

In the Forum he had a temple of which the doors stood open in the time of war, but were kept closed when peace prevailed. Augustus recorded with pride that during his reign the temple of Janus had been closed three times.

The worship of Janus was closely associated with that of Vesta, and they were often invoked during the same ceremony, though not at the same moment.

Flora, the goddess of flowers, had a temple near the Circus Maximus in Rome, and a priest of her own, the Flamen Floralis. Feasts called Floralia were held in her honour every year, and she was one of the most charming of those mythological beings who resemble the fairies of nursery lore.

Pomona, the goddess of fruit, was another amiable personage. Her husband, Vertumnus, was said to have wooed her in many various forms, as a reaper, a ploughman, a pruner of vines, before she would listen to his wooing. He presided with her over the changes in the rural year. Another agricultural goddess was called Ops. Every August a ceremony was held in her honour in the Regia, or ancient royal palace of Rome, at which only the High Priest, the Pontifex Maximus, and the Vestal Virgins were present. She was later identified with the Greek Rhea, but originally they were two different beings.

Quirinus, considering that he was one of the 'official' gods of the Roman city-state, and had not only a priest but a hill called after him, is a rather vague and colourless divinity. He was originally a god of the Sabine people, and in the later days of pagan Rome some said he was one and the same person as Romulus.

In a similar manner Tiberinus, a legendary king who was drowned in the Tiber, and Volturnus, the god of the rolling river, became merged into one.

T

The Pontifex Maximus was not necessarily a priest, though his duties were of a priestly kind, and included offering public sacrifices on behalf of the city-state. Julius Cæsar and all the Cæsars who came after him held this important post.

The actual priests were called flamens, and one was attached to the service of each of the principal divinities worshipped in Rome. Their chief was the Flamen Dialis, or priest of Jove, and they all wore conical hats of white leather and white togas edged with a purple stripe. No flamen might touch a corpse or look upon an armed force; and if during a sacrifice one of them was so unlucky as to lose his high white hat he had to resign on the spot.

THE AUGURS

Next to the flamens the most important figures in the religious life of Rome were the augurs, or foretellers of the future from signs and omens—whence our word ' augury.'

Various methods of divination were employed, and the augurs professed to be able to predict events from the flight of birds, the entrails of animals sacrificed to the gods, thunder and lightning, or even the manner in which chickens picked up grain.

There was a regular college of augurs, and military and naval commanders would take an augur with them as modern armies take their chaplains. On the occasion of a sea-fight between the Romans and the Carthaginians in 249 B.C. the Roman admiral was informed by the augur that the sacred chickens would not eat. " Then," said he, " let them drink." They were thrown overboard, and the defeat of the Roman fleet which ensued was regarded as the direct result of this wanton disregard of the omens.

Augurs who specialized in divination from entrails of animals were called *haruspices*, and a college of these founded by the Emperor Claudius existed until the fifth century A.D.

Macaulay, in his *Horatius*, describes when a " thunder-smitten oak " has fallen on Mount Alvernus,

> Far o'er the crashing forest
> The giant arms lie spread;
> And the pale augurs, muttering low,
> Gaze on the blasted head.

CHAPTER XXX

INTERPRETATION

FOR a long time after people had ceased to believe earnestly in the pagan gods most people ceased also to feel any interest in them. When Christianity took possession of the mind and heart of Western Europe the legends of the old beliefs were condemned as inventions of Satan, and not for many years did serious Christian scholars approach those legends with the true spirit of inquiry.

Certain of the pagans themselves had, however, made that approach in the days when the gods of Olympus still held sway over Greece, and, later on, over Rome. These men reasoned about things which their fellow-men regarded as too mysterious and perilous to be subjected to the cold processes of reason; they tried to find the inner meaning of the myths which were accepted as literally true; they interpreted many of those myths in an allegorical and symbolical sense; and they thereby incurred the hatred of the orthodox. It is always dangerous to be born ahead of your own time, as Anaxagoras, one of the earliest of the rational mythologists, found to his cost.

In the fifth century B.C. two schools of thought existed, which showed that the old legends were no longer accepted unquestioningly by men of vigorous intelligence. One of these was called the Eleatic, as it arose and flourished in a Greek city of lower Italy, Elea by name, and its teaching was that there is only one Supreme God, eternal, unchangeable, beyond the comprehension of the human mind, and in no respect resembling a human being in form or character. This implied a denial of the popular belief in various gods none of whom was morally the superior of the poor mortals who worshipped him. The other school of thought, called the Ionic, was also destructive of faith in the old divinities; but it taught that the force behind the visible world was not divine, but some such natural force as fire or water.

One of the earliest philosophers who approached the ancient myths in a critical spirit belonged to the Ionic school. This was

Anaxagoras.   The other followed the Eleatic theory.   That was Empedocles.

ANAXAGORAS, EMPEDOCLES, AND LUCRETIUS

Anaxagoras was born at Clazomenæ, in Ionia, in the last year of the sixth century B.C.   He spent thirty years in Athens, enjoying the friendship of Pericles, Euripides, and other great men of the Golden Age, but his philosophical views offended the more narrow-minded Athenians, by whom he was condemned to death. Pericles interceded for him, and the sentence was commuted to one of life-banishment.   In 428 B.C. he died at Lampsacus, on the shores of the Hellespont.

We are not concerned here with the scientific theories of Anaxagoras, which were remarkably sound, and included a foreshadowing of the Atomic school of thought—*i.e.*, that school which teaches that all substances are merely masses of atoms, a proposition endorsed by the scientists of our own day—or with his doctrine of the *Nous*, or ' shaping spirit,' which he believed to pervade all nature.   What annoyed his critics far more was his openly expressed scorn of the oracles, and his ideas about the gods, whom he did not accept as real and active beings, but regarded as personifications or symbols of great natural or spiritual forces.

Empedocles was a Sicilian physician, who flourished towards the middle of that remarkable century, the fifth before Christ.   His ideas were influenced both by the Ionic and the Eleatic schools of thought, with a bias towards the Eleatic.   In his view the four elements, earth, fire, air, and water, are the realities underlying the names of Zeus, Hera, and so forth, given to them by man.   He believed that the whole universe is kept in movement by two fundamental powers, love, which unites, and hate, which separates, acting and reacting upon each other.   If Empedocles had held these ideas with cold sincerity he would not have fallen into the fatal error ascribed to him by ancient tradition—that of imagining himself to be a god, and therefore flinging himself into the crater of Etna that the rest of the world might share his belief.   The Greek poet Lucian declares that the volcano flung up the sandals of the presumptuous philosopher in order to show that he was mistaken.   Matthew Arnold, in his poem *Empedocles on Etna*,

takes a more sympathetic view of this event, and thus sums up the
philosopher's theory concerning the pagan gods :

> Scratched by a fall, with moans,
> As children of weak age
> Lend life to the dumb stones
> Whereon to vent their rage,
> And bend their little fists, and rate the senseless ground;

> So, loath to suffer mute,
> We, peopling the void air,
> Make gods to whom to impute
> The ills we ought to bear;
> With God and Fate to rail at, suffering easily.

> .   .   .   .   .

> Nor only, in the intent
> To attach blame elsewhere,
> Do we at will invent
> Stern Powers who make their care,
> To embitter human life, malignant Deities;

> But, next, we would reverse
> The scheme ourselves have spun,
> And what we made to curse
> We now would lean upon,
> And feign kind gods who perfect what man vainly tries.

A third thinker who allegorized the ancient myths was the
Roman poet of the first century B.C. Lucretius. He is believed
to have studied at Athens the philosophies of Anaxagoras and
Empedocles, though his own conclusions were far more pessi-
mistic than theirs, and his bitter materialism was like a foretaste
of the disillusioned scepticism of our own day. The tradition—
immortalized in a poem by Tennyson—that Lucretius died raving
as the result of a love-potion given to him by his wife was probably
baseless, and may have been the invention of some early Christian
anxious to discredit an unbeliever.

Although this poet denied the existence of any god or gods, or
any sort of spiritual or moral force behind the visible universe, his
moral code was more austere than that of many comparatively
respectable pagan believers, to say nothing of that of the beings in
whom they believed. He held, as many modern mythologists
hold, that when primitive man beheld the sea, the budding trees,
the cornfields, and the vineyards he instinctively created in his
own mind Neptune, Ceres, Bacchus, and so forth, through the

whole range of life and nature, explaining what would otherwise be imcomprehensible in a series of unconsciously allegorical stories woven round imaginary beings of more than mortal power. It is when he himself is interpreting in this light some of the myths of the antique world that he reaches the highest peaks of poetry.

LATER INTERPRETATIONS

As time went on, and Christianity entrenched itself even more steadfastly, any thinkers who troubled themselves with pagan tales tended to look at these in one of two ways—either as allegories or as distortions of actual history. This later school of thought is known as Euhemerism, and its origin is to be found in the works of a certain Euhemerus, who in the fourth century B.C. declared that he had discovered a mysterious island in the Indian Sea called Panchaia where there were quantities of ancient inscriptions setting forth the lives and deeds of the earth-born kings and heroes who after death were raised to the rank of gods and honoured as such. This view appealed to Christian philosophers like St Augustine, who welcomed the proposition that any myths which were not devised by the Evil One were in sober fact mere exaggerations of actual history. Either theory demolished their supernatural glamour.

Exponents of Euhemerism would have it that Æolus was a seafarer with an unusual knowledge of the winds; Atlas, an astronomer; Pegasus, a pirate who sailed faster than any of his rivals; Danaë's shower of gold became the money with which her guardians were bribed; and Prometheus, instead of making men, made images of them out of clay.

A reaction against this theory next set in, and another school arose which reverted to the allegorical idea, but carried to such extremes that it defeated itself. For if all myths were parables there must have been in early times a caste of teachers who were also poets and philosophers, and who set forth to instruct their fellows consciously and deliberately by means of these parables. Nobody who knows anything about the antique world will affirm that such a caste existed.

Interest in the whole question deepened as the nineteenth

century advanced, and folk-lorists and philologists flung themselves into the fray. The science of comparative mythology developed, and learned men like Professor Max-Müller built up a
theory, based upon the pervasion of what were called the ' Indo-
Germanic ' group of languages by the dead but important Sanskrit
tongue, according to which practically all myths were of Aryan
origin. Sanskrit—a perfectly real and most fascinating language
—was said to be the creation of an Aryan race living in the uplands
of Central Asia at some vague and remote period. From them
were descended practically all the races of Europe, except the
Magyars, Finns, Basques, and Lapps, and many Asiatic groups,
such as the people of Persia, Armenia, and Northern Hindustan.
Evidence for their common descent was to be found in similarities
of languages, especially in those words denoting peaceful occupa-
tions, from which it was adduced that their ancestors had dwelt
side by side in tranquillity for many generations before dispersing
—and quarrelling—in other parts of the world. In the field of
mythology the Aryan theory offered a simple explanation of the
well-known fact that a great many nations had the same—or very
similar—gods, heroes, and myths at periods in history when there
cannot possibly have been any communication between them,
either by land or sea. (At a later date seafarers and merchants
were great disseminators of legends and fables.) Stranger still
are resemblances existing between the classical myths and the
beliefs of savage peoples still living in remote parts of the world.
Much fascinating information upon this subject will be found in
The Golden Bough, by Sir James G. Frazer. The word ' Aryan '
as a term to denote race has recently fallen into disrepute among
the scholars of every nation except one, and the existence of Max-
Müller's pastoral people (from whom all ' Nordics ' may trace
descent) is no longer an article of belief in any country but
Germany.

For a long time the Aryan interpretation held the field. And
incidentally there grew up a school of thought which recognized
in practically every widely diffused legend what was called a ' solar
myth.' From Herakles to little Red Riding Hood there was
hardly a solitary figure in folk-lore or fable who was not declared
to be an allegory of the sun's struggle with darkness. A variant
of this theory was the ' vegetation myth.' Herakles there appears

GREECE
OF THE MYTHS
English miles

0 10 20 30 40 50 60

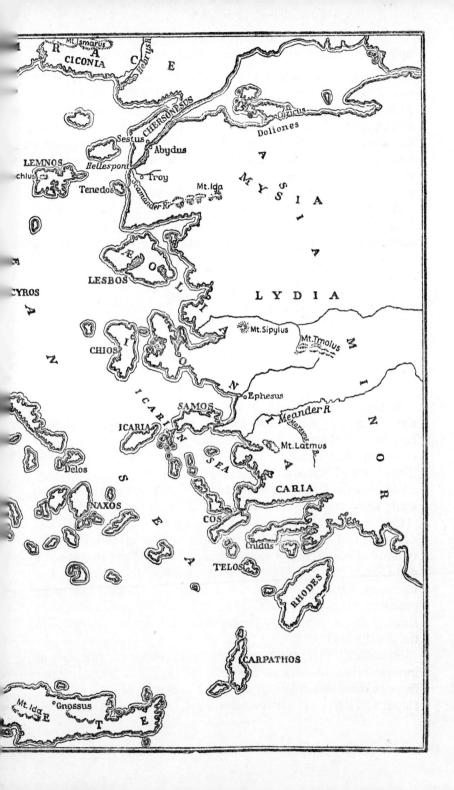

not as day fighting with night, but spring contending with winter
—and the same, of course, applies to Red Riding Hood.   The
philological theory was so poetical and so attractive, and the magic
of language played so large a part in its composition, that there
was a certain reluctance to discredit it; nor can it be said that it is
wholly discredited even now.   No longer, however, does it hold
the field.   The present-day scholar has, in some respects, reverted
to Euhemerus, and to the idea that most myths are based upon
historical reality.   The common origin is discerned, however, not
in any Asiatic upland, but in Egypt.   This is a hard knock for the
few who still cling to the Aryan hypothesis, for the Egyptians were
definitely *non*-Aryan.   According to the latest ideas,

> gold miners, pearl-fishers, and other seekers . . . have carried ' the archaic
> civilization ' step by step from land to land across Asia, from island to island
> across the Pacific, till even the Indians of Ohio practise meaningless rites and tell
> irrational tales that once had meaning and reason for Egyptians.

SOME INDIVIDUAL MYTHS

Whatever school of interpretation we incline to, it is clear that
the principal myths fall into certain main groups, associated with
certain natural forces, heavenly bodies, etc.   Without going so far
as to say that Herakles, Œdipus, Orpheus, Sisyphus, Perseus,
Theseus, and Jason are all personifications of the sun, we may
admit that the legends associated with Apollo have a solar origin,
while those telling of his twin-sister Artemis are not incorrectly
classed as lunar myths.   Again, though it was absurd to detect in
every hero an image of vegetation striving to overcome the harsh
tyranny of winter, it is obvious that the story of Pluto, Persephone,
and Demeter *is* derived from the alternation of the seasons.   The
Cyclopes, like the Cherubim and Seraphim of the Bible, were
probably Thunder and Lightning, and the glow upon the peak of
Etna no doubt gave rise to the myth of the forge of Hephæstus in
the depths below.

Fortunately there are some fables which admit of both sorts of
interpretation, the folk-lorist's and the fabulist's, without other
theories being automatically ruled out.   Such is the lovely tale of
Cupid and Psyche.   The folk-lorists tell us that it may have been

invented, or have come almost spontaneously into existence, to explain certain curious marriage customs practised among primitive peoples all the world over. Among some such peoples it is unlawful for a husband to see his wife's face until some time after her marriage, and brides are often veiled to this day; other tribes forbid a bride to pronounce her husband's name (*cf.* the legend of Lohengrin), and many superstitious beliefs cling round the bridal ceremony and the return of the man and wife to their own home. On the other hand, the name Psyche means both a soul and a butterfly; and, as we have said already, this story may be interpreted as an allegory with a happy ending—the reward of true love after trial, error, and tribulation. Our old friend the solar mythologist recognizes in Cupid the sun-god seeking in Psyche the goddess of dawn. So every one finds what he would.

To sum up. Many theories have been formulated as to the origin of the best-known and most widely distributed myths, and almost as many have been discarded. Ancestor-worship, fear and wonder, the desire to propitiate mysterious forces, the necessity of explaining existing customs, the natural instinct to glorify great men after their death, the human tendency to clothe thought in figurative language—all these factors have combined to create, almost as if by a natural process of growth without the intervention of any individual mind, the great body of mythology which formed the religion of the ancient world. Neither Wordsworth nor any other poet will ever again

> Have sight of Proteus rising from the sea;
> Or hear old Triton blow his wreathèd horn,

but there is no human creature in any part of the civilized globe who—unless at his peril—will neglect, disparage, or disregard the myths of Greece and Rome. Being ignorant of them, a man is ignorant not only of the history, the thought, the poetry, and the art of the vanished pagan world which still has so much to teach us; he is also wilfully and profoundly ignorant of the literature and the art of the world in which he lives to-day. The common speech of educated people, the metaphors, images, and allusions of authors, speakers, and thinkers, become full of meaningless phrases; picture-galleries abound in pictures which suggest stories, but can tell none; even the symbolical sculpture of the market-place presents a series of enigmas; and the whole form and colour of the composite mind of civilization is blurred and dimmed if the beliefs and legends of these distant days are suffered to slip into oblivion.

> Much have I travell'd in the realms of gold
> And many goodly states and kingdoms seen;
> Round many western islands have I been
> Which bards in fealty to Apollo hold.
> Oft of one wide expanse had I been told
> That deep-brow'd Homer ruled as his demesne.
>
> KEATS

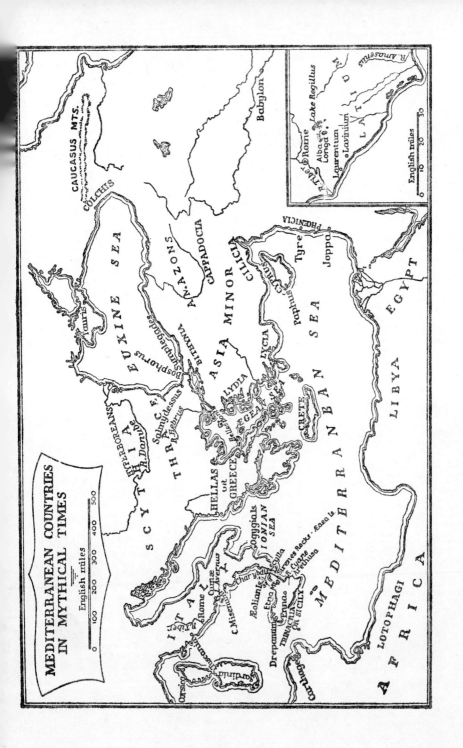

MEDITERRANEAN COUNTRIES
IN MYTHICAL TIMES

English miles
0   100 200 300 400 500

CAUCASUS MTS.
COLCHIS
EUXINE SEA
AMAZONS
CAPPADOCIA
CILICIA
PHOENICIA
Tyre
Joppa
ASIA MINOR
LYCIA
LYDIA
CYPRUS
Paphus
BITHYNIA
Bosphorus
Salmydessus
R. Hebrus
THRACE
SCYTHIA
HYPERBOREANS
R. Danube
Taurus
HELLAS
or
GREECE
AEGEAN SEA
CRETE
MEDITERRANEAN SEA
IONIAN SEA
Oggygia Is.
ITALY
R. Tiber
Rome
Cumae
L. Avernus
C. Misenum
Aeolian Is.
Charybdis
Etna
R. Acis
Scylla
R. Cyane
Arethusa
Drepanum
Eryx
Enna
TRINACRIA
or SICILY
SARDINIA
Corsica
Carthage
AFRICA
LOTOPHAGI
LIBYA
EGYPT
Babylon

LATIUM
R. Amasenus
Rome
Alba Longa
Lake Regillus
Lavinium
Laurentum
R. Tiber

English miles
0   10   20   30

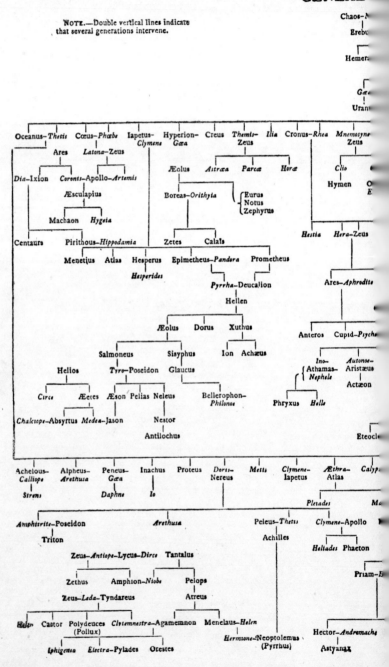

NOTE.—Double vertical lines indicate that several generations intervene.

Chaos-N

Erebu

Hemera

Gæa
Uran

Oceanus-*Thetis* Cœus-*Phœbe* Iapetus-*Clymene* Hyperion-*Gæa* Creus *Themis*-Zeus Ilia Cronus-*Rhea* Mnemosyne-Zeus

Ares   *Latona*-Zeus   Æolus *Astræa* *Parcæ* *Horæ*   Clio   Hymen

Dia-Ixion *Coronis*-Apollo-*Artemis*   Boreas-*Orithyia* ⎰Eurus Notus Zephyrus⎱   Hestia Hera-Zeus

Æsculapius

Machaon *Hygeia*

Centaurs Pirithous-*Hippodamia* Zetes Calaïs   Ares-*Aphrodite*

Menetius Atlas Hesperus Epimetheus-*Pandora* Prometheus

Hesperides   *Pyrrha*-Deucalion   Anteros Cupid-*Psyche*

Hellen   *Ino*-Athamas-*Nephele* *Autonoe*-Aristæus

Æolus Dorus Xuthus   Actæon

Salmoneus Sisyphus Ion Achæus   Phryxus *Helle*

Helios *Tyro*-Poseidon Glaucus

Circe Æetes Æson Pelias Neleus Bellerophon-*Philonoe*

Chalciope-Absyrtus *Medea*-Jason   Nestor

Antilochus   Eteocl

Achelous-*Calliope* Alpheus-*Arethusa* Peneus-*Gæa* Inachus Proteus *Doris*-Nereus *Metis* *Clymene*-Iapetus *Æthra*-Atlas *Calypso*

Sirens   *Daphne*   *Io*   *Pleiades* Ma

Amphitrite-Poseidon *Arethusa* Peleus-*Thetis* *Clymene*-Apollo

Triton   Achilles   *Heliades* Phaeton

Zeus-*Antiope*-Lycus-*Dirce* Tantalus

Zethus Amphion-*Niobe* Pelops   Priam-

Zeus-*Leda*-Tyndareus Atreus

Helen Castor Polydeuces *Clytemnestra*-Agamemnon Menelaus-*Helen*   Hector-*Andromache*
(Pollux)

Iphigenia *Electra*-Pylades Orestes   *Hermione*-Neoptolemus   Astyanax
(Pyrrhus)

TABLE

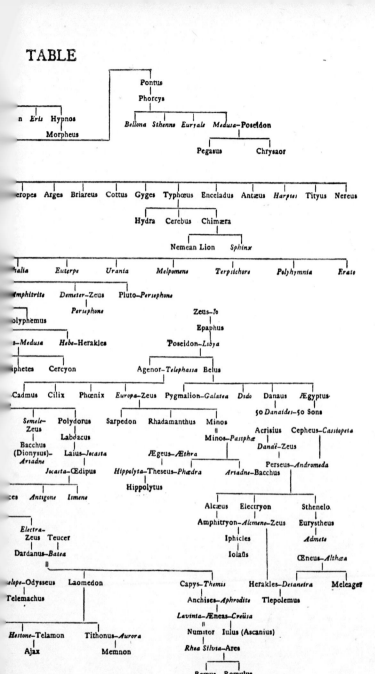

GLOSSARY AND INDEX

A

U

PAL-A-ME′DES. Bearer of summons from Menelaus to Odysseus, 190

PAL′A-TINE HILL. One of the seven hills on which Rome was built, 82

PAL-I-NU′RUS. Pilot of Æneas, who was drowned, 274, 276

PAL-LA′DI-UM. Statue (or shield) of Athene, supposed to have fallen from heaven, 40, 115; stolen from Troy by Diomed, 225

PAL′LAN-TI′DES. The fifty nephews of King Ægeus, 146, 147

PAL′LAS. Son of Evander, leader of the Arcadians, 279, 282. 2. See Athene

PAL′LOR (Terror). Attendant of Ares, 80

PAN. God of nature, father of Silenus, 34, 47, 75, 102

PAN-ATH-E-NA′I-A. Greek festival held in honour of Athene, 40

PAN′DA-RUS. Son of Lycaon, 200

PAN-DO′RA. First woman; created in heaven, she brings evil into the world, 22, 23, 24, 169

PAR′CÆ—see Fates

PAR′IS. Son of Priam and Hecuba, brother of Hector, 187; judgment of, 187–188; carries off Helen, 198–199; at Troy, 202, 203, 205, 224; death of, 225

PAR-NAS′SUS. Mountain in Greece sacred to Apollo and the Muses, 24, 25, 57, 58

PAR′THE-NON. Temple dedicated to Athene at Athens, 40

PAR-THEN-O-PÆ′US. One of the Seven against Thebes, son of Atalanta, 179, 180

PA-TRO′CLUS. Friend of Achilles, Greek chieftain in the Trojan war, 191, 196, 207 et seq., 218, 220, 224, 246, 263

PAX. Goddess of peace, who nurtured Plutus, 95n.

PEG′A-SUS. Winged steed created by Poseidon from the blood of Medusa, 90, 139, 183–186, 294

PEI-SIS′TRA-TUS. Son of Nestor, who befriended Telemachus, 231, 232, 252

PE′LEUS. One of the Argonauts, 161; joins the Calydonian Hunt, 165, 166; husband of Thetis, 187; father of Achilles, 190, 210, 212, 222, 224, 246

PE′LI-AS. Son of Poseidon, father of Alcestis, 43, 91, 156, 162

PE′LI-ON. Mountain in Thessaly, 158

PE′LOPS. Son of Tantalus, 99, 172, 265

PE-NA′TES. Roman gods of hearth and home, 288

PE-NEL′O-PE. Wife of Odysseus, mother of Telemachus, 165, 190, 229, 234, 251 et seq.

PE-NE′US. 1. River - god, father of Daphne, 45. 2. River used by Herakles to clean the Augean stables, 127

PEN′THE-US. King of Thebes who banned the cult of his cousin Bacchus, 102, 103, 104

PER′DIX. Name sometimes given to Talus, nephew of Dædalus, 148n.

PER-I-PHE′TES. Son of Hephæstus, 86

PER-SEPH′O-NE. Same as Kore or Proserpina; goddess of vegetation, daughter of Demeter, wife of Pluto, 49, 68, 76, 94, 95, 96, 113, 114, 151, 246; carried off by Pluto, 95, 107–109; search for, by Demeter, 109–114

PER′SEUS. Son of Zeus and Danaë; slays Medusa, 123, 137–140; and Atlas, 140; rescues and marries Andromeda, 140–144; slays Polydectes and Acrisius, 143; founds Mycenæ, 144

PHÆ′A. Giant sow slain by Theseus, 147

PHÆ-A′CI-ANS. People who dwelt in Scheria or Phæacia, 161, 236–238, 249–250

PHÆ′DRA. Daughter of Minos, sister of Ariadne, wife of Theseus, 151; loves Hippolytus, 153, 155, 183

PHA′E-TON. Son of Apollo and Clymene, 42, 53; drives the sun car and is slain, 53–56

PHA-E-TU′SA. One of the Heliades, Phæton's sisters; changed into a poplar-tree, 56

PHE′MI-US. Minstrel spared by Odysseus, 263

PHID′I-AS. Famous Greek sculptor, 32, 40

PHI-LE′MON. Husband of Baucis, host of Zeus and Hermes, 27, 28

PHIL-OC-TE′TES. Friend of Herakles, 134, 225, 231

PHIL-Œ′TI-US. Faithful neatherd of Odysseus, 259, 262

PHIN′E-US. 1. Prince betrothed to Andromeda, 140, 142–143. 2. Blind king who was persecuted by the Harpies, 159

PHLEG′E-THON. River of fire in Hades, 96, 97, 244, 276

PHO′BOS (Alarm). Attendant of Ares, 80

PHŒ′BE. 1. One of the Titanides, daughter of Uranus and Gæa, 14, 15. 2. Daughter of Leucippus, 170. 3. See Artemis

PHŒ′BUS—see Apollo

PHŒ′NIX. Son of Agenor and Telephassa, brother of Europa, 30

PHO′LUS. One of the Centaurs, host of Herakles, 126–127

PHRYX′US. Son of Athamas, brother of Helle, 156, 157; children of, 160

PHY′LE-US. Son of Augeas, 127; joins the Calydonian Hunt, 165

PI-RE′NE. Fountain on Mount Helicon, 184

PI-RITH′O-US. King of the Lapithæ, friend of Theseus, 130, 151; joins the Calydonian Hunt, 165

PLE′IA-DES. Seven of the nymphs of Artemis, daughters of Atlas, 63

PLEX-IP′PUS. Uncle of Meleager, 166, 167

PLU′TO. Same as Dis, Hades, Orcus, or Aïdoneus; god of the Lower World, son of Cronus and Rhea, 17, 19, 42, 94, 95, 96, 130, 138, 152; visited by Orpheus, 49–50; and Persephone, 76, 95, 96, 107–109, 113; kingdom of, 95–97, 275–277

PLUTUS. Blind god of wealth, son of Ceres and Jason, 95n.

PO-DAR′CES—see Priam

POL-I′TES. One of Odysseus's men, 243

POL′LUX—see Polydeuces

POL′Y-BUS. King of Corinth, husband of Merope, 172, 175, 176

POL-Y-DEC′TES. King of Seriphus, host of Danaë and Perseus, 137, 143